THE
REAL ESTATE
REHAB INVESTING
BIBLE

THE
REAL ESTATE
REHAB INVESTING
BIBLE

**A Proven-Profit
System *for* Finding,
Funding, Fixing,
and Flipping Houses . . .
Without Lifting
a Paintbrush**

PAUL ESAJIAN

WILEY

Contents

PART IV   Owning and Growing a Business of Rehabs   241

Introduction

The Decision

Real estate is the best thing that ever happened to me.

We face constant decisions as we grow up and learn how to allocate our time. One thing was very clear when the moment came for me to decide what I wanted to do with my life: real estate would play an integral role in my future. Everyone I knew or read about in the real estate industry seemed to have the opportunities that I desired.

I certainly knew what I did *not* want to do. My inner voice made it crystal clear that I would not be happy working nine to five in an office, trying to climb my way up the corporate ladder, with other people telling me when to work and what to do. I wanted to work with my friends and family and have fun on the path to my personal and financial goals—and I felt that I could create this reality. This is what initially interested me in investing in real estate—specifically rehabbing real estate as a residential redeveloper. I knew I wanted to focus my time, energy, and resources on what I wanted to do.

This book will not offer a get-rich-quick scheme; however, you will get rich if you're willing to put in the work, planning, time, energy, and resources to accomplish your goals. While I cannot make you work harder, I am going to share the techniques and systems that I use in my own business, which will allow you to work much *smarter*. I will show you that you can make money on your first rehab deal if you follow my system and put in the work. Experience and commitment to following this system will dramatically reduce the time it takes to become successful and make profits on each and every rehab deal.

According to *CNN Money*, the average working American earns approximately $50,000 a year. You, on the other hand, can take the knowledge, systems, and education provided in this book to make at least half—if not more than—the average annual income on your next rehab deal. The concept is simple and outlined throughout the book as follows:

Find = Identify and analyze distressed property in Chapters 3, 4, 5, and 6.

Fund = Leverage money and write offers to acquire the property in Chapters 7 and 8.

Fix = Execute my seven-stage rehab system in Chapters 9 through 16.

Flip = Implement a sales process and account for every dollar of profit, as shown in Chapters 17, 18, and 19.

This book is about more than just making money. I have found rehabbing to be one of the most fulfilling things that I can do with my time to have a social impact. Breathing life into vacant, dilapidated homes can improve an entire neighborhood's look and feel. Hiring local contractors, spending money on materials and renovating properties doesn't just stimulate job growth; it also has an immediate impact on the local economy. Rehabbing properties has a significant social impact on our communities and homeowners across North America.

As a residential redeveloper, it's important to understand your role in your community. Your actions can impact the entire area. Pulling and paying for permits with the city or county and placing a once-distressed property back on the local municipalities' tax roll generates revenue in the form of property taxes. Listing your finished rehab with a real estate agent, selling with a stager, closing with an attorney or escrow agent and financing a loan, creates jobs for everyone involved. Of course, there is the satisfaction you will receive by providing a beautiful house to someone who will make it a home. All in all, mastering the craft of rehabbing real estate by perfecting residential redevelopment is an asset and tool that has a beneficial impact on both you and your community.

I am fortunate to be a mentor, coach, partner, and friend in an amazing real estate education company through FortuneBuilders, Inc. My partners and I have devoted our life's work to documenting, improving, sharing, and coaching all of the real estate principals and systems I will share throughout this book. Through our active residential redevelopment company, CT Homes, LLC, we execute and share the strategies and systems on a daily basis that I will be teaching. My partners and I started teaching and sharing these tools in order to make our first local market more efficient so we could do more deals with more investors. Teaching our competition allowed us to develop an amazing network of confident investors; as a result, we all did more deals and helped each other build our businesses. FortuneBuilders, Inc. has taken this approach on a global scale and has the largest committed investor community. Throughout the book, you will hear some stories about this amazing community that is successfully improving houses and neighborhoods across North America.

Now is the time to make a positive impact on your community, master the rehab craft, create wealth, and improve your financial future. When you make your first $25,000 profit on a rehab, you will see the power this system has to change your life and the lives of those around you.

So let's get started!

AN OVERVIEW OF THE SEVEN-STAGE REHAB SYSTEM DESCRIBED IN THIS BOOK

As you move through this book, I will get into the specifics of all seven stages of a rehab. Here is a brief overview of my system and how it differs from other real estate rehab books and gurus.

Stage 1 is all about gathering information pertaining to a particular property. You must perform your due diligence by taking pictures inside and out, measuring everything, and identifying all the work and improvements that need to be made. Basically, this means that you take as much time as you need at the house on your first visit after owning or controlling it. Determine what it will take to turn that house into the most desirable property in the neighborhood.

Stage 2 involves reviewing all of your notes, the list of improvements that need to be made, and pictures of the house. You'll use these items to put together a detailed scope of work, a document where you'll write out every improvement, work needed, finish material and item number with price that your licensed and insured contractor will install and execute once they start work on the property. The scope of work is your written manifesto of exactly what you want done to the property.

Stage 3 consists of developing a contractor and job-bidding system to identify qualified, licensed, and insured contractors. Just as we take time to find the right property before we make an offer and close, we have to perform the same extensive marketing and analysis process to find the right contractor who will complement our system—which in turn will make you successful on the rehab. It's critical to remember that 50 percent of your rehab's success is determined by the quality of the team and, specifically, the contractors you hire to get the job done.

Stage 4 introduces and explains how to execute the paperwork that will keep you on time and on budget with your contractor. The following six critical documents are essential to your success as a rehabber and can protect you from any complications and liability that may arise:

1. **Independent contractor agreement:** This document is specifically designed to provide clear communication between you and your contractor. You have to articulate and explain why there is a penalty for failing to meet a deadline. It should spell out why they have to add you as an additional insured on their insurance policy with minimums to keep you safe.
2. **Final scope of work:** The final scope of work outlines, in writing, exactly what needs to be done to the property.
3. **Contractor payment schedule:** The payment schedule ties payments to specific benchmarks and milestones to incentivize continued and ongoing work until the house is complete.

4. **Insurance indemnification form:** This is a stand-alone statement re-iterating the insurance needed by the contractor.
5. **W-9 form:** This form will permit you to properly 1099 each contractor at the end of the year for his tax responsibility.
6. **Unconditional lien waiver:** The unconditional lien waiver is to be signed upon completion of the work and before you hand over the final check!

Stage 5 is the rehab itself. Wow, look at how much work we have already done in stages 1 through 4 and we have not even yet pulled the first shingle off our property! Truthfully, our success at the end of a rehab is directly correlated to our preparation and successful implementation of our rehab system. You need to avoid mistakes before they happen—and this system will help you do precisely that.

Stage 6 and Stage 7 have everything to do with buttoning up your paperwork while simultaneously implementing an impressive selling system and marketing blitz. Now that the rehab itself is complete, you must conduct the contract closeout and prepare to market and stage the property for sale. These are the final steps you need to take before you receive your first check. After all, if you finish a rehab and can't get it sold, you can't expect to make profit! Stick with me, follow my systems, and leverage the knowledge I will share with you and you will be well on your way to your first check.

PART

I

Getting the Rehab

Before we can implement our Seven Stage Rehab System, we need to market and find properties that need renovation. Once we find a rehab property, we have to do a proper deal evaluation to determine whether it's a good deal. After we determine it's a good deal, then we have to finance or pay for the rehab property. Throughout all these steps we will need to have the knowledge and confidence to estimate repairs and write a proper purchase and sale contract to control and close on the deal. Part I and the following nine chapters prepare us for all these steps, provide a system to implement, and most importantly will give you the confidence you need to move forward with writing an offer on your first or next rehab deal.

CHAPTER 1

How to Make a Profit On Your First Deal

You may think that you need to have a lot of money to break into the real estate industry—but that couldn't be further from the truth. Neither prior knowledge nor a bank account full of cash is a requirement. Yes, you can take advantage of more opportunities if you have both experience and money. However, we all have to start somewhere. In the words of one of my coaches, "Every master was once a disaster." No one knows what they're doing right at the beginning. But we all start somewhere.

MASTER REHABBING NOW

One student of mine, a professional football coach named Scott Squires, was overworked and traveling nonstop. Although he enjoyed his job, it did not provide him with the personal or financial freedom that he desired. He wanted to spend more time with his three kids. Scott took the first step to having that kind of life by participating in our real estate coaching program. He had absolutely no real estate experience, but he started following the principles laid out in this book. His first deal in Southern California was a HUD home that he purchased for $350,000. He ended up spending $13,000+ in rehab costs and sold the property for $415,000. He bought, rehabbed, and sold the property within 84 days and made a profit of $49,000—which allowed him to spend more time with his family and leave his day job. If you want to hear Scott walk you through his first deal, you can listen to his story here: www.fortunebuilders.com/video-case-studies/scott-squires.

A mere two years later, Scott sent me a text message telling me about his latest deal at the time: using my rehab system, Scott made a profit of $216,000 on one deal! By following the same rehab system I share in this book, Scott no longer travels for work—and he is able to spend as much time with his family as he wants.

You're likely wondering at this point if my system can truly apply to your situation—perhaps even convincing yourself that this just won't work. You may be thinking that Scott is an isolated scenario—real estate success can occur anywhere and to anyone. Imagine instead the success you will enjoy once you commit to your own goals. If you apply the principals, knowledge, and enroll coaches and mentors to successfully move forward, you *will* experience the results you desire.

How does a full-time radio DJ and a high school science teacher with no real estate experience make money on their first rehab in Richmond, Virginia? Jeff and Joanna Anderson got their first deal from a marketing campaign I will share in this book. They financed the purchase price of $80,000 with a hard-moneylender (which you'll learn about in Chapter 7, "Financing Rehabs"). After spending $61,000 on the rehab, they sold the property above their asking price for $215,000. That is a $45,400 profit—on their very first project. Check out Jeff & Joanna Andersons first rehab profit here http://www.fortunebuilders.com/deals/jeff-anderson/.

If you enjoy learning, self-improvement, and making large amounts of money, then you have come to the right place. Again—I am not offering a get-rich-quick scheme. It takes hard work, commitment, and a positive attitude. More importantly, it requires you to take action *now*. So let's get you started on making your first real estate rehab profit!

OUR BIGGEST OBSTACLE

To make progress, you must take advantage of the knowledge I share throughout the next 22 chapters. It is entirely up to you to start achieving your personal and financial goals.

The biggest obstacle you will likely face is fear. People are afraid to fail, to be unprepared, that it'll be too difficult, that they won't have enough money. Some people even fear *success*. These are all legitimate concerns; but the way you handle this fear will dictate your future as a residential redeveloper.

> Work finally begins when the fear of doing nothing exceeds the fear of doing it badly.
>
> **—Alain de Bottom**

Most people see fear as a stop sign—but really, it's a pay attention sign. That twinge of worry in the pit of your stomach is a signal to pay attention to what you don't know, what you need to know, and what you are already familiar with. Think about an opportunity that you knew you wanted to take, but didn't. What held you back? How will that be different this time around?

Once you change your perception of fear, you will notice countless opportunities. More importantly, you'll spend your time and energy more productively. Instead of avoiding fear, you should welcome fear with open arms. When you identify fear, then you have just identified what you need to learn and gather more information to move forward with confidence.

You don't have to know all the answers; you just need to have access and be willing to approach those who do. Henry Ford was not the best mechanic, nor did he know every detail about building a car. However, he had no equal when it came to recruiting the smartest and most talented individuals. The people you surround yourself with are integral to your success as an investor.

MY STORY

Whenever I sit down for a lecture, read a book, or take advice from someone, I always ask myself: Why should I be listening to this individual and what credentials do they have that make them an expert? Since you're likely wondering the same about me, let me share some statistics regarding my experience in the real estate industry.

Over the last decade, I have managed over 1,000 residential real estate transactions. I have spent over $35 million—from renovation materials to contractor fees for single-family homes—in states from Connecticut to California and everywhere in between. I currently manage and operate an eight-figure investment portfolio for my partners and me through real estate.

I know what it takes to begin at ground zero. I started with no money and zero real estate or construction knowledge, yet was able to create successful real estate transactions and a thriving real estate business.

When I graduated college, I had a degree in Agricultural Economics—earning what many may consider a degree in farming. Then I went through an entire year without a job. I initially took a job as a bar back and after a ton of hard work, finally became a bartender. The only things I ever flipped before houses were cocktails and dreams!

There were a few things that allowed me to bridge the chasm between bartending and rehabbing:

Step One: Embrace every learning experience that presents itself and read material relevant to your goal.

Step Two: Enlist the help of coaches, mentors, and professionals.

Step Three: Do not allow failure to impede on your inevitable success. And yes—you will fail. However, the sooner you embrace that failure, the sooner you can overcome it. If you fail with knowledgeable mentors and coaches supporting you, you'll find it much easier to pick yourself up and keep moving forward. Too many believe that a single mistake will lead to their demise. But allowing yourself the liberty to make minor mistakes only moves you closer to achieving your goals. Some of my best students did not let the fear of failure keep them from their goal of making money as a new real estate investor.

My First Rehab

The first rehab property I purchased was on Mead Street in New Haven, Connecticut—and I remember it like it was yesterday. We purchased it on a Saturday morning foreclosure auction. My partner and best friend since junior high, Than, and I dispatched to different auctions that morning with our last bit of money scrapped together into a bank check that we needed to take part in the bidding process. I ended the day without success winning any bids—and then got a call from Than, telling me he won the bid for Mead Street for $75,000. I then asked what seemed to be the next logical question: "Where are we going to get the money to close on the property in 30 days?" I guess he gave me his best shot at a logical answer: "I don't know."

This was our first lesson in using leverage to get our real estate business going. We employed a very technical fundraising application called dialing for dollars—that is, we literally called every number in our cell phones to raise the money needed to close on this property. What we were not able to borrow from friends and family we borrowed against our credit cards, increased our credit amounts, and got cash advances. This approach may not work for everyone; but it was all we had, and we wanted that deal.

Once we closed, we estimated a rehab budget for the property and set out to find and work with contractors to get the job done and put us in a position to sell the finished house. We probably made every mistake a rehab investor could make. We did not use a scope of work; we did not use contracts with all of our contractors; and we certainly did not develop an organized, well-thought-out payment schedule that would motivate our contractors to complete the house on time and within budget. However, we were lucky enough to sell the house for more then we estimated—and enjoyed a net gain of $27,000.

I have to ask myself when I look back, "How on earth did we make money on that deal?!" Neglecting to have a true system in place can get you in trouble—and it usually does. In the business of rehabbing, you can make a lot of money—and you can lose a lot of money.

The difference between the two lies in following a proven path, implementing a system that others have used successfully, and enrolling other people to support and help you achieve results. This will give you the confidence of accomplishing a known outcome each and every time.

Before our first rehab on Mead Street, Than and I started with the idea of buying multi-family rentals. I thought we would kick our feet up, collect rent, and call it a day. So the first properties I bought as an investor were rentals. I was immediately made aware of the problems landlords encounter on a daily basis. In short, being a landlord was not fun when you are not good at it. More importantly, I was on a path to get rich slowly, if at all.

I was constantly chasing tenants for rent and had made the mistake of buying buildings that had years of deferred maintenance. This approach forced my partner and I to reevaluate our business model. How could we make large sums of money in a three- to six-month period of time? Unlike rentals, rehabbing did not create monthly cash flow. However, when you completed a rehab job and sold it, the profit potential was 30 times that of a monthly rent check. This is why it is so important for you as a real estate investor to do the business niches in order. Start by making money rehabbing, then move those profits into long-term, passive income rentals.

In 2004, we enlisted the help of a couple crews and completed multiple rehabs and wholesale deals. By our third year, we set out to complete 100 deals a year. At this stage, we had built systems, hired team members, enrolled coaches and trainers and we wanted to really test our model. After three short years, we surpassed our goal and completed 104 deals, with the majority of them being rehabs.

When I got into real estate, I was learning a discipline that I could use to make money anywhere and at any time. But more importantly, it served as a vehicle for the lifestyle I wanted to live—in California, closer to my family, by the ocean, and able to wear flip-flops during the week. We call this *lifestyle by design*. Thus, in 2009, my company and I moved from New Haven, Connecticut, to San Diego, California. I now live in a beach community, wear flip-flops whenever I want, and can walk from one of my houses to work, the ocean, or my offices in just a few blocks. Lifestyle by design!

Your Turn

Write a paragraph of what your lifestyle would look like if you had 100 percent control over where you lived, with whom you worked, when you worked, what you wear to work, and so on. This vision exercise will get you excited about moving forward with the goals you have for yourself and the results they can produce.

THE OPPORTUNITY

Have you ever been driving or walking somewhere and noticed a property that needed some love? You know—the one with a front lawn taller than your waist or that needs an exterior paint job and siding more than you need a haircut.

Our first myth to dispel is that you can make a profit on *any* house. You can only make a profit on the right house—the one that needs work, has a problem to be solved, and has an owner who is motivated for you to create a win-win to buy it. When you find the right house, you can then implement the seven-stage rehab system without lifting a paintbrush.

In every market—up or down, buyers or sellers—there is always someone telling you that now is not a good time to invest in real estate. Ask yourself the following three questions when you hear that advice:

1. Does this person make 10 times more than I do financially?
2. Does this person have the lifestyle and freedom of time that I desire?
3. Is this person even experienced and currently making money in real estate?

Ninety-nine percent of the time the answer to these three questions will be no. Everyone has an opinion. If I listened to everyone who told me that now is not the right time to get into real estate, I would still be at my first job.

THINK LIKE AN INVESTOR—NOT A CONTRACTOR

Each level of income you desire demands a different version of you. If you approach rehab as a do-it-yourself hobby, you'll see that in your return. Your time is not best spent painting the house yourself to save money. This is a trap that prevents many would-be investors from actually getting to the next level. The next level is when you spend less time on one deal, make more profit on that deal, and spend your time on things that are more important than real estate.

My golden rule on rehabbing real estate is, "Never get your hands dirty." Our job is to find motivated deals, raise money, and manage a successful rehab. You are in the business of turning money. How quickly can you put one dollar in so you can get three dollars out? When this becomes second nature to you, you will realize that rehabbing is a vehicle for multiplying your dollars. When you save money by doing the work yourself, you are slowing down the job, putting out sub-par work, and missing other opportunities while you are working on site.

Basically, by getting your hands dirty, you slow down the opportunity to get your money back sooner. Ultimately your job is to put one dollar out of your pocket as an investor and see how quickly and efficiently you can bring two dollars back in your pocket.

Put your contractors in a successful system; this shows respect for their time and ability. Make it clear that you are not an errand boy or girl to fetch materials for the house. You must have enough confidence in yourself to truly understand where your time is best spent—and the following chapters of this book will show you just that.

CHAPTER 2

Never Lift a Paintbrush

Why Doing It Yourself Is the Biggest Mistake Most Rehab Investors Make

WHERE MOST INVESTORS FAIL

We all have to file taxes. Imagine what would happen if everyone you knew, regardless of their profession, did their own taxes—with no help from a CPA or accountant. Let me give you an example. Your passions and talents lie elsewhere, but you have to allocate 6 to 12 hours of your time filing your taxes or more. Yes, you may save a little money, but you are sacrificing something that is more important—and you aren't functioning at your highest nor making the best use of your time.

As we discussed in the previous chapter, a rehab investor should not be performing work on the house. Rather, you should focus on activities that will make you, your contractors, and your entire team more money: finding deals, funding deals, fixing deals, and flipping deals. Concentrating on these high-priority tasks will positively impact everyone involved in these projects.

For fun, let's assume that you are already working on your first rehab project. Because I have been there, I've included the following potential mistakes you will make *if* you do not implement the strategies in this book.

THE STORY OF HOW TO DO EVERYTHING WRONG

By the time you get your first rehab deal, you are going to be so excited that you may forget how valuable your time is as an investor. For the first month, you will be driving friends, family, and co-workers to your new rehab project without realizing how much time you are wasting. You neglect to think things through, prepare, or identify the contractors and work that need to take place. Before you realize it, you'll have burned a month and countless visits to the house by not being prepared and organized with a system. In financial terms, you just paid for a month's worth of holding cost. After loan payments, utility bills, taxes, insurance, and maintenance you have nothing to show for everything you have done up to this point.

By the time you finally make a few decisions, you hastily hire a contractor. Unfortunately, you failed to interview, prescreen, and check the contractor's referrals; and you did not set up the proper working relationship through the six critical documents. And you hired your friends, mothers, sisters, and sons.

The contractor starts the job with a point and shoot scope of work, meaning you walked them around the house while pointing with your index finger and verbally telling them what you want done in each room. You don't write anything down, let alone even consider having them sign the six critical documents that will keep them within the rules, timeline, and budget necessary for you to succeed.

Finally, the job starts. However, the contractors require 50 percent of the agreed upon price as a down payment before they'll start working. So you pay them. Since the only leverage you have over any contractor is the money you have not yet paid them, you're in trouble. What incentive do they have to get the work done on your timeline or hit your milestones now that they already have half of the project money in their pocket?

As the rehab gets started, you are eager to participate and get your hands dirty. You proceed to ask the contractor what you can help with, at which time he gives you a list of supplies to pick up from Lowe's or Home Depot. While you may think you are helping, you just turned yourself into a $10/hour errand boy/girl.

The job reaches approximately 25 percent completion and the contractor explains that he ran into some unexpected costs and work that he needs more money for. Remember, you already paid 50 percent of the contractor's fee up front and they have only completed 25 percent of the work. Now they are asking for more money and you pay them another 30 percent of the fee to keep working. You're getting yourself into quite a hole here.

The contractor gets back to work and swiftly completes another 10 percent of the project. Their immediate progress allows you to feel good about your decision. However, the contractor happens to find another job and client that is willing to pay them another 50 percent down payment. He takes on the additional client and gets 50 percent of the money and now has an obligation to someone else's project. In the meantime, no one is working at your house.

Growing concerned, you call the contractor who gives you one excuse after another as to why they are not at the project site, and promises to be at your property the next day. However, they are once again a no show the following day—after you've continuously called and left numerous voicemails.

You now have a house that is 35 percent complete after having paid out 80 percent of the cost of the job. You have a contractor that no longer answers your phone calls and sends you straight to voicemail. Then again, why *would* they answer your calls? They already have a 45 percent profit margin (80 percent of the payment minus 35 percent of work completed) without ever having to set foot in your house again.

You might wonder why I know exactly how a situation like this unfolds. I know, because this exact situation happened to me. I have made the mistakes that you should not make! That is why I am so passionate about sharing my system and years of experience rehabbing properties—to help people do it the right way from day one. Ultimately, the outcome of my example situation resulted in the hiring and firing of multiple contractors to finish the house. By the time my project was complete, I had already gone way over budget and was months past my deadline. I have lived and learned from my past mistakes—and am hoping you will too.

You might also wonder if it's possible to make money in the scenario I just described. Sometimes. However, making money in a situation like this can potentially be more dangerous—because it can lead you to believe that this is the experience you have to go through when rehabbing a property. It provides a false sense of confidence that you were actually the reason the deal made money, when it's truly just a matter of time before you tie up on a deal and lose everything.

Most investors fail when they neglect to focus the majority of their attention on their highest and best use as an entrepreneur—when they do not respect the fact that there is an assembly line-style system they should follow to produce a systematic, repeated known result that I like to call a *rehab profit*. Follow the system I share with you on *every project* and you will turn a profit.

THINK LIKE A BUSINESS OWNER, NOT A CONSUMER

A consumer focuses on what things cost; a business owner focuses on *what things are worth* and the value they can bring into their life. A consumer doesn't spend money they don't have. A business owner spends other people's money on anything that will bring value back to their business and life by utilizing leverage. A consumer is paralyzed with fear of delegating work that won't come out as good as they can do it. A business owner can't wait to delegate and have someone do the job better than they did so they can focus on growing other areas of their business.

Up until this point, you've likely spent your life thinking like a consumer. You need to start making the shift to a business owner's mindset. The two biggest challenges will be a need to reevaluate your perception of time and leverage. Please fill in the blank: "Time is _____." Let me guess, you answered money. (I know, because I can read minds.)

Ninety-nine percent of us are programmed to believe that time is money. This is simply not true. Can you give me an example of when you were able to spend your money to get more time back in your life? When did the money you acquire allow you to go back and buy time so you could spend it with a loved one who is no longer here? Unfortunately, none of us can give an example of when money bought time. This is because time is not money—time is *everything*!

There is one level playing field for the rich and poor, the haves and have nots, the privileged and the unprivileged: We all operate with the same 24 hours in a day. The differentiating factor between people is how they use their time to determine what they accomplish and achieve.

You must also reevaluate your definition of leverage. A successful residential redeveloper leverages everything. They leverage money by establishing, accessing, or finding credit to borrow funds and further their business. They leverage coaches, experts, advice, and information to reduce their learning curve. They leverage licensed and insured professional contractors to help them complete an amazing rehab.

My friend and coauthor Michael Gerber explains the three stages of being a business owner, outlined in Figure 2.1. We all start in the first stage as a technician. This is when we are actively doing the work that the business requires, running errands, producing and creating our product and everything in between. The second stage requires you to become a manager,

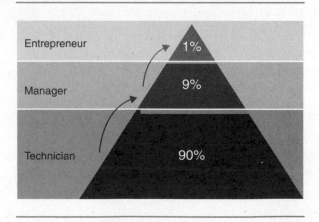

FIGURE 2.1   Three Stages of Business Ownership

delegating to others, while embracing the responsibility of achieving the end result. Finally, the third stage deals with becoming a true business owner—an entrepreneur. This is when you own a business that *works for you* instead of having a business *you* work for!

VALUE YOUR TIME BY OUTSOURCING MWA ACTIVITIES

An MWA is a minimum wage activity. MWAs are jobs you should outsource and remove from your daily schedule as your time becomes more valuable so you do not get stuck as a technician in your own business. As an aspiring real estate investor, creating successful habits is critical to undertake early on in your career. Some options might be to hire a cleaning service for your home, or pay the $12–$20 charge to have the grocery store deliver groceries you order online. There are countless ways to let others complete the menial tasks we all need to complete in our lives, so that you can free up your time to concentrate on moneymaking activities. The next time you are completing a chore, ask yourself if you can hire a service to create more time and get your next $25,000 profit deal.

DEFINING A RESIDENTIAL REDEVELOPER

A residential redeveloper is a more credible title than a flipper or a rehabber or just some house dude. A residential redeveloper renovates the eyesores in a given neighborhood and produces quality housing that everyone can be proud of. A residential redeveloper creates jobs within their community. A residential redeveloper is someone who takes pride in their work, their community, and creates a social impact on every house with character and integrity.

It does not matter if you want to consider this as a part-time endeavor to make the occasional rehab profit or if you want to go fulltime and increase your earnings potential beyond anything you have ever imagined. Being a residential redeveloper is all about the mindset, working smarter and not harder, making the best use of your time, and delivering the best product (a finished rehab) the right way (pulling permits and following all code compliance), and delivering a home to families that will take care of it for years to come.

Time is everything. Do not fall victim to the do-it-yourself mentality. Start thinking like a business owner starting today. Leverage money, resources, systems, mentors, and anything else that is available to get you to your personal and financial goals. Through adopting this mindset and attitude you will transcend from the technician in your own business to a true entrepreneur who enjoys the benefit of owning a business, rather than most technicians who have a business that owns them.

CHAPTER 3

Finding Properties to Rehab, Professionals to Work With, and Opportunities to Explore via Network Marketing

Luck is when opportunity meets preparation.

—Lucius Annaeus Seneca

Any business owner knows that if you cannot or do not know how to market, you won't be in business for long. And finding killer rehab deals has *everything* to do with marketing. A good deal is a targeted opportunity to which we can add value as an investor. In the next few chapters, I'm going to share with you some viable online, offline, and network marketing strategies to find deals.

So what is the secret to landing a good deal? It begins with finding a motivated seller. If a seller's house does not need repairs, if they have no timeline to sell, or if they don't have pressing situation to solve financially or personally, they don't need to sell their house to a rehabber. Remember, if you cannot add value to the situation as a rehab buyer, then you cannot create a win–win. Making an offer on a house in perfect condition and listed on the Multiple Listing Service (MLS) for top dollar is *not* how we create value as a rehab investor.

You must constantly market for deals to buy, money to raise, contractors to work with, and sellers to sell to. Thus, network marketing is the first strategy we describe, as it requires no up front money to get started.

Network marketing is an extremely cost-effective and proactive form of marketing, limited only by your willingness to move your feet and your mouth to interact with the people around you. The overall goal of network marketing is to promote your business and educate the masses on how you may be of service to them, or vice versa. You are establishing these relationships so that those with whom you network can benefit from your product, services, and business opportunities. These relationships can lead to additional business, either directly or indirectly through a referral.

There are tools that can help you manage all of the relationships you form. A customer relationship manager program, otherwise known as a CRM, can help you organize your contacts and automate your ability to keep in touch with them. This technology accelerator allows investors to maintain a working rapport with all of their contacts and leads. Like so many others, real estate is ultimately a business built upon relationships—specifically, in terms of how many connections you can make and being prepared when your next opportunity presents itself.

The longer you introduce yourself as a real estate professional who can buy and sell properties, borrow money and secure it against real property, or hire and pay contractors, the more network marketing referrals will come your way over time.

THE POWER OF NETWORKING

How do I find great deals? How do I find money to fund my deals? How do I find someone to clean a house I just purchased? The answer to these and countless other questions is networking. Every successful investor has a passion for their business and cannot wait to talk to people about the opportunities they have to offer. If you do not tell people what you do—no one else will! No one can sell the opportunity of working with you better than *you*; and no one knows what your new business can do for them if you don't tell them.

One of the great aspects of working in real estate is that everyone, at some point, will need a place to rent or buy. You should have no trouble initiating a conversation and finding common ground; everyone needs a place to call home. And as a real estate investor, everyone is now a potential client and customer!

My favorite place to find and prospect for buyers of our rentals or rehabs is *everywhere*. Whenever I'm out at a restaurant, I always ask our wait staff professional if they own or rent. Subsequently, if they rent, I simply inquire if they would like to enjoy the rewards of homeownership. Merely by making conversation, I can create a lead for a potential buyer on my next rehab home.

Recognizing Opportunities

The key to successful networking is to recognize great opportunities when they present themselves. Are you taking advantage of networking opportunities in your everyday life? It can be easy to miss out on the ones you assume aren't relevant to your business. However, any community where you have built a reputation provides an opportunity to network. Even members of a non–real estate related community or group of which you are a part of know you and your work ethic more than an investor or stranger that you just met. This kind of opportunity is unique to your search, as you have already spent time building and created a mutual respect with these community members. Remember, now that you are in the business of real estate, everyone will need your service at some point, so let them know about the opportunity you have. All of your contacts are a valuable asset to your real estate business. And you will find that many people are actually looking for the opportunities that your business can provide.

Power Players

As a rehab investor, there are several people who you should constantly be networking with and directing your marketing efforts toward. You will want to align yourself with people who have achieved success on the road you are now traveling. A lot of your networking will involve finding individuals who have been where you want to go—and those who can help get you get there.

You will need to enlist the help of several experienced individuals for your team to grow and work efficiently. Each person you come into contact with while doing business becomes a part of that team. For instance, the success of your contractor is directly correlated to the success of your renovation business. It all trickles down and everyone must rely on the team. Figure 3.1 shows the power players that you should be using in your network-marketing model.

WORKING WITH OTHER INVESTORS

Many investors actually get their start by teaming up with other investors and taking the deals that they may not want or can't get funding for. A version of this is wholesaling. There are two different types of investors out there: beginner investors and advanced investors. You want to network with both.

Beginner

New investors should jump at the chance to partner with other investors. Beginners in real estate often find deals that they need assistance in assembling. I've encountered countless beginners who needed education on how to structure a deal, or who don't have enough cash to fund it. Both parties involved in such collaboration create a win–win by adding value and establishing a long-term relationship to move forward with. Whether it's knowledge, capital, or

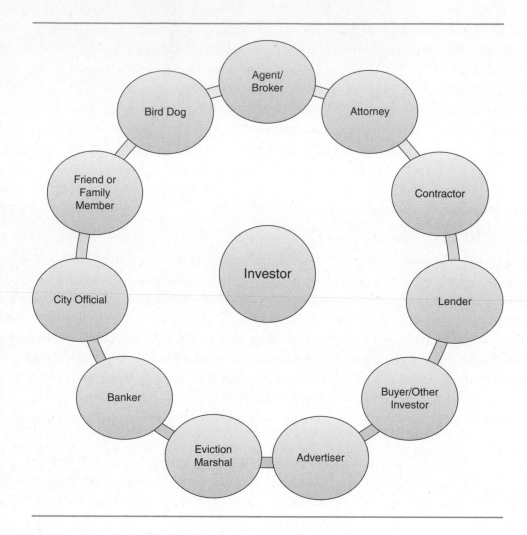

FIGURE 3.1   Players in the Networking Marketing Model

simply time and effort that you can commit to a project, you always need to bring something to the table to increase the probability of them doing business with you.

Advanced

You will also need and want to interact with successful real estate investors who have gone through it all. If a seasoned investor has too many deals in their pipeline or a bigger project that demands their attention, you may be able to purchase their next property; in return, they get a wholesale profit. Many experienced investors are willing to partner and offer expertise or funding.

It's important to exercise caution when entertaining the idea of a partnership. You need to carefully think through any collaboration you make. You should avoid partnering with someone with whom you do not have a long-standing relationship. The best approach is to sell a deal to or buy a deal from someone so each party can take their own risks and control their own destiny without any disputes. You also want to make sure the numbers work when purchasing a property from a wholesaler. Any good wholesaler will always leave enough profit for the rehabber. The key to building a relationship with other investors is to add value to their business through performance or knowledge shared.

Mortgage Brokers

Networking with good mortgage brokers is critical to your rehab business; they are an integral part of your team who can help you with your financing needs. More importantly, a good mortgage broker can give you referrals for good deals to buy, and also refer potential buyers who are not yet working with a mortgage professional.

Mortgage brokers are also valuable advertising partners. Because they aren't directly competing with you for a deal, they can complement your marketing efforts—and you can split the costs. For example, you can send out a direct mail piece with pictures of your houses to sell on one side and information regarding the mortgage brokers' business on the other. This allows potential buyers to see the house that is for sale and inquire about any financing they may need. A conventional licensed mortgage broker cannot pay you a referral fee for sending them business, but they can split marketing costs with you on your next campaign to find buyers or sellers.

Real Estate Agents

As a residential redeveloper, you'll need to add real estate agents to your team. They can provide a very solid source of leads for buying and selling homes. Many investors dismiss the notion of working with an agent when they get their own agent license and do the work themselves. Even if you do obtain your real estate license, you must remember that you are first and foremost an investor, not a Realtor. I do not have my license, so I depend on very good, investor-minded real estate agents to work with.

Obtaining your own license is not necessary. I have successfully completed hundreds of transactions despite not having mine. The key is to seek out, identify, and enroll real estate agents who will simultaneously build your business. There are many agents who will contact you even before they list a property if they know you are a serious player in the business.

You want to cater to agents' needs as much as they are catering to yours. Your goal is to become their go-to contact—an authority in your area of renovating properties. Let Realtors know you are not afraid of homes that need work and renovations. Working with investors gives agents the opportunity to realize repeat business and multiple commissions. Agents have the opportunity to transact numerous deals a year with your assistance. By acting as a dual agent in a transaction, representing both the buyer and the seller, they earn both sides of the commission. An agent will come to see you as a very valuable contact with whom they will work hard to keep. Letting good Realtors know that you will potentially give them the listing of any rehab property they deliver to you is a huge benefit and a way for a Realtor to get paid on the same house twice.

Attorneys

Whether they are foreclosure, probate, eviction, or divorce attorneys, these individuals are some of the most important people with whom you can network. Think about how many potential sellers, lenders, and buyers they encounter during their daily course of business. These power players come into contact with clients who are often in need of disposing a property, or may be in a situation where they are truly motivated to sell—especially if they're going through a situational motivation such as a divorce. Additionally, attorneys will have information about properties in foreclosure and those who are going through probate.

And let's not forget about the other major reason to network with attorneys: *money*. Attorneys are a great source of private funds. Even if not lending themselves, they know and facilitate transactions for private lenders. I made the mistake early in my career of failing to discuss potential funding opportunities with my attorney, who had already closed dozens of deals at the time. I most likely missed out on several chances to identify a new lending source because of my failure to recognize my attorney as a source of funding.

You can absolutely incentivize your attorney by paying a referral fee of .5 to 1 percent on any person to whom they introduce you who actually lends you money. Once you do get a responsive attorney, make sure you communicate with them on a regular basis and send them business and referrals as well. Eventually, they will introduce you to someone with whom you can create a working rapport.

Contractors

Contractors often come across information regarding properties that need work, which makes them a valuable source of leads for rehab investors. Their line of work gives them a lot of access to the properties that may be of interest to you as a residential redeveloper. They also interact with the people who own homes and investment properties who may be interested in selling. If you can actively network with good contractors, you can develop a mutually beneficial relationship. I will be discussing the importance of a reliable contractor and the contractor interview system in much more detail in subsequent chapters.

City Officials

Periodically, a city will hold an auction to dispose of nonperforming loans on its books (tax foreclosures) and to raise capital. While purchasing these homes is usually a very time consuming and tedious process, it offers hidden deals. Your chances of buying properties are greatly enhanced if you are able to develop a relationship with local officials, since they look for competent business owners in the area who add value by improving the community. They know that you can not only buy these properties, but also provide job opportunities to local residents. City officials know what is going on in neighborhoods and towns, and are in the loop about future plans—powerful information for an investor. They can also tell you about the fire damaged, condemned, and torn-down properties in a given area. This is one of my favorite networking leads and relationships for my residential redevelopment business. Here is a list of some city officials and departments to network with.

Building Officials
- Building inspector
- Plumbing inspector
- Electrical inspector
- Compliance inspector
- Plans examiner

- City planning department
- Economic development administration
- Fire department
- Health department
- Housing and living city initiatives
- Tax collector

Eviction Marshals

Eviction marshals may not be the first networking source that comes to mind, but it is definitely one you'll want to remember. Property management is not easy. You will encounter plenty of landlords who are tired of fixing toilets and leaky pipes. When they come across individuals who don't pay rent on top of all the other nuisances, you just may find a motivated seller and a deal. Eviction marshals have a good handle on situations where owners of such a property may be ready to give up and look for a buyer. I have networked very successfully with them in the past.

Family, Friends, and the Community

These people should already know what you do. You should always be offering the same service to your friends, family, and neighbors as you do to others. They will want to help you and may know hundreds of others who may be in need of your real estate services—or at the very least, need advice in real estate. As an investor, you will automatically become an authority when it comes to real estate. A lot of people will seek you out for advice and rely on you for guidance. As long as you let everyone you know that you are the go-to for their real estate needs, you will start to benefit from this networking.

Bankers and Hard Moneylenders

Rehab investors should always look to network with people who have money. It is extremely advantageous for your business to choose the right financial backers and establish relationships early on in your career. A solid track record will be invaluable when you're pursuing loans or lines of credit with a bank or lender with whom you have been doing business for years. Personally, I have had the most success in working with hard moneylenders that specialize in lending money to rehabbers. These individuals know the risk and lend money on distressed properties at a higher cost than a traditional bank. Most importantly, they are valuable people to have in your network because they work with other investors who are looking to buy deals. Hard moneylenders have a lot of rehab clients that are approved with funding but need someone to sell them their next deal. And this is where you can wholesale a deal and create another great relationship. I am proud to share our hard moneylending company that was built by investors for investors, www.GrandCoastCapital.com.

Most conventional banks do not like the risk associated with rehabbing houses. However, local banks that are in the process of growing are more likely to entertain ideas and conversations on how to finance your future deals or business with a line of credit or another creative strategy. Remember, a new bank that is trying to make money has to actually lend money to make money—so why not lend to you?

Of course, banks are another source of prospective opportunities. This is especially true with smaller institutions, where you are more likely to connect with a lending representative in the REO (real estate–owned) department. Banks want to lend money, not hold real estate—which makes them a great source of properties to purchase. It is important to note, however, that it can be quite difficult to buy properties directly from a bank without first going through an agent.

Bird Dogs

A bird dog is someone who simply looks for properties that may need repairs and tells you the address. While these individuals do not technically work for you, they act as your eyes around town and can be anyone from family members to your postal worker. Bird dogs are wholesalers with limited knowledge, who do not put properties under contract; they generally give you leads on properties they know are for sale or in need of repair in return for a fee. This is essentially a finder's fee for bringing you a lead that you wouldn't have otherwise found. Depending on whether or not you buy the property, typical bird dog referral fees range anywhere from $250 to $1,000.

It is up to you to determine whether or not the properties that bird dogs identify are viable rehab candidates. I have personally bought, rehabbed, and sold multiple deals that my cable guy brought to my attention. People in this profession are perfect bird dogs; they drive around town fixing cable boxes and satellite dishes for many people. Let individuals with jobs like this know what you do; give them your card and make sure they let you know any property that needs work and looks like a deal.

BECOMING AN EFFECTIVE NETWORKER

Networking is the art of making and utilizing contacts for your business. The goal is to create and maintain a list of people who can directly increase the quality and efficiency of your business. Networking is a two-way street. If you can help another person and they can help you, you'll build a relationship quickly. Always offer value first by asking and seeing how you can help them meet *their* business goals. This will make it more natural for you to share what you do and what you need. It's a numbers game: the more people you meet and connect with, the better networker you will become.

Finding Networking Opportunities

You can extend your network sufficiently by involving yourself in local events. Although day-to-day interactions should always involve networking, events—like the ones I've listed below—allow you to focus *specifically* on this task. You can take advantage of several opportunities, both online and in person:

In-Person Networking Opportunities

- **Auctions**, both large and small, are an excellent place to find other investors in your area. You will also inevitably run into serious cash buyers, as auctions require these kinds of people to attend. It is essentially a party where every investor is a buyer and has cash to purchase properties. I love going to auctions—not to bid on the properties, but to meet all the buyers who have cash to burn!
- **Local Real Estate Investor Association (REIA) meetings** are another opportunity to network with real estate professionals in your market. Each city typically has REIA meetings you can attend. Try to get to know those who are leading the REIA meeting; these individuals have spent a large amount of time in this organization and are likely to know the right people. You can also benefit from joining the small subgroups that meet weekly to discuss the business.
- **Homebuilders Associations** usually consist of builders and suppliers. This is a good place to network and meet potential contractor and builder referrals.
- **Local Landlord Associations** can also be a great source to locate buyers for your multi-unit rehab properties, as well as to network with other landlords.
- **Home or Trade Shows** can help you find a ton of real estate business. Even if you don't have a booth to set up, you can take the chance to speak with a lot of people. Figure out who the big guns are at each show and exchange cards with everyone you can.

A good rule of networking is: don't try to talk to the whole room. Try to connect with about three or four new people, and find a reason to *follow-up* with them, and this is what usually leads to opportunities for real estate investors.

Online Networking Opportunities

- **Meetup.com** is one of the most popular networking platforms for both formal and informal groups. The site enables you to find out about any real estate meetings and networks close to where you live. You can also start your own Meetup for others to join. Some networks have over 1,000 members. Most Meetups have networking events where you can meet great connections within the industry.

- **Yahoo! Groups** is an excellent resource and one of the world's largest collections of online discussion boards. Yahoo! Groups offers free mailing lists, photo and file sharing, and group calendars among their many great features. There are dozens of these investor groups across the country.
- **Facebook Real Estate Groups** are a great source to meet a ton of people who are all interested and doing real estate.
- **LinkedIn** is a great business oriented social networking site to identify professional team members.

PERFECTING THE PROCESS

Networking can be a difficult habit to develop. You have to keep at it constantly to notice a difference. Once you understand the basic concepts, there are a few things you can do to improve yourself and your business. You can't simply wait for networking opportunities to present themselves; you must create them. You can also work on how to become a better networker by understanding what's most important—*rapport*.

Joining other local real estate investing groups can be an excellent way to add to your real estate education and make new connections. But, think how powerful it would be if you ran your *own* real estate investing group—especially if there isn't already a club in your area. Starting your own network-marketing group for real estate investing will position you as the go-to expert in your area. People will come to you to buy deals, sell deals, and inquire about all types of opportunities. It makes you a preferred partner for other industry professionals, compelling them to seek you out and only do business with you. The influence you gain from hosting a group will allow you to demand better terms on a variety of services like loans, contractor work, and title services.

Key Personality Traits

Whether dealing with buyers, sellers, contractors, Realtors, attorneys, or even your own business partners, you are going to interact with a wide variety of people and personalities, so it's crucial to begin by understanding *yourself*. It is difficult to try and interact with someone else if you don't. The following is a list of five traits that represent a good networker; see which ones you encompass and which ones you will need to work on:

1. **Enthusiastic.** If you aren't excited about what you do, how do you expect anyone else to be? Walk into a room with your head held high and show passion for what you do.

2. **Amiable.** To make it in this business, you have to be a nice person, friendly, and polite. If you find you are dealing with a rude person, keep your cool and move on. Don't let anyone see you being anything but respectful.

3. **Generous.** Have a giving spirit. Don't always think about what's in it for you, but rather what's in it for the person you're dealing with. Again, the more you give to others, the more they will want to give to you.

4. **Trustworthy.** You'll have to be reliable to build trust. Do what you say you're going to do when you said you're going to do it. We call this *completing our agreements*. Never say something you are not going to follow through on.

5. **Persistent.** Good networkers always follow-up. Make some quick notes regarding key points of your conversations so that you can follow-up the next day and stay fresh in everyone's mind.

Tools Needed for Networking

While network marketing doesn't involve online advertisements or outdoor signage, you will require a few tools to execute your strategy in an efficient and effective manner. You can use the following tools in a variety of ways to promote your rehab business.

Business Cards

A business card is a *must*, and the most common networking tool. Designing high-quality business cards can improve your business's image and make a memorable impression. This is the best way to leave a piece of marketing behind for a new contact to remember you. Even if you don't end up working with the person who received the card directly from you, they may pass along your card or your name to others who may end up working with you.

When it comes to business cards, focus on *asking for them* rather than handing them out. Most people put a business card in a pile and never get to it. However, if you get business cards and send an introduction email the next day, you have done what 90 percent of people don't do: the first step of establishing a relationship.

Elevator Pitch

Making a unique impression is the best way for a person to remember you. Develop a 30-second commercial, often referred to as an elevator pitch, to explain what you do. You may have different pitches depending on different objectives. Here is a simple system to deliver for any elevator pitch.

- Ask an initial enrolling question: "You come here often?"
- Acknowledge and pay a compliment: "I have seen you here before and you are always very well dressed"
- Share how you can add value or help them: "I work with sellers who have disrepaired homes that need work that they have a hard time selling. I have helped a dozen homeowners out of tough situations and helped them identify better housing."
- Convey the benefits of networking with you: "If you ever refer or have a seller that you refer to me and I purchase the home, I always pay a marketing and referral fee to you."
- End on another enrolling question that they will always say yes to: "Do you like making money through simply referring leads?"

Credibility Packet

Building credibility and trust is extremely important in this industry, and not something you can do overnight. People are skeptical, especially when it comes to real estate investors. They will question your ability and may not completely understand what it is that you do. You want to make sure you are always documenting your successes and building your credibility packet, which is simply an album representing your work. It can include pictures of projects, renovations, and even families moving into your homes. You have to be able to *show* how you serve your customers, not only talk about it.

A credibility packet should also feature your due diligence in each project. All of our new students leverage the credibility of our system and the national network of which they are a part. Anyone starting will want to seek out a coach and a community to accelerate this tool.

Credibility packets are relatively inexpensive, but provide great value. Some items to include are:

- A description of who you are.
- Company credentials.
- The benefits of working with you.
- The different ways to work with you.
- Property showcases.
- Client testimonials.
- Professional testimonials.
- An FAQ section to handle the rest.

Social Media

Investment in a social media platform is no longer something you might do; it is a means of survival, something you *must* do. More and more companies are actually hiring fulltime social media strategists to account for the growing demand of a loyal following. Professionals and companies in every industry have adopted some sort of integration with social media. Many of these professionals are ones who you should have in your social network. At the very least, you need to set up and establish a presence on social media; a Facebook account is a good start.

You can establish relationships and deepen communication with those you already have a relationship with. People like fast responses, and social media offers the ability for you to do this. You can also get in touch with more people for referral purposes. It is also a key tool you'll leverage when marketing and selling finished rehabs. So do yourself a favor and begin setting up your social media presence immediately.

I recommend you create accounts and start networking on these social media sites:

- Facebook
- Twitter
- LinkedIn
- Google+
- Pinterest
- YouTube
- Blog
- Houzz (I love this one as a real estate investor—check it out.)

Always remember these important things when networking and building rapport:

- Understand what professions and people can benefit your business and in what way.
- Plan which networking events will help you meet your goals and objectives.
- Set networking goals for each meeting.
- Know your audience and understand what benefits you can offer them.
- Build relationships by showing genuine interest in people and in what they do.
- Follow-up on a regular basis to maintain the relationship.
- Help others succeed and they will help you do the same.

The sooner you start meeting other professionals and spreading the word about what you do—how you can help them and add value to their lives—the sooner other people will be adding value to your business. And that is the power of networking. To organize all the professionals you meet in your real estate business, I will share a simple tool for Excel that saves and organizes your networked leads. To download and use my Master Contact List for Your Team, go to www.RehabInvestingBible.com/resources. This list will give you the template and title of all the different professionals you will need to meet and network with over time.

CHAPTER 4

Use a Stamp to Find Properties to Rehab

Direct Mail Marketing

Direct mail is one of the most powerful and proven marketing tools today. It is also one of the most inexpensive and efficient ways to generate leads for your real estate business. To find profitable deals on a consistent basis, it's imperative to utilize direct, one-to-one marketing, as it can award you opportunities that other rehab marketing strategies often neglect.

Direct mail is such a powerful tool because it is *measurable*. You can track responses and measure your ROI (return on investment) with ease. Unlike advertising, it's also traceable, inexpensive, and provides results that are tangible. When developing your rehab marketing plan, it's important to create a cost-effective system that can predict the number of leads coming into your pipeline each month. This chapter gives you the tools necessary to create a successful marketing campaign. I've implemented this proven system in my own business, yielding profitable rehab deals.

DIRECT MAIL SIMPLIFIED IN THREE PARTS

Who?

This is the most important aspect of the direct mail campaign. Forty percent of your success is correlated to whom you specifically target. There are several types of lists that investors use to complete this task that we can divide into two categories: urgent and not so urgent.

The urgent category list includes homeowners who are in more of a rush to sell their homes, possibly because they are facing a timeline or loss. These include pre-foreclosure lists, 30/60/90-day-late lists, bankruptcy lists, fire damaged and code violation lists, and tax lien lists. It is important to note that a large portion of the leads from urgent lists will be time-sensitive. So the earlier you reach these clients, the better.

The not-so-urgent category consists of homeowners who may not need to sell their home, but are still motivated. These are inherited property lists, absentee/out-of-state homeowner lists, probate lists, expired listings, and free-and-clear lists. However, keep in mind that although the not-so-urgent list may not have an underlying need to sell, they can end up becoming some of your most profitable deals. Much like the urgent mailing lists, timing is crucial; you never know when the seller may be ready. Therefore, following through with a multi-letter drip campaign is important.

What?

What type of marketing pieces are you using for your mailings? The way you approach someone can impact their response. In my experience, prospects on the urgent list respond better to a professional mailing on company letterhead. The homeowners' credit and livelihood are often at stake, so they want to feel like they are working with an experienced professional. On the other hand, not-so-urgent homeowners are often more likely to respond to a personal touch. At times, mailing them a less professional-looking yellow letter is often more effective than a postcard or letter on company letterhead.

How?

How do you send out your direct mail? There are two ways: you can fulfill yourself, or leverage and pay a fulfillment company. Obviously, compiling your list in-house will be more cost-effective, but you will more than likely only be able to handle fulfilling two to three mailing lists at a time, as it is very time consuming. However, if you outsource your campaign to a fulfillment company, it is automated for you. While your costs will be higher, you no longer have the stress and frustration of fulfillment. When you outsource, you're also able to implement multiple campaigns.

SEND YOUR MAILINGS CONSISTENTLY

Consistency is essential when it comes to direct mail marketing. Once you have effectively implemented your strategy, it's crucial to send your direct mail campaigns at regular intervals. Once you have everything in place, you can track each campaign's effectiveness. One of the biggest mistakes real estate investors make is sending out just a few mailings and then throwing in the towel. They are called campaigns for a reason. You need to implement them three to six times before you can determine whether they're working in your favor. If you have gone to the expense of purchasing a prospect list or spent the time to compile one, you owe it to yourself to exhaust all possibilities before giving up. It is infinitely better and economically smarter to send a letter or postcard five times to 1,000 people than to send one letter to 5,000 prospects.

STEP 1 TO A SUCCESSFUL DIRECT MAIL CAMPAIGN: DETERMINE YOUR BUDGET AND PLAN

Determining a budget for your direct mail campaigns is crucial to your real estate investing business.

What is a reproducible and realistic budget that you can utilize every single week? Although you may not have an answer initially, you will want to make a few response rate and budget assumptions to determine an approximate return on investment up front. This will allow you to evaluate whether or not your marketing campaign expenses are justified. It may be out of your comfort zone to spend money that you can't immediately substantiate, but it's all about setting a goal and committing to the process.

The best way to organize your direct mail campaigns is to prepare them all at once and categorize them by date. Tuesdays are the best days for mail to arrive, as it is usually the lightest mail day of the week. Your mailings are more likely to stand out with less competition, so time them wisely.

STEP 2: IDENTIFY YOUR TARGET MARKET AND OBTAIN YOUR LISTS

Defining your target market is all about choosing your audience and sourcing the list to which you will mail. Before you even begin writing, it's crucial that you understand your target audience. Your marketing message should reflect the intentions of those with whom you are seeking to connect. For example, if you are focusing on single-family homes in pre-foreclosure, your message shouldn't include information about buying tax lien foreclosures. Irrelevant information can distort your intended message. You want your prospects to feel as though you understand their personal situation. Each individual piece of your direct mail campaign should speak directly to its reader.

There are many different niches you can target when formulating your direct mail campaigns:

- Bankruptcy
- Eviction
- Divorce

- Probate
- Attorneys (i.e., bankruptcy, probate, divorce)
- Fire damaged/code violations
- 30-60-90-day overdue payments
- Vacant property/absentee owner
- Free and clear properties
- FSBO (for sale by owner)
- Pre-NOD (notice of default)
- Expired listings

Remember, each one of these lists you have the ability to bring value and create a win–win to put a deal together. If you cannot create a win–win, you should never move forward with a deal. With that said, you can combine some of the prospects on these lists and send them the same mailers. For example, 30/60/90 day lists can be combined with pre-NOD. Additionally, fire-damaged property leads can be combined with the code enforcement violation list. As long as the target list and messaging are congruent, you can distribute the same mailer.

While there are many different campaigns and lists to target, there are a few that have been particularly beneficial to me as real estate investor and residential redeveloper. The following illustrates which lists have favored investors and how you can obtain them.

Absentee Owners

An absentee owner is someone who owns but does not live at the subject house. You know a property has an absentee owner when you check the recorder's office and see that the tax bill is being sent to a location that is different than the subject property. Direct mail campaigns geared toward absentee owners have the potential to bring in consistent leads. More importantly, this type of lead is abundant in just about any market.

Absentee owner leads are gold mines, as the average landlord lasts only a few years. There is always going to be a huge number of landlords wanting to sell their property, and a constant turnover in landlords means money in your pocket. Landlords usually have very little emotional attachment to their property, which makes it easier to do business with them. In addition, some of these properties are owned free and clear, which can be a huge benefit to you.

Absentee owners can also be inherited owners who live out of town or state. In these cases homes left to other family members who no longer live in the area only become a financial and management burden. These are great opportunities to create a win–win situation. These are also great deals to rehab because they typically have not been maintained or kept up over the years since the owners and families live out of town.

There are a number of different places where you can find absentee owner leads, including:

- Directly from your county, list brokers, county websites, and so on.
- Local tax assessor's site (which is more than likely very accurate).
- Local or national list provider (for a fee).

Probates and Inherited Properties

A probate is the legal process that settles a deceased person's final debts and formally passes their property's legal title to the intended heirs. More often than not, the heirs to an estate would much rather receive cash than deal with an old property. Inherited properties are usually vacant, and therefore encourage instances of vandalism, theft, or illegal occupancy. Therefore, most owners can't wait to rid themselves of these headaches. This provides an opening for you and your business to offer the heir or group of heirs a quick and beneficial alternate solution. Probate records are accessible to the public, which makes it easy to see how much estate a given individual has left, who the beneficiaries were, and what they received.

This campaign is a little different from the others, as few states actually have a commercially produced probate list. As a result, you more than likely have to manually compile the list yourself. However, since there are a limited number of providers that supply a probate list, fewer people are marketing to this particular group. The ratio alone gives you a competitive edge over your competitors. You can locate these records by:

- Monitoring probate court information at your county courthouse or town/city hall.
- Searching for postings in a local publication, or tracking them online at the courthouse website.
- Local or national list provider (for a fee).

The probate process is different in every state, so there is no 100 percent, universal method that works to get the list manually at every courthouse or town hall. Likewise, every county courthouse or town hall has different methods of recording the information.

Preforeclosures/Notice of Default (NOD)

It's fairly easy to obtain preforeclosure and notice of default leads. Every time a lender starts the foreclosure process, they are required to file the necessary paperwork. These public-knowledge documents provide the following information:

- Owner's name.
- Address of the property being foreclosed on.

- Mailing address of the owner (if tenant occupied).
- Balance owed to the lender.
- The lender and loan number.
- Length of delinquent payments.

It's important to note that most states have different requirements for the information contained in their foreclosure filings. You're not going to get the same data from state to state. However, depending on the list provider, some also have access to additional local information related to the property.

Types of Foreclosure Lists

- 30-, 60-, and 90-day lists. This is when the homeowner is one to three months behind on the mortgage, *before* the *lis pendens* or NOD (notice of default) has been filed. It is not public knowledge at this stage; only the homeowner, lender/bank, and credit agencies know about it. These are also often called pre-NOD lists.
- *Lis pendens*/NOD (notice of default) filings. This is when the lender files the necessary paperwork and the foreclosure process begins. The information becomes a matter of public record at this stage. The only downside with NOD leads is that anyone can get their hands on them. Therefore, most of your competition will also be sending their marketing and information to them as well.

Focusing on preforeclosures helps to eliminate more of the competition with foreclosure leads. These grant you access to private information regarding prospects who may be in financial stress. When a homeowner falls behind on their mortgage payments, delinquencies are reported to the credit bureaus and impact the credit report. This information is not public, but you can obtain these leads through companies that have access to credit agency information.

Here are a few ways you can find preforeclosure and foreclosure leads:

- County Recorder's office. Although most cities and counties have this data filed electronically, others may not. This would require you to go to the courthouse and pull the files manually. This is the most difficult, labor-intensive way to collect the information, but it can also get you the leads faster than the other alternatives.
- Do an online Google search. Start by searching for *local foreclosure list provider* and your county or city name; then expand your search to the state level. You can also search any local publications in your area for these listings.

- Title company. Contact a local title company in your area and inquire about foreclosure leads. Not all title companies or closing attorneys offer this service, but some do. Those who offer this service may even provide it for free if they expect to do business with you in the future. However, the only downside is that the list may be a little old by the time you get them, and the homeowner will likely receive other letters and postcards before yours.
- Local or national list provider (for a fee). They compile information on homeowners in default and sell it privately, generally with a small monthly subscription fee.

Expired Listings

An expired listing occurs when a listing agreement between a seller and a licensed real estate agent expires. They usually indicate problems involved with the sale of a property. For whatever reason, the house was on the market for sale, but didn't sell. This creates an opportunity for real estate investors to help homeowners. Immediately after the contract with the real estate agent expires, investors are permitted to step in and make an offer directly to the homeowner.

Once you've compiled your leads on expired listings, quickly send out your marketing piece to that homeowner. It's important to keep in mind, however, that agents have access to this data as well. You will be competing with other agents who may be mailing that same homeowner to acquire the new listing, or other investors just like yourself. It is imperative that your marketing materials stand out from the rest.

A Few Facts About Expired Listings

- Time changes circumstances: A seller becomes much more motivated the longer their property takes to sell.
- You'll be competing with Realtor postcards: You won't be the only one who has access to expired listings. You'll also be competing with other Realtors soliciting the seller with their marketing campaigns, and with other investors like yourself.
- Short timeline: Because the property failed to sell within the seller's projected timeline, they may become much more motivated to sell and willing to negotiate.

You will need to work with a Realtor/agent who has access to the Multiple Listing Service (MLS) in order to obtain expired listings. The agent can send you a current list of expired listings in the database. Oftentimes, they can set up a search for expired listings that automatically sends them to you each week.

Delinquent Tax/Tax Lien List

Obtaining a delinquent tax or tax lien list can be a very affordable source of income for your real estate business. Most of the time, delinquent property owners have taxes and other pressing issues to address—making a quick sale their ideal solution. However, it's important to understand your particular area's policy regarding back-tax liens and how frequently they are pursued. Some municipalities rarely foreclose on homeowners who are behind on taxes; delinquent taxes may not be a large motivator for a homeowner to sell their property in that particular area. So, delinquent tax lists may not be the best target list to pursue. When it comes to obtaining the delinquent tax/tax lien list for your campaign, remember that there are always different rules involved for different cities and towns.

You can locate tax-lien lists by calling the tax collector's office in your designated area and inquire about the list of homeowners who are a year late or more on their taxes (in some states only). If available, they may require a small fee for the list.

Fire Damaged/Code Violations

I personally like to market and identify these properties as a residential redeveloper. Code violations are when your local building department fines a homeowner each day they do not improve or repair the property that is deemed to be a safety hazard to the community. This means that each day an owner has this property but does not improve the property, it costs them money. These are great opportunities to create a win–win situation for a rehab buyer.

Fire-damaged properties are typically too much work for the average rehab investor. This creates an opportunity to have less competition on these deals. Remember how we discussed that fear is not a stop sign but rather a pay-attention sign that you need more information so you can take advantage of the opportunity. Take a look at one of the fire-damaged properties that this campaign took advantage of. If you have fear, you will skip this deal and I will get it!

STEP 3: SET UP YOUR MULTI-LETTER, DRIP MARKETING CAMPAIGN

Once you have your target list in place, you can execute your drip marketing campaign, which you'll use to maintain consistent contact with your prospects over an extended period of time, using various outreach methods. This approach is designed to continuously place your company and message in front of your prospect. I have found that homeowners go through three primary stages when coming to terms with an unplanned real estate decision like having to move because of work or financial distress: Stage 1 is denial; if you send a direct mail piece in this stage, you will not get a response. Stage 2 is anger; good luck having a positive conversation in this stage with a seller. Finally, stage 3 is acceptance; if one of your direct mail pieces is in front of the seller at this point, you are in a good position to get a response and have an opportunity to put together a deal.

I've outlined an example of what a direct mail drip campaign can look like. Keep in mind that this is just an example; you can and should tweak it to fit your target list and budget.

First mailing: You can start your direct mail campaign with a postcard, since these are an easy and inexpensive way to kickoff—especially when mailing a new list for the first time.

Second mailing: Follow-up with a second piece to the same list. This time, send a yellow letter expressing your interest in buying the property with cash. The color will stand out more than a traditional letter and hopefully elicit a greater response rate.

Third mailing: Send a letter that uses a handwritten font to give it more of personal feel. This letter should not sound like it's coming from a big company. You can write or print it on any kind of paper or letterhead, such as plain white printer paper, notepads, and so on.

Fourth mailing: Send a professional letter on company letterhead.

Fifth mailing: Send a letter that specifically cites the benefits of working with your company. For example, buying as is—namely, in any condition—means the seller can leave junk behind, and so on.

Postcards

A postcard is a simply designed mailing piece with your basic information that lets sellers immediately know how they can benefit from working with you. You should utilize the small space efficiently to excite the seller and to get them to understand how you can remedy their situation.

Postcards are inexpensive, give the message up front, and don't require stamps or envelope stuffing. Make sure that you include a compelling headline, information about how you are going to solve the homeowner's problem, and your contact information. Here are some tips to make your postcard more appealing:

- Make it personalized by using a handwritten font on the prospect's name and address on the envelope. Chances are, they will be less likely to throw away mail pieces that appear to have their name and address handwritten on them—even if it's from a stranger.
- Use unique and interesting stamps, since these generate some curiosity from your prospects. The longer they look at your postcard, the better chance they'll grasp and remember your message.

Yellow Letters

A yellow letter should use handwriting or a font that emulates handwriting on yellow legal or notebook paper, and be sealed in a handwritten envelope. This marketing piece is designed to be as nonconfrontational as possible; it should look to the seller as if it were coming from a friend. Yellow letters have a fantastic response rate; they are probably one of the most effective mailers to utilize.

Key Components of Any Direct Mail Piece

Headline

Your headline is the single most important thing at the top of your letter or on the front of your postcard or envelope. You must ask yourself when you look at your mail piece, "What catches my attention?" If your answer isn't the headline, make some tweaks. Your headline should be clear, catchy, and bold, and should catch the attention of homeowners who have vacant properties or a major workload to improve their property. Strong statements pique curiosity and interest and prompt a seller to call, email, or go to your squeeze page website.

Examples of Headlines

- Need a Creative Way to Avoid Foreclosure?
- Your Property Sold in 10 Days … Guaranteed!
- How to Sell Your House in 27 Days or Less
- I Can Buy Your House—CASH & Close in 7 Days!
- Fire Damage, No Problem—We Want Your House!

Commonality/Empathy Statement

You may sense frustration and apprehension in marketing to distressed sellers. However, there is a good chance they are looking for somewhere to turn. The opening statement should encourage sellers to face their problem, while the commonality piece makes them understand that they are not alone and that you genuinely want to help them by providing a solution to their problem.

Examples of Empathy Statements

- Every year, hundreds of thousands of people face foreclosure. Unfortunately most have no idea what options are available to them.
- Our company specializes in solving complicated real estate problems and will assist you with finding solutions to any real estate dilemmas you may encounter.

- We've helped hundreds of people just like you get out of this same situation.
- You're not alone with your tenant problems. Thousands of evictions are filed each and every day.

Offer/Benefits

Never assume the seller knows the benefits of what you're offering; you need to break it down for them. How are you going to help them? What is your unique selling proposition (USP) that sets you apart from the rest? Including information like, "We've been helping fire-damaged homeowners for years," or "We specialize in solving real estate problems on tough renovations and difficult improvements for homeowners." This will let the homeowner know your company specializes in improving homes that are in physically distressed conditions.

Examples of Offer/Benefit Statements

- Homeowner saves money amounting to thousands of dollars.
- We buy all houses in as-is condition — in any condition, and any location.
- There's no need to schedule multiple showings with nonserious buyers.
- We can make offers within 24 hours.
- We specialize in solving real estate problems for local homeowners in your area.
- We specialize in fire damage, mold remediation, and lead abatement.

Your offer should be tailored towards getting the reader to take action immediately. Remember, your prospects are constantly wondering, "What's in it for me?" Step into their shoes and imagine why they would choose to do business with you. Then craft the proposal around those reasons. A better solution is necessary for someone who needs to sell his or her property fast.

Call to Action

Your mail piece *must* have a call to action that urges the homeowner to act quickly. It should be time-sensitive to create a sense of urgency. This process should be goal-based; that is, you're telling the seller exactly what you want them to do. Convince them to "call today for more information" or "visit your website for a free report." These are a few of the most common call to actions.

Examples of Call-to-Action Statements

- Please hurry! I need to buy two houses this month! Call me today!
- Call today! I REALLY NEED TO SPEAK TO YOU!
- Act now! Let me help you before it's too late.

Contact Information

While this might seem like a no-brainer, many people forget to add their contact information. This should be prominent and positioned right below your call to action. Provide your name, mailing address, phone number, fax number, email, and website address directly following the call to action.

Guarantee

Companies are afraid of guarantees, but people *love* them. This will help your prospect feel comfortable and build trust that you really want to do right by them.

Examples of Guarantee Statements

- Guaranteed cash offer in 24 hours or less
- Guaranteed offer on any condition house
- Guaranteed site visit on your house for an offer

All of these elements are essential to your direct mail campaign. Together, they create a very powerful reason for a homeowner to call you for more information on selling their property.

STEP 4: SET UP YOUR INBOUND SYSTEM

Before you even think about sending out a direct mail piece, you must decide how you're going to handle responses. You need to have your lead intake systems in place prior to sending out any mailings. Are you going to take phone calls in your office? Are you going to use a call center? Or are you going to send your prospects to your website to submit information to you that goes into your database? We've listed a few ways below.

- Call center: Create a script and intake form so phone representatives can answer calls for you 24/7 and email/fax you the lead sheets for your review.
- Google Voice: A virtual service that can be redirected to a third-party number (your cell or office). The system also records and transcribes the voicemails and emails them to you for review at your convenience.
- Website squeeze page: If you're going to be using a website response option, be sure to use easy-to-type URLs, such as www.webuynational.com.
- Utilize a squeeze page website designed specifically to capture your prospect's name, contact info (email/phone), and address of the subject property they're interested in selling by offering them something for free. Once you've added this name, it should go into your

database, automatically triggering a programmed email sequence that kicks off as soon as the name comes in. This will build rapport for you and your company without taking any time or energy out of your day. You are leveraging technology to communicate the benefits of working with you.

STEP 5: FULFILLING YOUR CAMPAIGNS

Now that you've compiled your mailing lists and created your mail pieces, you're ready to fulfill your campaigns. Let's discuss the difference between outsourcing and in-house fulfillment.

Many investors choose to start by fulfilling their campaigns themselves, especially in the beginning. This approach may save you some immediate money, but you will more than likely be able to handle only two to three mailing lists at a time. A lot of investors become easily overwhelmed with the time that in-house fulfillment requires, so they eventually decide to outsource their campaigns to an outside mail-fulfillment company. Using a fulfillment company provides a turnkey solution to sending your mass mailings to the public. Although it will cost more, you eliminate the stress and frustration of fulfillment, and it's easier to implement multiple campaigns. An alternative to using a professional mail house is to hire someone to handle your campaigns in-house.

Typically, smaller mailings—such as expired listings, tax lien, and probate lists—are much easier to fulfill yourself. Some of the larger lists, such as pre-foreclosures, inherited properties, out of state owners, and absentee owners will more than likely require a mail house to fulfill.

System to Outsourcing (Fulfillment Company)
- Research and locate a direct mail fulfillment company to do your campaigns.
- Give them the marketing pieces to use as templates or use what they have.
- Save mailing list in database. This makes it easy, because when someone calls from your marketing efforts, you have their information readily accessible in the database.
- Provide the fulfillment company with your mailing list each week.
- They create and send out the mailers for you.

STEP 6: TRACK YOUR MAILINGS AND STAY ORGANIZED

Tracking and evaluating your direct mail campaigns effectively will allow you to determine where your money is best spent. The last thing you want to do is spend money and time on a direct mail campaign that did not produce any leads that turned into deals. Test and measure your marketing on a weekly and monthly basis, so you can make the necessary adjustments to produce results.

As we've discussed, most prospective sellers will not respond until the third or fourth time they receive a direct mail piece. If you don't develop direct mail systems, you'll have no effective way of ensuring that you reach your prospective sellers each and every week. Establishing these systems allows your campaigns to run on autopilot—and allows you to focus your efforts on meeting with sellers to buy properties.

Make sure there is a way of tracking the response rate for every piece of direct mail you send out. This is the only way to determine whether it's working like it should. Without proper tracking, it will be difficult to spend your marketing dollars wisely. This will improve your response rate and increase your exposure, therefore allowing you to make wise decisions with your marketing dollars.

It's also crucial not to have unrealistic expectations with your response rate. It's okay if only 1 out of 100 mailings gets you a handful of phone calls, and it is normally expected that 8 to 10 percent of your mailings will be returned because of bad addresses when sending bulk mail.

Postcard Response Rates
- The average fulfilled postcard has the lowest response rate.
- Expect a .5 to 1 percent response rate.

Direct Mail Response Rates
- Expect a 1 to 2 percent response rate on good direct mail. A 3 to 5 percent response rate would be amazing.
- You should be sending out around 3,000 mail pieces every month on average (Note: If you're fulfilling your mail in-house, you probably won't be able to manage that volume. However, 3,000 monthly mail pieces is standard when utilizing a mail house to fulfill your campaigns, as well as running three to four drip campaigns at once).

Consistency is the key here. Keep in mind you will likely get responses from your first mailing—but, often it takes a little more persistence to get through to some prospects. Assuming all sellers are going to be ready to sell the first time you send mail to them is shortsighted. Many people won't respond until the third, fourth, fifth, or even sixth time. Sometimes, sellers will look at your mail piece for a year or more before they pick up the phone to call you. In that case, *you* want to be the one still mailing to these folks when they finally become motivated; and they will remember you because your message has been in front of them several different times. Remember, timing is everything and circumstances change over time.

Here are a few tips that can help raise your response rates:

- Use live postage and handwritten notes.
- Use colored envelopes or odd sized envelopes.
- Adding objects in your mail to create lumpy packages will differentiate your mail from others'.
- Stamps sometimes outperform metered mail.
- Personalize the direct mail copy with the seller's name and the property address that you are interested in.
- Colored stationery/mail piece/letterhead (see-through window).

You always want to track your results based on the goals you set for your marketing campaign. For example, if you wanted to increase traffic to your website or grow the number of inbound calls, establish mechanisms that allow you to determine if web traffic or calls increased and by how much. If you wanted more homeseller leads, how many homeseller leads were generated?

Tracking your results starts with one very simple question: "How did you hear about us?" You must ask this question at every interaction (inbound call takers, web forms, etc.). I'd also recommend adding a unique response tracking system (i.e., website landing page for that specific direct mail piece or a unique toll-free number, etc.).

Direct mail marketing is one of the most cost-effective marketing techniques we can apply as residential redevelopers looking for our next opportunity and deal. It is a targeted marketing approach and can be very effective for testing and trying different marketing campaigns. Send more than one letter to a potential buyer, mail often, and follow-up. Direct mail is a targeted and very effective form of marketing to implement and find your next rehab deal.

CHAPTER 5

Finding Properties to Rehab

Online Marketing Secrets

Though the online world may still be foreign territory for some individuals, most people now find clicking and typing to be as natural as walking and breathing. The Internet is where they shop, read reviews on restaurants, or see what's going on this weekend. It's where they meet friends and maybe even their soul mate. We can and do use the Internet almost everywhere and almost all the time.

This has led to a fundamental shift in the way homeowners market their homes for sale, and how buyers search for homes. According to a 2013 collaborative report by Google and the National Association of Realtors (NAR), 90 percent of homebuyers searched online during their home buying process. Searches related to real estate on Google grew 253 percent since 2009. Therefore, having an online presence that will generate leads and sell your houses quickly is no longer an option; it is an absolute *must*.

DEVELOPING A COMPANY WEBSITE

Although making phone calls and talking to people in person is a crucial element in building your business, you need to establish a foundation first and building a professional company website is the cement in that foundation. In this day and age, having a website for your real estate investing business is a necessity. In most cases, when someone gets wind of a product or a company, the first thing they do is look it up on the Internet. You need to make sure you are taking advantage of your target audience's tendency to do their research online. If you send out direct mail that only lists your phone number as a source of contact, you neglect a significant percentage of potential leads.

Website Advantages

- Lead generation: You can actually find motivated sellers online if you have a website they can view and where they input information. You can use online marketing to generate leads from motivated sellers and build a buyers list in an automated, time-efficient manner.
- Credibility: When you tell people you have a business, the first thing they do to check if you are legitimate is confirm you have a company website. Searching online is the litmus test for credibility these days. Seeing your company website and reading online reviews makes people comfortable doing business with you.
- List your products and services: A website provides a place to list and display all of your finished rehabs for buyers, private investors, and other real estate professionals to check out what you have to offer and see the caliber of work you do. Listing your projects with a detailed description, photos, virtual tour, and a map allows you to be selling your house 24 hours a day!
- Multiple streams of income: As your website gets more and more traffic, you can start offering referrals, affiliate links, and advertising on your website to bring in additional streams of income to your investing business.

I highly recommend using a content management system (CMS) to help simplify everything associated with publishing your written content, enabling search functions, allowing edits, managing the layout of your website, and many other helpful things you may not be aware of.

There are a few different CMS options to choose from:

- Wordpress.com currently boasts almost 70 million sites. It is popular because it is easy to use and free of charge. This service has been around since 2003 and has gained the most popularity among users. WordPress is a great starting tool to help with web design and functionality. The average set up time is around five minutes.
- Wordpress.org is web software used to create a website or blog and allows you to get what's called a domain name (yourcompany.com). You have to install a hosting company (like HostGator.com) and costs start around $4 a month. Set up takes around 30 minutes.
- Realeflow.com is a web software and platform specifically designed by real estate investors for investors that allows for website, content, and contact management.

Five Main Components of a Good Website

Of course, it isn't enough to just have a website. You have to have a *good* website. This is the most persistent communication vehicle you have with prospective buyers and sellers, so you want it to represent your company well. There are five main components you want to keep in mind when creating your own website for your company:

1. **Content.** Write your website content as if you were speaking with your visitors face-to-face, since this will make them feel comfortable. Make sure to cover the main elements, such as the property descriptions, the prices, and the benefits. Always remember what people are searching for and make sure to use those words in your content. Use targeted marketing copy in order to speak directly to your prospective buyer. For example, if you want to target homeowners who need a quick sell, try using the following title: "Sell Your House in Nine Days!!"

2. **Flexibility and Customization.** When you are creating your site, pay attention to the control panel and make sure you understand how to customize your content. You'll have to make changes frequently, so this has to be an option.

3. **Simple Navigation.** No one wants to work hard to find the information they're seeking. The whole point of using the Internet is to speed up this process. Your website should therefore be a place where visitors can get in and out when they're in a hurry. Usually, there is a navigation bar along the top of the screen or along the left side of the page. This should be simple to use and not over-cluttered.

4. **Multimedia.** A growing number of people prefer video over written content nowadays. You will need written content for your site to come up on the search engines; however, you should begin to consider using video on your site as a means of keeping up with the times. This is a great opportunity to take a tour of a rehab and show what you did and where you did it. Video allows you to show people that you're an expert. Of course, you always want the photographs of your property to be top notch as well. Give people a reason to browse.

5. **Lead Capture Ability.** Although you should have a separate site for lead capturing all together, you should always include an area to collect names and emails on your main website. Figure 5.1 shows an example from the CT Homes, LLC website. Notice how we offer a free newsletter and real estate information? People will visit this page for information. In order to obtain their email address, we need to prompt them to do so by offering additional free material.

Overall, your website should do three things:

1. Showcase your company.
2. Showcase your properties.
3. Capture names and emails.

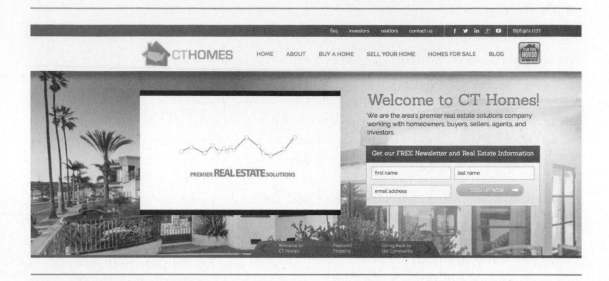

FIGURE 5.1   CT Homes, LLC Screenshot
Source: CT Homes, LLC.

Website costs can vary depending on what you need. The costs start when you pick a domain name (www.yourdomainname). You then have to pay to host the website and to provide ongoing maintenance.

Having a main company brochure website is important for credibility, but you really need multiple websites to capture the opportunities presented by buyers and sellers. Three websites are better than one. Therefore, you want to have separate sites for your buyers and your sellers. By directly speaking to your prospect, you can eliminate distractions and confusion on your website. If someone visits knowing exactly what they are looking for and gets lost in the content, they may leave. Secondly, you will avoid running into negotiating problems with sellers. If a seller is able to see that you are trying to buy their home to turn around and resell it for a profit, you will create headaches and conversations that could reduce the probability of putting the deal together. Ultimately, the three websites strategy will force you to learn and understand how to drive traffic to multiple sites. Additionally, it will give you a more effective online presence.

However, if you are looking to concentrate specifically on driving traffic, you want to use what is often referred to as a *squeeze page* or a *lead capture page*. This type of website has one job and one job only: to generate leads. It is referred to as a squeeze page because you are trying to squeeze out information. When a person visits a squeeze page, they are required to provide their first name, last name, email, and zip code. Squeeze pages are single-action

FIGURE 5.2 Seller Squeeze Page

websites. Once the information is submitted, it is added to your list and they receive an email. Once they complete this initial step, it is a good idea to then have another form where the person is prompted to fill out additional information. If you put a complicated form up front, people are less likely to fill it all out. However, once they've committed to the simple form, the likelihood of them continuing increases, giving you more information.

Figure 5.2 shows a simple example of a seller squeeze page to illustrate the simplicity.

CREATE AN ONLINE PRESENCE

There is a difference between a website and a web/online presence. Your website is where you serve a purpose and interact with potential leads. An online presence is your overall existence on the World Wide Web. When someone searches for you on the Internet, what will they find? Some people only have social networks such as LinkedIn, Twitter, or Facebook. Others may have blogs, which we'll get into later. If you want to be a successful real estate investor, you should have all of this and more.

Creating an online presence is all about boosting your exposure and creating a stellar reputation. It's not only how you market your business, but how you portray your own personal brand. You can enhance your presence by establishing a website as your base, and then building off of that base with links to drive traffic to your networks (social media profiles, squeeze page, blog, etc.).

Developing an online presence is not a tremendous undertaking. It's something you can gradually accomplish in three simple steps:

1. Create a well-designed website to develop your brand and reputation.
2. Cross-link social media profiles, squeeze pages, and agent websites.
3. Use social networking to communicate with clients, post pictures, and deliver new properties.

Driving Traffic

Once your website is up and running, you have to start on the most important part—putting it to work. You not only have to be out there; you must be actively promoting your website and getting people to notice that you are out there. You need to drive visitors to your website. Thankfully, there are a few strategies you can implement in order to do so.

One of the most basic means of driving traffic to your website is to include the web address on *all* of your advertising and marketing pieces—business cards, direct mail, newspaper ads, billboards, flyers—everything and everywhere your name goes, your website goes as well.

There are also more advanced techniques for driving traffic to your website. The basic components of today's Internet marketing campaigns are known as PPC (pay-per-click) and SEO (search engine optimization). Both of these serve to increase your online traffic and your site's overall success.

There are multiple ways you can monetize the success that comes with website traffic. For example, you can offer banner advertising opportunities for vendors (title companies, contractors, lenders, etc.). You can even start listing other investor's properties on your site for a flat fee or a marketing fee (if a buyer came through your site), or even charge buyers a small nominal fee to access your exclusive listings, not available to anyone else.

The first thing you want to consider when trying to funnel online traffic to your website is where the traffic is currently congregating. One major aggregation of online traffic is Google, which hosts about 80 to 85 percent of all searches. When you look at a search result in Google, you see 10 results that populate on the first page. There are also paid listings on the right-hand side from Google AdWords. Every time someone clicks on a Google AdWord listing, the company advertising has to pay a fee. These advertised listings can also appear above the top 10 listings; however, because they are advertisements, most people ignore them. Your best bet is to be in the top 10 organic listings that are produced by a prospective search. Every time someone clicks on your organic listing, it is 100 percent free.

Now that you know a little about search engines, you need to understand how to improve your ability to use it to your advantage.

Search Engine Optimization

Search engine optimization (SEO) is the traditional method of helping websites rank on the top of the results list. SEO is not paid advertising; therefore, when you need to move up the search result ladder, you can work on getting your website more content specific. By adding key words such as geographic information and target niches, you can cater to the people who are searching for information relevant to your topic.

As with your other efforts, you want to monitor your progress to see what works. Search for yourself every so often and see how you're ranking. Remember, this is not something that happens overnight and could take a few months. Once you get things rolling, however, you will continually receive traffic. Search engines can be picky when finding relevant content, so here are some helpful SEO tips:

- Make sure to place in relevant content. Content is determined by the theme, the text on the page, and the titles and descriptions.
- Don't overstuff keywords. Search engines see this as spam.
- Keep your website's performance optimal and working properly. Also make sure that your site is easy to navigate and provides a quality user experience.
- Make sure to display content that can link to other sites as reference to prove your credibility.
- Don't place too many ads and make it difficult for people to find content they are looking for. This can prompt visitors to change their minds and leave.

The number one thing required for building and sustaining your online presence is *consistency*. You must make marketing a daily and weekly activity. Once you have effectively implemented your websites, regularly update your content with new properties and new deals you are working on. Keeping things fresh will not only help drive traffic to your website, it will help it stay there. The more you share about yourself and your business, the stronger your presence—and the greater your business's success—will be.

Increase Your Conversions

A conversion rate is the number of potential leads that actually end up on your buyer/seller list—the people you convert from browsers to buyers. This turns what you have (visitors) into what you don't (leads). In order to have a successful website and a strong online presence, you have to maximize your conversions. You need to look at not only the volume of visitors to your website, but the quality as well. It only takes 20 seconds to lose a website visitor if you do not instantly capture their attention and engage them. You can have a thousand people click on your page, but if they all leave before receiving your message, what's the use?

Your ultimate goal is to expand on your buyer/seller list. Many investors tend to focus energy on getting traffic flowing, and end up forgetting or neglecting what to do when it actually does. You need to have the necessary tools in place to convert your visitors. If a website has a low conversion rate, it is typically a fairly simple problem that can make a world of a difference and improve the bottom line when solved. Here are a few tips to improve your website's conversion rate:

- Keep it simple. The more difficult you make your website to use, the fewer leads you will convert. A well-designed page is accessible. Have someone on both a PC and a Mac computer try to access your site and make sure it works properly on all browsers.
- Be open and honest. If you are listing a property, make sure to include all the necessary details such as list price, square feet, bedrooms, baths, and lot size for example that a buyer or seller would want to know.
- Don't info dump. Although you want to keep your visitors informed, you don't have to overload them with *too* much information. The same is true when you're requesting information; don't burden the visitor with questions they don't want to answer. Gather the small pieces first (name, email) and collect the rest when they've invested a little more time on your webpage.
- Establish credibility. Having a web presence is your chance to prove your worth. Most people are extremely cautious when buying or selling real estate. It's important to establish trust with your audience right off the bat. Include an About Us section so that your visitors can easily read about your company and your background. Having testimonials from prior leads

can help to calm the nerves of a first-time homebuyer, or someone who may have had bad experiences in the past. Don't forget to include a phone number to call in case a question arises. Design and content also play a part in trust. A poor design will automatically signal an unprofessional feeling. Take pride in what you do and how you are represented.

- Be memorable. A good site will include good information and not just be an online catalogue. Figure out what sets you apart from the competition, and flaunt it.

Pay per Click

Pay per click (PPC) is an Internet marketing formula that is used to put a price on online advertisements. These ads are the sponsored links that show up when you perform a web search in Google or other search engines. This Internet advertising model is used to direct traffic to a website. PPC programs require the online advertiser to pay Internet publishers an agreed-upon rate for when an ad is clicked. This rate is paid regardless of whether a sale is made.

Typically, PPC works like an auction. Advertisers place bids on keywords or phrases that they believe will target the audience. This allows advertisers to reach a target population while only paying when their ad is clicked. The major heavyweight in this industry is Google AdWords, which we've touched on briefly. With Google AdWords, you can even show your ads on specific days of the week or hours in a day. This is an easy and cost-effective way to get traffic flowing. PPC marketing can also be very low risk because you are always in control of every dollar you spend, and you only pay for results.

Create a Blog

Another way to help you drive traffic and increase your SEO is to have a blog. Short for web log, a blog is a personal website where you express your opinions on a regular basis. Think of it as a journal that is available on the Internet. In real estate investment, you can blog about a house that you are rehabbing and update it each day. Constantly communicating with your potential buyers or sellers is part of your work. You will find that as you go, people will become addicted to reading what you are doing and actually get excited about a property that they've yet to step foot in.

Blogging not only offers traffic generation but SEO benefits as well, both of which are ongoing. For example, if you write about a foreclosed house in California, and someone searches for foreclosures in California, guess what shows up? Keep in mind that once a post is made, it will keep working for you forever, unless you take it down. Compare that to any other type of marketing you may be considering for your real estate investing company. Then take into account the number of ways each of your blog posts can be shared and spun to attract more traffic and generate more real estate investing leads. This includes syndicating your blogs to your social media profiles, and even using them to increase the effectiveness of your email marketing campaigns. Although you are encouraged to first try blogging for free and on your own, you can certainly hire a professional writer if you run into trouble finding things to write, or even how to put your thoughts into words. Most investors do start out by hiring ghostwriters to blog for them or they simply repost articles and other investors blog posts.

Tracking and Retention

You need to know whether or not your marketing efforts are bringing in leads. Therefore, it is imperative to have the right tools in place to measure your success based on the goals that you've set. Many people make the mistake of only tracking small pieces of information. You need to know if web traffic has increased or decreased, and by how much. If you want more homeseller leads, you will need to know how many were generated. The percentage of repeat visitors tells you whether you are engaging visitors early in the process and bringing them back. A high bounce rate indicates pages that are failing to deliver on their promises. There are several free and user-friendly options to get you started on this. Some of the most popular options are Google Analytics, Alexa, StatCounter, and Sitemeter. Make sure to do your research and figure out what works best for your business.

SOCIAL MEDIA AND ONLINE COMMUNITIES

When looking for a simple and effective marketing technique, look no further than social media. Some real estate investors may be skeptical about incorporating social media sites into their marketing plan, but this method has become one of the most efficient means of marketing a real estate business. If you haven't heard of Facebook, Twitter, LinkedIn, Pinterest, or Instagram yet, then you are missing out on some major opportunities to find buyers, sellers, and even potential funding partners.

Social networking sites provide more than an opportunity for you to capture leads; they are also a source of limitless marketing for your company, yourself, and most importantly your credibility. Remember, there is a lot of stress involved with buying, selling, and even renting. People are more inclined to turn to social sites for recommendations. Getting your name out there shows potential buyers, sellers, and partners who you and your business are. It also positions you to receive comments and endorsements from other people, which only serves to enhance your reputation. Here is a brief overview of the most popular social media sites you should utilize:

- Facebook is the largest social network currently available. It is a private social space for people to communicate with friends, family, and even coworkers. You are able to friend others in order to have access to what they display on their page; in return, they can see what you have on your page. Facebook also offers analytics tools to help you track the traffic you are creating. Some businesses have spent a substantial amount of money convincing people to "like" their page. You also want to use Facebook to put a face to your name as an investor. When people type your name into a search engine, your Facebook account is typically one of the first items to show up. When creating your personal page, make sure that it is professional, yet has a bit of charisma as well.

- Twitter allows you to network and connect with other users, celebrities, brands, and trending topics. This platform is a common place for self-promotion. You can regularly tweet (post) a microblog of 140 characters or fewer about your company, which can ultimately draw attention to your website. The key here is to tweet often with short, helpful, and targeted information. There are hundreds of tweets sent a day, so don't get lost in the mix.

- LinkedIn lists your previous work history, skills that you have, and recommendations from those who have worked with you in the past. It is essentially your online resume, and you want to keep this as accurate and up-to-date as possible. This is another common site that will pop up when someone types your name into a search engine. Think of it as a more professional measure of your credibility. Here, you'll have an option for a status update you can use to drive traffic to your website.

- Pinterest allows you to "pin" images to your own virtual corkboard. Each pin is placed into a category that you can create—such as fashion, music, recipes, and so on. Once you've pinned something, it is available for the rest of the social network to then pin and add to their boards. When you click a pin, you are directed to the website from which it was originally pinned. For example, if you pulled a picture of a remodeled kitchen from a specific website, the pin would be a picture of the kitchen, and the link would go back to the specific website that holds that picture. You can create unlimited boards to highlight all the unique parts of your company. You could highlight boards by different rooms of the house such as bathrooms or kitchens. Place a link on your website to allow others to pin it and your fans will generate traffic for you.

- Instagram, which is owned by Facebook, is strictly a picture-sharing platform that you can use to highlight your properties and services in a very aesthetic manner and to show a behind-the-scenes look into your business. Many use this platform as a push tool as well.

Listings, open houses and tours are the main stepping-stones toward making a sale in the real estate world. This website is an ideal tool to use to make those steps much easier.

The key is to integrate all your social media into your preexisting marketing campaigns. For instance, if you're blogging, automatically post each new article on Facebook. You should also include links to your social media pages at the bottom of your email and the bottom of your website.

In order to improve upon your skills and network in the industry, use social networks to search for your contractors, your real estate agents, your investors, or any of your other key players. Sites like LinkedIn or Meetup provide spaces for real estate professionals to connect and learn from one another. There are even specific group settings such as the National Association of REALTORS on LinkedIn that are great places to connect with specialized professionals in the industry.

Once you have a new listing that you need to move within a few months, follow this simple process:

- First, announce your new listing on Twitter.
- Second, add your new listing to your Facebook profile and/or your company page
- Third, update your status on LinkedIn to introduce your listing.
- Fourth, post a picture of your listing on Pinterest and Instagram with a link to your company website.

CRAIGSLIST MARKETING

Craigslist is one of the many free online classified forums where you can find great deals.

Organized by either city or region, Craigslist unites buyers and sellers throughout hundreds of communities, and is an oft-used tool for buying anything from concert tickets to furniture and even houses. This particular classified forum sees an average of over 50 billion users each month. Craigslist gives you the opportunity to both market your properties and services, and provide links to your websites and social media pages. Remember, this is free marketing, which means you have open range to try out a variety of different techniques. There are countless ads you can produce, so it is a great way to start having your business working for you.

Searching for Deals

When searching for great deals on Craigslist, you can actually respond to house-for-sale ads yourself, instead of just waiting for people to call you. In order to generate leads, head into the apartments/housing section where you may find individuals listing properties for rent. Most often, these are properties from homeowners who may be facing financial distress and are trying to rent their properties as a last effort to save them.

The exact search terms are important when searching for seller leads on Craigslist. Instead of just searching for generic terms like houses for sale that focus just on the actual property, you should use search terms that are geared toward locating the motivated seller.

- Motivated seller
- Rent to own
- Take over payments
- Owner will finance
- Seller will carry second
- Need to sell quickly
- Lease option
- Owner desperate
- All offers welcome
- Considering all offers
- Will sell on terms
- House must go
- OBO (Or Best Offer)
- Please help
- Homeowner must sell
- Below appraised value
- Will sell for what is owed
- Assumable
- Flexible seller (or terms)
- Desperate to sell fast
- Creative financing okay

Create Your Ad

Craigslist is a surefire way to generate seller leads, but it can be a minefield if you don't know what you're doing. We've been running Craigslist ads for years and have tested and tweaked what works and what doesn't. So now that you've created your account, you're ready to compose the copy for your ad. Here are a few key tips.

- Create an attention-grabbing headline/title. The body of your advertisement can be incredible—but if the prospect doesn't even click on the ad, then it is worthless. When posting ads, it all starts with a captivating, attention-grabbing headline.

   Here are a few examples:
   - Having a Hard Time Selling Your Property?
   - Looking for Three Houses to Buy This Month!
   - Owe More Than Your Home Is Worth?
   - I Buy Houses Cash and Close Quickly!
   - Sell Your House in 7 Days or Less

- Include a CTA (call to action) in your ads. Make sure your prospects have an opportunity to reach you. You can either include your phone number or links to your website.

- Include images in your ads. When browsing listings, most people want to see if the ad has an image before even clicking the title. Craigslist also allows them to filter their search where they have the option to only browse ad listings that have images.

Make sure the text you include in the body of your ad is concise yet captivating. You'll need to give users a reason to click your ad and take action; here are a few examples.

Having a Hard Time Selling Your Property?
We buy houses, all sizes, shapes and conditions. We're the (your area) premier real estate buying company and can make you a cash offer for your house immediately!
Give Bob a call at xxx-xxx-xxxx

Need to Sell Your Home?
I BUY HOUSES
CASH FAST
CLOSE IMMEDIATELY
Call Bob @ xxx-xxx-xxxx
Or visit my website at www.yourwebsite.com

Looking to Buy Three Houses Immediately!
Yes, I am looking to buy houses in your area and can buy them CASH. No financing contingencies, and I can close quickly!
Give me a direct call on my cell xxx-xxx-xxxx

Typically, your classified will run for one week and automatically be taken down. Because of that, there are two things you need to do with your ad once created: repost and renew. After about three to four days, you'll see the option to do so. But keep in mind that Craigslist rules and regulations are always changing, so make sure you stay connected and up to date with the website.

When posting your Craigslist ads, it's vital to track the effectiveness of each ad you run. It's important to do your own testing and track your responses, as you will need to know what works and what doesn't. Tracking gives you the opportunity to tweak your messages, times the ads are placed, and so on.

Here is a recap to start your online presence:

1. Build your primary website.

   Establish credibility, showcase your company and properties, and include a name-capture tool.
2. Create squeeze pages.

   Keep it simple to generate more leads. Create separate pages for your buyers and sellers.
3. Increase your online presence.

   Work on boosting your conversion rate by fine-tuning your website. Be consistent with everything you are doing online and never stop learning.
4. Drive traffic.

   Understand SEO and how to pull yourself into the top 10 results. Start writing a blog, be passionate about it, and track all of your results.
5. Join social media.

   Set up accounts on all the big-time social media sites. Post regularly, share links to all of your sites, and constantly network.

Creating, maintaining, and having a presence online is a necessity to leverage all the benefits of today's online real estate opportunity.

CHAPTER 6

The Three-Step Rehab Deal Evaluation Process

I've structured the rehab deal evaluation process into three distinct steps, so you can quickly identify whether or not a particular opportunity is worthwhile. Your time is valuable, and you don't want to waste it.

During my first year of rehabbing, I thought every seller I spoke with had to turn into a deal. This caused me to spend a lot of time and energy working with potential sellers who never came through. Because of these false starts and miscommunications, I spent some time developing my Deal Evaluation Process. I share this with you to prevent you from wasting time—and to put you more quickly on the path to making more money.

STEP 1: PHONE ANALYSIS

Before you can evaluate a rehab deal, you've got to have a lead—that is, a prospective seller. This takes place while you are on the phone with a prospective seller or real estate agent. Locating a lead and then using a system to take down and organize the Seller's information is critical. My students and I use a Seller Lead Sheet to gather all necessary information and determine if the lead is hot, warm, or cold. To get a copy of the *seller lead sheet* I use, visit www.RehabInvestingBible.com/resources and you can download it for free.

This first step in the deal evaluation process requires you to ask a variety of deliberate questions to gauge the seller's motivation. For example, you'll need to inquire as to whether the property is in disrepair or in need of any updates to make it marketable and livable. Sometimes a person who has lived in a home for years will not realize it is in need of major repairs and will incorrectly inform you that no repairs or updates are needed. In cases like these, you are instantly back at square one.

In order to save time and get as much info on the property as possible, a better way to ask the question is: "If you were going to stay in the house for the next 5 to 10 years, what would you want to do to the house?" Suddenly, they'll tell you how the bathroom is outdated, the heating system doesn't quite work properly, the shag carpet has to go, and so on. By engaging their personal interest in the house, you are encouraging a more productive response. Asking better questions during your phone analysis with the seller will result in more detailed and honest answers—which saves you both time and frustration.

Here are some critical questions to ask and information to gather on the subject property.

Seller's Contact Information

Always confirm and know who is on the title and who can legally sign a purchase and sale agreement with you in order for you to purchase the house.

- Property Owners':
  - Name(s)
  - Phone number(s)
  - Email address(es)
  - Fax number(s)
- Contact person for owner if there is one.

Realtor's Contact Information

If the seller is working with a Realtor, you must get this information and bring the agent in on all communication you have with that seller. You will most likely be working with the agent to put the deal together moving forward.

- Real Estate Agent's:
  - Name(s)
  - Phone number(s)
  - Email address(es)
  - Fax number(s)
- How long has the property been listed?
- What price is the property listed at?
- Has the price on the listing been dropped?
- Have there been any offers on the property?
- What price did the offer(s) come in at?
- Why did the seller not accept the offer(s)?
- When does the listing expire?

General Property Information

This is the critical information you need to determine the value of the subject property compared to homes that have sold or are listed in the same area.

- Property address
- Type of property—single family, duplex, commercial, and so on.
- Style of house if a single family
- Square footage of property
- Number of bedrooms
- Number of bathrooms
- Lot size
- Garage and how many cars it holds
- Type of heating unit
- What type of fuel for the heating unit—gas, oil, electric?
- Does the property have a view or is it located in a special area?
- What amenities or special features does the property have?
  - Hot tub
  - Pool
  - Sauna
  - Wine cellar
  - Putting green
  - Library
- What subdivision is the property located in?
- What school district is the property located in?

Current Status of Occupied or Vacant Property

Is the owner currently living in the house or is it vacant? You may be able to walkthrough the house with contractors if it is vacant; this will allow you to complete your scope and fully prepare to start the renovation as soon as you close. To get details on this, ask:

- Does the seller currently live in the property?
- If yes, for how long has the seller lived in the property?
- When is the seller planning on moving out?
- If no, how long has the property been vacant?
- Who was living in the property before it was vacated?
- When is the last time the seller has been inside the property?

Current Status of a Rental Property

When buying multifamily units to rehab, you have to determine who or what tenants will come *with* the house to know what units you improve.

- How many tenants live in the property/unit?
- What is the current rent for the property/unit?
- Is there a security deposit for the property/unit?
- How long have the tenants lived in the property/unit?
- How long is the current tenants lease for the property/unit?
- Are the tenants in any Section 8 program or other government subsidized program?
- If they are Section 8, what portion of the rent is Section 8 covering?

Property Condition and Repairs Needed

What repairs does the property need?

- Has the property been updated in any way in the past few years?
- What would you estimate the ballpark repair cost to be if this property were to be updated or remodeled?
- "If you were going to stay in the house, what would you improve?"

The Seller's Motivation

Without motivation, you do not have a viable, win–win deal for you and the seller. So uncovering and understanding this motivation is critical.

- What is the seller's reason for wanting to sell at this time?
- What does the seller need to solve their current situation and move forward?
- How quickly is the seller looking to sell the property?
- What is his/her ideal closing date?
- What will he/she do if the property does not sell?

Current Debt against the Property

This tells us whether there are additional costs from late payments that will increase the deal's price. It also allows us to consider potential finance options on how we will acquire the subject property.

- What does the seller currently owe in total against the property?
- Does that include all liens and mortgages?

- Is the seller current on their payments?
- If not, how many months behind?
- What is the seller's monthly payment on the loan?
- Does that payment include taxes and insurance?
- What is the interest rate for the loan? Is it fixed or adjustable?
- When was the loan originated?
- Is there a prepayment penalty on the loan?
- Who is the lender?

The Seller's Lowest Price

This is when you have to ask the tough question of how low of a price the seller can agree to if you can close with cash and take the property as is, knowing you will do all the clean out and improvements as the rehab buyer.

- What is the bottom-line price the seller will take for the property?
- Is that price flexible?
- How did the seller establish this price?
- Could the seller do any better if you made them a cash offer?

Once you have gathered this critical information, you start to determine the as-is and after-repair values to understand if you are on track to a good deal.

Online Property Value Websites

While you're walking your lead through the Seller Lead Sheet phone interview, look up the property on Zillow (www.zillow.com), Redfin (www.redfin.com), Trulia (www.trulia.com), or a similar site. Use this to compare the estimate of online market value against what the prospective seller says he or she wants for the property. If you are a real estate agent or have access to the Multiple Listing Service (MLS), you can see the value by pulling comparables from the MLS as well as using the preceding sites. (We'll cover the MLS in more detail later on in the next section.)

STEP 2: DESKTOP ANALYSIS

If you received satisfactory answers to your questions during Step 1 and have decided that the subject property has potential, you're ready for Step 2. This should take place after the initial phone call with the seller, but before your in-person meeting. This is the largest part of the deal analysis and will determine whether or not you visit the subject property. This is also when you'll discover that 80 to 85 percent of the leads that come in are not hot leads, and will require additional follow-up to make them appointment-worthy. The remaining 15 to 20 percent of your leads will more than likely be hot leads. For them, you will need to analyze the financial numbers and create packages of comparable sales of like-type properties (also known as comparables or comps) and buying-appointment folders.

There are five critical financial areas to understand in order to analyze the numbers of your potential deal. When done correctly, this will tell you precisely whether you should move forward with this property. The only piece you will not have exact at this point is the estimated rehab, since you still need to visit and physically walkthrough the subject property. However, you can get a rough idea of the improvement cost through your phone questioning and analysis.

1. Property Values and Pricing

After-repair value = What the house will be worth when fixed up.

Current as-is value = What the house is worth in its current condition and state.

Estimated repair cost = What you estimate the cost of improvements to be.

Purchase price = What you believe you need to offer on the house to make money.

Estimated hold time = How long you own the property from purchase and rehab to sale.

2. Financing Costs

First mortgage and private money cost.

Second mortgage and private money cost.

Borrowed rehab money cost.

3. Holding Costs

Property taxes = Tax rate on property.

HOA and condo fees = If applicable for condominium or Homeowners Association.

Insurance Cost = The cost of insurance you will incur on the rehab.

Utility Cost = The monthly carrying costs, such as:
- Gas bills
- Water bills
- Sewer bills
- Electricity bills
- Miscellaneous holding costs

4. **Buying Transaction Costs**

   Escrow and attorney fees.

   Title insurance and title search costs.

   Miscellaneous buying costs.

5. **Selling Transaction Costs**

   Escrow and attorney fees.

   Selling recording fees.

   Realtor fees.

   Transfer and conveyance fees.

   Home warranty.

   Staging costs.

   Marketing costs.

   Miscellaneous selling costs.

These are the five financial areas to which you must pay close attention when estimating the outcome or costs of your potential deal. Our coaching students leverage our deal analyzer software, which allows them to plug in three numbers and spits out an answer in seconds. With practice and awareness, you will improve every time you analyze a deal by the numbers. Most importantly, you will avoid the deals that don't make you money. To get a copy of the *deal analyzer software* I use, visit www.RehabInvestingBible.com/resources.

Look Up the Property Tax Card

Before you start researching comparable sales of like-type properties you must confirm the information the seller, agent, or third party gave you about the property by pulling a property card. You can find this piece of information for almost any property in the county records where the property is located. These are typically available online in most states, and contain details about the property including: sale price history, ownership history, assessed value (for tax purposes), the heated square footage, the number of bedrooms and bathrooms, and much more. This is a good place to look for any inconsistencies between what the seller told you and the official tax records. Don't be afraid to call the seller back and verify information prior to meeting if need be.

Look Up the Property on the Multiple Listing Service (MLS)

The Multiple Listing Service to which real estate agents have access is a great tool for gathering information for your deal analysis. The MLS will tell you the number of bedrooms and bathrooms, square footage, the sales price, average days on the market, information on the area the property is located, and much more.

I always encourage new investors or someone on your team to get licensed as an agent to gain MLS access. As mentioned in an earlier chapter, I am not a licensed real estate agent, but I have sought out, developed, and maintained connections with some of the best investor-focused Realtors around. While MLS access is generally limited to real estate brokers, their agents, and appraisers, you can access much of the information on a variety of public websites (you'll see a more complete list in the section below). However, the MLS is a preferred tool because it is generally more accurate and current than most online real estate sites.

You can find all kinds of information in the MLS for the subject property, including the prices that similar properties in the area sold for in the past. The MLS and the list of other sites below also have pictures of the house interior and exteriors, which shows you the condition and work needed on the property before you make a visit to the physical location.

Any properties you use as comparables for your subject property should be within a half-mile radius and sold within the past six months or less. You must also make sure you are looking at similar home *styles,* with approximately the same square footage, and the same number of bedrooms and bathrooms.

Look up Other Valuation Sites

Although working with a real estate agent or getting your comps from the MLS is the strongest way to support value, there are other valuation websites that can be very useful, such as:

- Zillow (www.zillow.com)
- Redfin (www.redfin.com)
- Trulia (www.trulia.com)
- SiteXdata (www.sitexdata.com)
- RealQuest (www.realquest.com)
- HomeGain (www.homegain.com)
- Homesnap (www.homesnap.com)
- FlipComp (to see if FlipComp is available in your area, visit www.flipcomp.com)

The information from the preceding websites, in addition to the information you gain from a seller when you complete the Seller Lead phone call, will give you an initial barometer about the details and value of the subject property. However, you'll want to dig a little deeper to confirm these numbers.

A few tips when doing your desktop evaluation: If the prospect wants a dollar amount that matches or exceeds the online market value from comparables, or is not much under, you'll immediately know that the deal is unlikely to meet your profitability goals and needs further discussion if it's going to benefit both you and the seller. Not all properties will result in a deal. If there is not a driving motivation, it may be best for that seller to explore the option of listing the property on the MLS and seeing what, if any, price will be offered on the open market.

If the lead gives you a price that is significantly less than the market value you found online, there is a strong indication that it is a hot lead. In this case, you should push for an immediate appointment to meet with the seller and get an in-person look at the property. I have a 50 percent rule in my office. If I am on the phone with a seller and the requested sale price is 50 percent lower than the online value I see upon property look up, I'll set an appointment. These are the opportunities that are most likely to pay off for everyone involved.

I highly recommend that you use two monitors, or a laptop and a desktop, when you're doing quick property lookups. Have a website open, like Zillow or the MLS, on one screen and your database on the other screen to increase efficiency in analyzing deals. Remember, if you can't figure out if it's a deal within 24 hours or less, someone else will.

Classify Your Leads and Follow-up

Running comparables will tell you whether or not you should even move forward with the next step in the deal evaluation process. Next, you'll need to determine which type of lead you're dealing with: Hot leads, warm leads, cold leads, and agent-referral leads. Here's a brief description of each:

- Hot lead: This is a lead that makes you feel so good that you want to set an appointment for an in-person meeting—the sooner the better.
  TIP: This is a lead you more than likely set an appointment with on the first phone call.
- Warm lead: This is a lead who compels you to make a verbal offer before you set an appointment for an in-person meeting. The response will determine whether or not it's worth your time to meet with the lead.

- Cold lead: This involves an unmotivated seller who is ambivalent to your interest in the property, or whose price doesn't make financial sense for you.
- Agent-referral lead: This is a seller with low motivation and who has time to market and sell their property on the open market. These are deals that are not listed on the MLS that you can refer to a Realtor with whom you work. This allows the seller an outlet to see if their property sells on the MLS and at what price.

Create a Comparables Package

If you've decided you have a good lead and the property is worth an in-person visit, then it's time to compile all the information you've gathered into what I call a comparables (or comp) package. This helps you determine your final after-repair value appraisal at the property.

The following criteria are the critical pieces of information you need to evaluate the subject property and the comparables:

- Types of comparables
  - Sold, deposit, and active.
- Type of property
  - Same as the subject property.
- Sale date
  - Within the past six months.
- Radius search
  - Less than a half-mile radius from the subject property.
  - Must be in the same city.
  - Ideally in the same neighborhood, subdivision, and school district.
- Square-footage range
  - 80 to 120 percent of the square footage of the subject property.
- Bedrooms and bathrooms
  - Same as the subject property.

These are the base criteria for searching and viewing your comparables to determine the value of your potentially finished rehab on the subject property. Once you have analyzed and pulled this information together, you are ready to create the comp package. It should contain the documents you will use to help determine your offer when you meet with the seller at the property, including:

- Property card—A printout of the property card that has details about the property.
- MLS comps—If the property is listed, you want to have the listing sheet printed out with all the property information. You also want to print out each individual comparable property you are using to estimate the value of your subject property.
- Map of MLS property comps—In most multiple listing services, there should be a map view that plots the comparables you selected and merges that data onto a map you can print out.
- Additional comparable websites—On websites such as Trulia, SiteXdata, RealQuest, Home-Gain, FlipComp comps, Zillow.com, and Trulia, you can possibly find sold comparables that were not found within the MLS.
- Deal Analyzer for Flips—I use a template Excel spreadsheet I created to estimate the profit potential of a deal. This helps me formulate an appropriate offer. To get a copy of the *deal analyzer software* I use, visit www.RehabInvestingBible.com/resources.
- Property Repair Sheet—This is the sheet I use to get a quick estimate of repairs. To get a copy of the *property repair sheet* I use, visit www.RehabInvestingBible.com/resources.

Preparing for Your Meeting with the Seller

The easiest way to lose a deal is to arrive unprepared to a seller meeting. I've provided you with the information you need since I can recall doing exactly the opposite when I started out. The seller was asking good questions when I arrived at the meeting and I didn't have good answers. I wasn't all that upset, however, and remember leaving the meeting not really caring that I had failed to close the deal together. A few months later, I bumped into a friend and fellow investor at my local real estate club. She had actually met with the same seller but had better information and understood all the comps and had a better grasp on the after-repaired value of the subject house. My friend and fellow investor put the deal under contract and closed on that deal. She then completed an easy rehab and sold the project for a $34,000 profit. Needless to say, that was the last time I went into a seller meeting not prepared.

Create a Buying-Appointment Folder

You need a complete comp package so you make a very accurate value determination when you compare the property before meeting with the seller. You want to make sure you have the documents within the buying-appointment folder so you are ready to sign a contract at the kitchen table when you get the seller to commit to selling the property. I once had a seller commit to the deal verbally, but I'd accidentally forgotten the second page to my Purchase and Sale agreement. So, I ran back to my office to pick it up, and during the 15 minutes I was gone the seller changed his mind. Let that be a lesson that you must always stay organized and always be prepared!

The buying-appointment folder contains all the necessary paperwork to sign a contract with the seller, including:

- Purchase and Sale agreement—The contract used to control the property.
- Backup Purchase and Sale agreement—A backup contract used to control the property.
- Additional creative contracts (e.g., owner-finance, subject-to, etc.).
- Authorization to release information from mortgage company—The document you need signed by the seller to speak to their mortgage company on their behalf.
- Property disclosures—Standard documents the seller signs to disclose property defects.
- Authorization to release information from the bank—The document you need signed by the seller to speak to their bank on their behalf.
- Affidavit of Purchase and Sale agreement—The document that protects your contractual interest in the property that can be recorded on the land records.
- Leave-with-seller credibility packet—This packet has information about your company that you leave with the seller in case they aren't ready to accept your offer yet.

I always recommend using the standard local Realtor purchase and sale agreement when you meet with a homeowner. Most people and professionals are familiar with the Realtor Association contract in your area, so it is the path of least resistance. Make sure you have several contracts with you, including creative contracts such as owner financing, subject to, and options contracts. You never know when you will need them. *Always see your local investment attorney/title company to have these documents created or reviewed*.

STEP 3: IN-PERSON ANALYSIS

This stage of the deal evaluation process starts 30 to 45 minutes before your meeting with the seller, and it extends to your in-person meeting in his or her home. During this stage, you will perform a prevaluation en route to your meeting. You'll then walk the property and see if it matches up to the seller's description while you determine a more accurate value. During the course of your meeting, it's imperative you take the opportunity to build rapport and trust with the seller.

Property Prevaluation

As you are driving over to your in-person meeting with the seller or Realtor, conduct a prevaluation of the subject property by driving by the following places:

- The closed comparables.
- The pending sales.
- The active listings.
- The subject property.

Once you've completed all your drive-by analyses, make sure you re-analyze your as-is value. It's important to check for inconsistencies with the subject property and the surrounding homes. This is the time to make sure your exit strategy is still the best option—after you've seen the surrounding area.

Buying Appointment

The meeting with a seller is an exciting event, since you just never know what you're going to find when you get to the property. You may discover that the property needs far more work than the seller let on; or you get the pleasant surprise of discovering that you've got a real gem that you'll be able to exit with minimal repairs.

The purpose of the buying appointment is to *build rapport* with the seller. You want to create a solid foundation of trust and goodwill that will help you successfully negotiate and close a deal—which you can accomplish by doing the following:

- Take control of the seller meeting by asking a lot of questions.
- Establish rapport by finding some common ground:
  - Kids
  - Sports
  - Local clubs and affiliations
- Build company value and credibility.
- Isolate and uncover seller motivation.
- Determine needed repairs.
- Adjust your deal analysis with your new information.
- Present an offer to purchase.

In Chapter 9, we will get into the details of estimating repairs and all the visual estimates you have to pick up on. With this deal-evaluation process, the training on estimating repairs, and our work with making offers, we are on track to put rehab deals under contract!

Adhering to a system to review, analyze, and evaluate your deals helps you save time and get more deals. Do as much homework and analysis before you get to the seller meeting so you are prepared and can handle any questions or objections the potential seller may bring up. Preparation is the key in analyzing and getting more rehab deals.

CHAPTER **7**

Financing Rehabs

How to Leverage Systems and Other People's Money (OPM) to Fund Your Deals

The biggest obstacle many real estate investors face when getting started with their first rehab is their inability to obtain financing for more than a handful of deals at one time. Mortgage lending restrictions can make things difficult and prevent investors from expanding their real estate investment portfolios. In order to capitalize on some of the best and most profitable deals, you will need to understand your financing options.

Financing is what makes the real estate world go round. Aside from getting a quality education, getting access to capital for your deals it of utmost importance to you as a residential redeveloper. Funding allows you to create leverage. To be successful, you need to be able to purchase properties with relatively small amounts of your own money. The question won't be about *how* to leverage when you're first starting out; the more pressing matter is finding the money to fund your first deal and get your business off the ground. The best part is: it doesn't even have to be your own money. As you learn how to raise money, you can borrow millions of dollars for your deals. Many new investors are relieved to find that you can acquire this money regardless of your current financing standings or credit score.

This chapter will explore a variety of financing options available to you throughout your investment career. From traditional to creative financing, I've tried them all and found out that it doesn't take money to make money. It takes a smart investor to use other people's money to make money. By familiarizing yourself with the methods outlined in this chapter, you'll be able to make better-informed decisions about which financing strategy will work best for your deal.

There are three types of capital needed in the business of residential redevelopment

1. Growth capital. This is capital for investments in your business education, systems, and technology accelerators so you can achieve results with more efficiency and more success.

2. Transactional capital. This is the capital you borrow and raise to buy and sell individual deals.
3. Operational capital. This is the capital needed to pay for your business cell phone, marketing campaigns, and other expenses for your day-to-day business.

Growth capital is the key. Your investment in this book is an example of growth capital. By taking the lessons contained in these pages, you will gain knowledge on how to start and raise money for your transaction capital, which allows you to buy your next rehab. Once you sell that first rehab, you can use some of that money to fund your next marketing campaign and other operational costs. The key is to *always invest first and foremost into growth capital*; this is where you'll get the resources and knowledge to tackle the other two capital requirements within your business.

FUNDING DEALS WITH PRIVATE MONEY

It didn't take long for my partners and me to realize we needed to do more deals. We needed better access to capital, so we had to create relationships with moneylenders. Developing these crucial relationships gave us the confidence to make more offers and do more deals. Not to mention, having access to additional funds insulated us from a lot of risk by giving our business more liquidity.

Private lenders can be just about anyone who is willing to listen to you and has money to lend. Oftentimes, you will create private lenders by actually teaching people how to make more than the half-percent return they are currently earning in their savings account. I love to give our private investors a good double-digit return. Who wouldn't want to earn 10 times more than what is in the savings account they currently have? You can let lenders know that every time they lend money, it is secured by real estate, which should be of great comfort to them.

Building cash reserves over the years also made us realize that private lending is an excellent way to earn a high rate of return from our rehab profits. Instead of just letting the money we earned from flips sit in the bank or buying our next property with the cash, we've discovered a way to actually lend our money for higher rates of return. We know how critical it is to have a debt fund for other accredited investors to lend their money alongside our own for a good risk-adjusted current return through Grand Coast Capital Group.

There are people out there with money who want to invest in something secured by a real asset. You have the chance to offer them the opportunity to invest their money in the real estate you want to buy. Private moneylenders can bring speed and efficiency to your transactions. Additionally, you will have much greater leverage when you purchase a property using private-cash funds. Many of the properties purchased by investors need a sale to take place within 10 to 14 days. Traditional banks require 30 to 45 days to close a loan and won't lend on rehab deals that are not livable, thereby making many traditional home sales fall out of contract due to financing. Being able to use cash allows you a much lower purchase price, and reduces your overall risk.

How to Use Private Money

Private lender funds will be primarily allocated to the purchase price and renovation cost. At the closing, the lender will receive a mortgage on the home along with a promissory note. You will then go about your normal renovation process. Many lenders will lend at a percentage of the after-repair value (estimated sales price upon completed rehab), typically 70 to 80 percent.

Here is an example of a deal with numbers:

- Purchase price: $150,000
- Estimated rehab: $25,000
- After-repair value: $250,000

Private lender at 70 percent of $250,000 = $175,000 private lender loan

So the loan from the private lender is $175,000 and covers the purchase price and allows you to finance the additional $25,000 needed for rehab. Again in this example, the private lender gets two documents:

1. A promissory note. This has all the details of amount, interest, timeline, and terms in which you will pay the money back
2. A copy of the lender's mortgage/trust deed. This is the actual security instrument that gets filed on the land records to secure the lender's interest and position in your property.

In addition to the promissory note and mortgage/trust deed, you will add the private lender to your property insurance as a loss payee. This way, if anything happens to the house, the insurance company will pay back the loan before they give you any money. This is important to understand, as it reduces the lender's risk when the proper controls are in place.

Once you complete the renovation phase, you list and sell the property. When you are able to close on the property with a buyer, the lender receives their principle plus interest payment. You want to make sure this process runs smoothly, especially with private moneylenders. Once you've been successful in doing your first deal with a private lender, it's important to build a long-term, mutually beneficial relationship so the lender will keep coming back to you.

What's in It for the Lender?

The private moneylender can benefit greatly from investing their capital. Essentially, investing private money is the lender's opportunity to become the bank and reap interest just like a bank would. A real estate mortgage/trust deed provides them with security instruments they simply won't get with other investments. Your lender also has added layers of protection because of how you buy and because of the fact that they only lend at a percentage of the after-repair value. They have recourse available to them in case you were to default on the loan. Your lender can relax while the money is secured by a real asset, which is the property itself.

You, on the other hand, provide them with an opportunity to make interest on their idle money. Typically, private moneylenders will want between 6 and 12 percent interest. In exchange for lending you the money for the deal, you will give them a promissory note and a mortgage or trust deed on the property. Again, they will be named in the insurance policy in case something happens to the property while you own it as a loss payee. Finally, some private lenders will want you to personally guarantee the loan, meaning your own house or other assets secure the loan—but everything is negotiable.

Lenders also love clients like you who repeatedly borrow funds because it gives them an opportunity to become a bank and reap interest. It is important to understand that both parties benefit from their involvement. There is no other investment vehicle like this.

How Do Private Lenders Fund Deals?

Most private lenders use cash held in most types of bank accounts. These can be accessed quickly and can fund your deals in minutes, instead of hours or days. Fees are generally minimal for wire transfers and cashier's checks. These can be checking accounts, savings accounts, or money market accounts.

Home Equity Line of Credit

A home equity line of credit is a very powerful source of funding that many people have and don't even think of. Unleveraged equity is dead money that isn't making any interest, and that you can easily tap into. It's a way to make sure you're in first position when we're ready to pull the trigger on a property.

For example, ask people if they own the home where they live—and if they answer yes, ask them what they think their house is worth and what outstanding debt it might have. Then teach them that banks love to lend up to 70 to 75 percent on second mortgages at the cheapest rates possible.

Illustration:

Bank appraisal value of house = $200,000

70 percent of bank appraisal ($200,000 × 70 percent) = $140,000

Less the homeowner's first mortgage = $80,000

Bank-issued home equity line of credit (HELOC) = $60,000

This homeowner just found an extra $60,000 through the education you gave them in getting a HELOC. By sharing this information, you teach people how they can make money with something they already have by borrowing from the bank at 5 percent and lending to you at 10 percent. That is 5 percent in found money!

Personal and Business Lines of Credit

Anyone with good credit and a stable income can obtain these personal loans and signature lines of credit from most banks or credit unions.

Retirement Accounts

More and more private moneylenders are using their IRA funds to invest in real estate. A self-directed IRA is essentially the same as a traditional IRA, but allows you to purchase a broader range of investments, including real estate. Most people do not know they can change custodians and invest their money into real estate notes and transactions.

Liquidated Securities and Investments

Investments are a way to put your savings to work earning more money. However, if your stocks and investments have not performed as you had expected, it might be time to consider other investments. As you know, you can liquidate stocks when you wish. Sometimes you need the money to purchase real estate.

HOW TO FIND PRIVATE MONEYLENDERS

Finding private money is not nearly as difficult as people think. While many people may not be actively looking to invest, they have money sitting around and may be open to investing with you if you just ask. After all, right now it's just sitting around not earning interest.

Private moneylenders can be anyone—friends, family, or perhaps others in your community who may be looking for a good rate of return on their money. There are those who have saved cash in their bank accounts or CDs, people whose businesses generate more cash than they need, people who saved money in a retirement account and want a safe return on their money—the list goes on. You might communicate with these people daily—and you'll never know they are interested in the opportunity if you don't ask. You have to spread the word about what you're offering. You will be amazed at who comes forward to express their interest.

Before you start reaching out to individuals to finance your deals, you've got to take the time to clearly determine what you're offering. Without a solid program, you can't expect a potential lender to jump at the chance to give you their money. What rates of return will you provide to private lenders? How long will they have to commit for? What is the minimum amount of investment you will accept?

Here is a good starting place to offer a private lender on your next rehab:

- Length of term: nine months.
- Annual simple interest rate: 10 percent.
- No monthly payments, all interest and principal is paid upon resale of the property.
- Security instrument is a mortgage/trust deed issued to the lender that is filed on the land records.
- Lender will be added to your rehab insurance policy as a "loss payee."

We've found that having a private money credibility packet for your business can be a valuable marketing piece when you are speaking with a possible private lender. You need to prove yourself to be a worthy investor when you first start out. This packet should include a little information about you, how the company was founded, and even your experience and education. You must demonstrate your knowledge, expertise, and even likability if you expect strangers to entrust their money to you. Use social media, blogs, and a website to build your branding and credibility. Having a professional private-lending guide will impress any lender. Make sure to include these items/sections:

- ☐ Personal company story
- ☐ Company leadership and team
- ☐ Mission statement
- ☐ Company credentials (including experience and certifications)
- ☐ Company business model (your overall investment approach)
- ☐ Transaction history
- ☐ Property case studies
- ☐ Testimonials

FUNDING DEALS WITH HARD MONEY

In addition to private money, you need to build a relationship with a hard moneylender. This is the most important money relationship you will make to move your business forward, even more so than with private lenders. Hard moneylenders are organized semi-institutional lenders who should be licensed to lend money to investors and rehabbers buying properties in need of repairs. They provide short-term, high-rate loans with fees that allow a real estate investor to purchase rehab projects quickly and easily. Usually, these are deals that investors might not be able to purchase otherwise through traditional lenders.

Unlike traditional bank loans, hard moneylenders offer short-term loans, and will also typically lend money for the costs of construction on a rehab property. This portion of funding is distributed in draws against work being done, and funds for rehab are usually set up on a payment schedule of work that has been completed. This is very similar to the payment schedule you would create for contractors for your rehab project. Draws and payments are paid after work is completed.

The name "hard money" does not imply that these loans are difficult to acquire; in fact, it's actually the opposite. While the terms and criteria for hard-money loans require more information, they are most often easier and more reliable than any other lenders. Hard moneylenders base their approval on the deal and the home first, and then they review you personally. This means that you may in fact qualify for a hard-money loan with bad credit, a pending foreclosure, or income that is difficult to prove if you have a great deal. The beauty of hard moneylenders is they understand the business: they focus on the deal, not the person looking to make it.

You're going to need to do some of your deals quickly, which makes hard money an extremely valuable resource for you. You can often acquire a hard-money loan quickly and close on a transaction fast (3 to 10 days to fund). Hard moneylenders offer a range of requirements as to how much they will lend, what types of real estate they will lend on, and minimum and maximum loan sizes. Typically, the loans are based on the comparison of the property value *and* the purchase price. Although all hard moneylenders lend on different terms, more often than not, they lend around 60 to 75 percent of the property's after-repair value. Working with a credible and reliable hard-moneylender is paramount to your rehabbing success. Our national hard-moneylending company, www.GrandCoastCapital.com, is a great resource for new and experienced investors to leverage and use throughout the country.

What to Know about Hard Money

Though hard moneylenders are more reliable than private lenders, hard money is more expensive than many other sources of funding. This is due in large part to the heightened interest rates trying to cover the higher risk. They are not based upon traditional credit guidelines, which protect investors and banks from high default rates. Fees for borrowing hard money are often three to five points (an additional up front percentage fee based on the loan amount), and 11 to 15 percent (or more) interest. Keep in mind that each hard moneylender will have different terms, so your terms depend on how the loan is structured.

Many hard moneylenders will only lend a percentage of the purchase price or that after-repair value—usually, around 70 percent of the value of the property. This will require you to fund the remainder of the purchase yourself, or obtain another type of loan, such as a private lender loan, to bridge the gap in second position. Also, since lenders want to get in and get out of deals rather quickly and want less risk, most hard moneylenders will only lend for 6 to 12 months. If you plan to rehab and resell the property in a timeline longer than one year, you'll need to line up less expensive private money, a credit partner, or wholesale the deal all together.

Lenders also look at the loan-to-value ratio (LTV) to measure the risk of their investment. The LTV for a hard-money loan is calculated by dividing the loan value by the appraised value of the property. The higher the ratio, the more difficult it is to get a loan.

Of course, it's important to remember that all lenders are different and specific criteria needed for approval depends on the lender. Due to losses suffered from hard-money loans, some lenders in the real estate industry have moved toward requiring decent credit scores, W-2s, and/or tax returns, your most recent pay stubs, bank statements, and down payments to reduce their risk; and some even ask for a personal guarantee on the loan as well. It really all boils down to protecting the lender's assets. However, there are still lenders in the market who only lend based on the property value itself, without all the additional qualifications that others now require. So you've got to make sure that you shop around to try to find the best lender for your business.

If you have a fantastic deal with a great profit margin, don't hesitate to call a hard moneylender. Five points may sound expensive, but when you look at your potential profit margins, it may be worth it. If you're not able to justify the five points, maybe your deal wasn't really a deal in the first place. Of course, we recommend that you use hard money with caution, and make sure you have multiple exit strategies in place before taking out a hard-money loan.

Financing Request Template Outline

This outline organizes the crucial information and data on your deal to make you look professional and provide all the necessary information to a hard moneylender, so they can make a quick funding decision to you as the borrower. The Financing Request Package (provided by www.GrandCoastCapital.com) should not be longer than five to seven pages. Here is the outline:

I. Cover Page

This contains the details about the subject property and you as the borrower.

II. Executive Summary

A brief narrative of the financing request that summarizes the transaction, including the property and loan specifics. The executive summary should be clear and concise, and gives the borrower the ability to sell the deal to the lender.

III. Property Description

This section should provide a complete physical description of the land, improvements, and the property, as well as any additional visual aids, such as photos, site plans, and so on. For development and construction financing, the borrower should include a detailed scope of work, broken out line by line, regarding the proposed improvements to the property and associated costs of those improvements.

IV. Location and Market Information

This section should educate the lender on the property's particular location and neighborhood, as well as include the general market information and economic drivers for the particular area and city. In addition, this section should include comparables (active and sold) that justify and strengthen the exit strategy proposed.

V. Financial Analysis

The lender is looking to review the assumptions made by the borrower when conducting their analysis, as well as any additional financial documentation that can prove the analysis.

VI. About the Borrower

This section provides a brief description of the company and the associated borrower(s), manager(s), or principal(s). The borrowing entity that is purchasing the property should also be included in the section. The lender is looking for company history and a track record, as well the backgrounds of the individuals in the transaction.

VII. Appendices

The borrower should provide all relevant additional documentation related to the particular transaction. The lender will typically request this additional information after initial review, but it is always good to have the information ready for the lender to review in order to expedite the underwriting process.

I have included the Financing Request Template from Grand Coast Capital Group. It is a proven system and layout that has helped investors raise millions of dollars in capital from hard moneylenders; you can leverage and use this moving forward. To get a copy of the *Grand Coast Capital Financing Request Template*, visit www.RehabInvestingBible.com/resources.

SELLER/OWNER FINANCING

When you engage in seller financing—also known as owner financing—you are borrowing money from the seller instead of a bank. You will make your monthly payments to the owner. This approach is one of the easiest and most cost-effective ways to finance a property, even if you have the credit and capacity to go to a traditional lender. For a seller to carry a first mortgage, they have to own the property free and clear—owing no mortgage and remaining in a 100 percent equity position.

The tricky part about this approach is that if you ask the seller directly, he or she is likely to say no. Sellers often reject the suggestion of owner financing because nobody has explained the benefits or proposed owner financing as a way to sell the home before. Most people don't sell a home all that often, so their knowledge is limited to conventional practices where the buyer goes to the bank to get a mortgage. However, a seller whose home isn't selling or is operating under tightened traditional lender guidelines might find owner financing to be a more attractive option. If a seller is motivated and has significant equity in the house, try offering full market price for the house. They have to agree to accept 100 percent of the purchase price, and then you sell them on the fact that you will be rehabbing and selling the property within 12 months, so they won't have to wait long for a full payoff.

Some pros and cons to using seller financing are:

Pros
- Zero money down is a possibility.
- Seller can unload the house, profit from interest income, and limit their tax liability by taking the sale proceeds in payments over a period of time.
- The seller may even offer you some favorable terms (no reporting to credit, small or no down payment, below-market interest rates).

Cons

- Savvy sellers may try to sell the house for more than it's worth.
- There may be something wrong with the house that the seller is trying to cover up by avoiding an inspector or appraiser's visit.
- Some sellers want large down payments and higher monthly payments.

SUBJECT-TO FINANCING

Another great strategy to use is subject-to financing. Using this approach means that you are buying subject to the existing mortgage that is already in place. The original terms of the mortgage are kept as is, including the name in which the loan was purchased. The only difference is that you are making the mortgage payments on behalf of the original seller until you decide on your exit strategy.

This is a great way to buy a house without ever having to apply or qualify for a mortgage. Usually, sellers who consider subject-to financing do so because they are behind on payments and aren't able to catch up. Others may need to move quickly because of personal life circumstances. The following scenarios will allow you to consider offering subject-to agreements:

- Foreclosure
- Illness
- Divorce
- Job change
- Behind on payments
- Old age
- Urgent need for cash
- Inheritance or probate
- Sudden need to move
- Owners don't want hassle
- Live in another part of the country
- Tired of dealing with renters

You may have heard of something called a due-on-sale clause, and you likely wondered: how can someone take over an existing loan and leave it in the homeowner's name when most mortgages have a clause that allows them to call the loan due?

As stated previously, banks aren't, and don't want to be, in the business of managing houses. They only want their payments. If the bank has a performing asset, they are not going to call the loan due in order to have a nonperforming asset. Because there is risk involved with subject-to financing, you want to make sure that you are using only this method in the right situation. Not every deal you come across will be an opportunity to introduce this option. To be clear, we are not assuming the loan—and some loan and mortgage covenants will have restrictions against assuming loans. Very few banks will ever call a loan due if it is being paid on time and performing. You must understand the possibilities of subject-to financing so you can recognize these opportunities when you see them. Any successful real estate transaction will cater to the seller's needs, and this situation is no different. There will be some cases where you will realize that a subject-to agreement is what would work best for your sellers and you.

The deals that are the best fit for subject-to financing are:

- Properties with existing or minimal equity
- Multifamily homes with cash flow
- Rehab properties
- Properties with minimal equity
- Basically any other type of deal where the numbers make sense for both parties

The pros and cons to using subject-to financing:

Pros
- You will own the house, but the loan will never appear on your credit report.
- You do not have to have good credit for this strategy.
- There is no limit to the number of houses you can own when the loans are in the other person's name.
- If done correctly, this strategy will provide monthly cash flow and equity.

Cons
- Do not take a property subject to unless you are 100 percent committed to the mortgage payments.
- If you don't make mortgage payments on time, you can hurt the seller's credit.
- There is a possibility that the lender could call the loan due.
- You own the home and cannot change your mind, even if the market changes and you can't sell the house.

- Make sure you check if there is prepayment penalty on the loan if you plan on selling the house in the next 12 months, so you don't get bit by that cost.

SELF-DIRECTED RETIREMENT ACCOUNTS

You can also get financing using the funds in your retirement accounts. In order to do so, however, you will have to structure the account as self-directed. For instance, if you were using your IRA, you would have to make sure it is a self-directed IRA. The difference between self-directed and traditional accounts is that traditional accounts limit what investments you can make. These restrictions are dictated by account guidelines and managed by a custodian. The second kind of retirement account you can use is a solo 401(k), which is similar to a self-directed IRA but is set up for your business as opposed to you as an individual.

You can use self-directed IRAs to fund rehab costs as well as the purchase. Leaving your retirement assets to sit in an account leaves an opportunity on the table. If you currently have a traditional retirement account that is not yet self-directed, you will want to contact a retirement account custodian who specializes in setting one up. He or she will be able to inform you of the steps necessary in order to move the funds in your old account to your new one—which will give you the flexibility to invest in the real estate of your choice.

The pros and cons to using retirement accounts:

Pros

- The profits you make on your real estate investments that go back into your retirement are tax deferred.
- This method enables you to enjoy the benefits of accumulating rental income within your retirement account when you purchase buy-and-hold properties.
- You have a safer and more tangible way of investing retirement funds than mutual funds or stocks.
- You can diversify your retirement portfolio in a variety of assets, such as condos, raw land, and commercial property.

Cons

- The IRS prohibits you from buying real estate for yourself if it's going to be owner-occupied. This means you cannot buy your personal residence out of your IRA. This holds true not only for you, but your spouse, children, and other relatives as well.

- There are significant IRS restrictions on certain types of real estate transactions.
- Any money earned from renting or selling the property *must* be placed directly into the IRA used to pay for it.

WRAPAROUND MORTGAGES

Wraparound mortgages are when the seller, who agrees to finance the sale of their property, incorporates the existing financing by wrapping around the current debt owed with the financing provided to the buyer. The structure is shown in Figure 7.1.

This type of loan is often used when an existing mortgage cannot be paid off. This enables the borrower to obtain financing from a second lender or seller. The new lender assumes the payment of the existing mortgage and then provides the borrower with a newer, larger loan that is usually at a higher interest rate. The borrower will make payments to the new lender on the larger loan, and the new lender will make payments on the original loan.

A wraparound is attractive to lenders because they can leverage a lower interest rate on the existing mortgage into a higher yield for themselves. Usually, but not always, the lender is the seller—making this a type of seller financing. In some states, escrow companies are required by law to inform a lender when a loan is being wrapped. If a wraparound deal on a nonassumable loan does close and the lender discovers it afterward, the lender may either call the loan, or demand an immediate increase in the interest rate.

The pros and cons to using wraparound mortgages:

Pros

- You do not have to deal with a bank.
- Your credit or income does not come into play.
- There is no mortgage originator, so you can avoid closing costs.

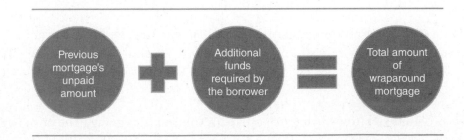

FIGURE 7.1 Wraparound Mortgages

Cons

- The buyer and seller have to depend on one another for a wraparound mortgage to work.
- If either of you fails, you both risk losing out if the property is damaged, foreclosed upon, or sold in a tax sale.
- Some mortgage contracts have a due-on-sale clause, which stipulates the lender must be paid when the property is transferred to a new owner.

Financing is an important part of real estate investing. As you can see throughout this chapter, we are in the business of creative real estate financing. When I started I did not have enough money to buy a house. What I learned and have shared with you is, it is not how much money you have, but how much education you have to leverage other people's money to fund your next deal.

CHAPTER 8

Writing and Making Offers

When it comes to presenting offers, knowing your numbers gives you the ultimate power. In fact, this knowledge is so critical that we've broken it down into a plug and play calculation. The maximum allowable offer (MAO) calculation is an effective method investors have used for many years. In its simplest form, your MAO is the highest price that you, as a buyer, can safely offer on a property. Using the MAO calculation eliminates the unknown and allows you to manage risk—which gives you the confidence to make offers without fear or hesitation.

KNOW YOUR OFFER

The MAO calculates backward from your profit potential. Since putting cash back into your business and your pocket are two of the main reasons you are rehabbing houses, identifying your profit potential is a good place to start. The calculation is a quick estimate that you can use when determining a rough valuation and initial offer on a property.

The MAO formula = (ARV × 70 percent) − Repairs

Here is how the formula works:

1. Calculate the after-repair value (ARV) by averaging the prices on recent and supported comparables.
2. Multiply this number by 70 percent or 0.7. (In many markets and price points 70 percent will not be an effective discount to actually get deals under contract. Higher price points and more competitive scenarios can warrant around 80 percent or more.)
3. Next, subtract your estimated repair cost to get your maximum allowable offer (MAO). Please note that the formula accounts for closing costs of 5 percent and a profit/error margin of about 25 percent.
4. The final number is the maximum allowable offer (MAO) as a rehabber you should offer the seller.

Now, let's plug in some numbers and see what the calculation looks like.

Known variables:

ARV	= $200,000
Repairs	= $ 30,000

STEP 1: Calculate your ARV
Determine what the market value will be.

$200,000

STEP 2: Create Your Profit/Error Margin
Multiply your ARV by 70 percent or .7.

$$\begin{array}{r} 200{,}000 \\ \times \quad .7 \\ \hline \$140{,}000 \end{array}$$

STEP 3: Calculate Your MAO
Subtract your estimated repair cost.

$$\begin{array}{r} \$140{,}000 \\ -\ 30{,}000 \\ \hline \$110{,}000 \end{array}$$

The MAO formula is the highest offer you can pay as a rehab buyer—which you can see is $110,000 on this deal. This means that, accounting for the 5 percent for closing costs and the 25 percent margin of error, you should not offer more than $110,000 for the property. Again, this is the highest offer price you can go up to, not your first offer price.

Always have an exit strategy in mind when working outside the calculated MAO. Identify the best way for you to make money and then do what it takes to make the deal. Always stick to your numbers and leave emotion out of the equation.

The MAO calculation eliminates guesswork and allows you to know your numbers every time you make an offer. That knowledge puts you in a position of power and allows you to make decisions and act confidently and quickly on offers.

MASTER THE ART OF SUCCESSFUL NEGOTIATIONS

Once you have a good idea of your preliminary offer, you should be ready to put on your negotiating hat. Negotiating is involved at every stage of investing, no matter how big or small the deal. So it should be no surprise that the success of a real estate investor depends on the development of negotiating skills. You can throw as many offers down as you like—but your ability to effectively negotiate with a seller will determine whether or not your offer is accepted.

Oftentimes, fear inhibits new investors from initiating a negotiation and prevents more experienced investors from achieving their ultimate goals. But the truth is that we've *all* actually been negotiators since birth. As infants, we cried to get our way; then we used hand signals, and eventually learned to use our words. We became experts in our teenage years, always evaluating our parents and figuring out what leverage we could use to stay out late or borrow the car—and when to use it. So, think of yourself as a seasoned negotiator—because in a way, you are. You negotiate daily with your spouse, children, friends, family members, and colleagues. And it's a skill you will only improve when you learn the right techniques and put them to practice.

DETERMINING THE SELLER'S NEEDS

Before you begin negotiations with a seller, you must first understand and address all of his or her *personal motivations* to sell. The better handle you have on this, the better you will be able to meet their needs and ultimately land the deal.

Beginning at your initial seller meeting, you should always try to evaluate the seller and their personality, and immediately begin building rapport. If there isn't a connection, it can be difficult to reach a positive outcome. Knowing what your seller wants and needs, and structuring your offers around those needs will give you a distinct advantage while negotiating. Understanding and directly addressing any concerns will allow you to be more successful at obtaining what you want out of the deal.

Researching the Seller

It is critical to conduct your research before attempting to make a deal with the seller. And in this day and age, information is at our fingertips. Conducting research is as simple as entering a name in an online search engine. Getting a feel for what their interests are can assist you in understanding the seller or agent before even meeting them. If your seller is active on the web, take a quick look at their social media profile to help you appreciate what he or she is interested in and help you learn more about their current situation.

Uncover the Seller's Hot Buttons

You will occasionally encounter sellers who refuse to cooperate or budge. In these cases, figure out how to uncover their hot buttons. Ask yourself: What is important to this person? What will prevent him or her from walking away from the negotiation? What are his or her emotional triggers?

Be an Active Listener

Listening is an art. Any negotiation requires you to be an active listener who tries to understand the seller's deepest motivations in order to discover their needs. Too many rehab investors blow a negotiation because they rush in and try to reach a conclusion without really understanding the seller's point of view. Someone who has honed their listening skills is able to concentrate completely on the other party. Make sure that you listen more than you speak during your conversations with the seller. As a result, you will more than likely uncover the seller's needs and concerns.

Be a Problem Solver

Typically, sellers call upon you because they need your help. They have a problem they need someone to fix and it's your job to immediately find out exactly what that problem is. You mostly ask questions like:

Why are you selling?

When do you need to close?

Where are you going next?

Have you made an offer on another home?

Have you missed any mortgage payments?

The answers will give you an idea of whether or not your seller is pressed for time or money. If they have children, you should try and determine the deadline for moving the children into a new school district if needed. Make sure to keep an ear open to understand how attached to the home the family is.

In addition to finding the seller's motivation to sell, you should also find their reasons for choosing to call you versus a Realtor, or trying For Sale By Owner. These details are important to have in your negotiation process. The more you know about the seller, the better prepared you are to enter into negotiations.

Occasionally, sellers may not divulge all information and may have issues they aren't being *exactly* honest about. Although a seller can make you aware of one specific problem, you may uncover other skeletons in the closet as you continue through the process. For example, they're not only behind on their mortgage payments, they are also going through a divorce or bankruptcy. The more you listen, the more likely you are to uncover any, and hopefully all, of the seller's real needs and concerns. Remember, you're not just trying to make a good impression; you're gathering info you need to put together a win–win to get your offer accepted.

Explain How You Can Help the Seller

After you've identified what brought the seller to the table, be authentic and show that you genuinely care about finding the desired outcome to their situation. One way to elicit this information is to discern what it is that they value. Is it time? Money? Health? Future security? For example, if your seller is going through a divorce, then they will more than likely be seeking a quick and painless process. Understanding their priorities will help you negotiate more effectively.

What Can You Offer the Seller?

Although money may be the first thought that comes to mind when thinking about what the seller is looking for, that isn't always the case. The buyers with the largest offers don't always win. Concentrate on a few intangibles when negotiating, and realize the success that can come with understanding your seller's hidden needs.

One of best ways to move things forward is to prompt your seller to make small commitments, and have a sense of urgency with selling the home. You can do this by offering little things like:

- Let them leave all the "stuff" and sell "as is." The distinct advantage we have as a residential redeveloper is that we are going to have to do a lot of the work on the house after we buy it. A lot of sellers are happy to hear they do not have to clean out or do any repairs to their house if they sell to you.
- Flexible closing and move-out dates. This is a way of getting your seller *time*. When they are looking move quickly, they will be grateful to save a mortgage payment, storage costs, or rent on interim storage or accommodations.
- Assistance with their move. Moving can cause major stress to a family. Offer to help them figure out what to do with existing appliances; schedule a moving truck, obtain boxes, and so on.

- Assistance with relocation housing. If a seller's move is unexpected, they may not have had the time to locate a new place to live. Remind your seller of your expertise and lend a hand in their search.
- Assistance with debt negotiation. If the seller is in financial trouble, you can offer to assist by setting them up with a credit repair program. Tell them that they are a client for life and have a positive result conversation. Advise them that after they establish credit, you can help them buy another home.

These are just a few examples of ways you can contribute that don't cost a large amount of money or time but that *can* help the seller to make small commitments to you. When you go above and beyond in this way, you stand out from the competition.

THE PROPERTY WALKTHROUGH

Once you've gotten a good idea of the seller's motivations, you should ask for a tour of the home if you haven't already done so. The property walkthrough is vital to your negotiations, because it enables you to see any needed repairs and determine the overall property condition prior to finalizing your offer. Point out anything that is noticeably wrong during your walkthrough, and take notice of structural problems, broken fixtures or finishes, obviously outdated décor, stains, major wear and tear, and anything broken or unusable—just to name a few. Don't be rude when pointing out the flaws, of course; but be certain that the seller is aware that you are in control of the assessment. You can use these necessary repairs to form your negotiations. After the tour of the property you can make the offer.

Remember, don't wait until you're on the property to decide what you want to offer. You should already have a good idea of what to offer based on your prior research before you even arrive for the walkthrough. You may need to adjust your number up or down depending on what you see, but a good investor always has a plan in place first. It's easier to steer away from an imperfect plan than to start from scratch.

PRESENT A STRONG OFFER

Presenting an offer is much more than just putting a number on the table. You're using your education, training, and creative real estate skills to help the seller make a commitment. Executing accepted offers during a seller meeting depends entirely on your knowledge, confidence, and overall ability to negotiate successfully.

You should never shoot in the dark when you are entering a negotiation. You have to know your terms and be crystal clear on exactly how much you can give and take. Where are you going to start? What is your final number? Never use the word *between* in a negotiation point, as in, "somewhere between 200 and 250." Without exact benchmarks, your targets are always moving and make it almost impossible to accept or deny an offer.

While presenting my offer, I focus on the fact that I am a *cash*, no-hassle buyer. A subconscious understanding of economics prompts many sellers to see guaranteed cash now as better than possible cash later—even if the guaranteed amount is less.

Be sure that you know in advance whether you are dealing with the seller directly or with another party, like an agent. Make sure all necessary parties are present at the time of the presentation. Typically, if there is an agent involved, you will be negotiating with them instead.

HANDLE OBJECTIONS EFFECTIVELY

The first step in handling an objection is to understand whether it is an actual objection, or just an excuse. If your offer is fair and holds value, the seller's hesitation likely stems from an overall lack of understanding—which would require you to provide additional explanation to put them at ease. Follow these key steps to effectively handle seller objections.

Recognize the objection.

You can uncover what is going on underneath the objection before confronting the issue by repeating the objection back to the seller to make sure you understood it correctly. You also want to make sure you are recognizing the question by following with a statement such as:

- Question: "I am concerned we won't be able to close on my timeline."
- Answer: "I understand your concern. However, we stick to our timelines with all closings."
- Question: "I am sad to sell this house and want to make sure it is rehabbed properly."
- Answer: "I totally hear you. Every rehab we take on is with highest quality team and materials."

Acknowledge the objection's validity.

This validates the concern and also compliments the person:

- "You bring up a very good point. Let's take some time to address that."
- "That's a very good question; in fact, it's the most common question that I receive."

Answer the question contained in the objection.

When answering the question that was outlined, make sure not to talk too much. Speak precisely and only enough to answer the question. Make sure that you keep your tone of voice positive and don't act as if you've taken it personally.

Support the answer.

Even after you provide an answer, you may still face some resistance. In order to keep things moving along, make sure you are able to support *your* answer as well. This should be natural for you since you've already conducted your research beforehand. Try convincing the seller to see things from your point of view. Make sure you are supporting your answer and not arguing their rebuttal.

Move On.

Finally, you need to quickly and effortlessly move on with the process—which you can do by ending your answer and then asking a question such as: "So, where are you relocating to again?" You aren't avoiding the objection, because you've answered it—you're just moving the conversation along.

Receiving a barrage of objections usually indicates that you aren't dealing with a very motivated person. If you find the seller to be too combative, don't be afraid to just let the deal go.

THE PURCHASE AND SALE AGREEMENT

Once you and the seller have come to a verbal agreement, it's time to put it in writing. The real estate purchase and sale agreement, also known as the contract, is a necessary tool in committing a seller to a negotiated agreement. It's crucial to have this document on hand and ready to prepare as soon as you have verbal commitment. Having it ready shows your level of confidence in the offer you've presented, which will compel the seller to stay committed.

Other than its obvious legal value, the contract has a psychological impact on the seller—as he or she is unlikely to seek other offers when they've signed a contract with you. If the seller does continue to shop around for offers, the purchase and sale agreement and deposit gives you a contractual legal interest in the property and, in most circumstances, protects your right to purchase prior to any other buyers.

Purchase and sale agreements come in different formats, and may sometimes be adjusted for certain situations. We do not recommend making changes to the contract without the supervision of an attorney or title company. Visiting a real estate investment attorney or title company in your area will make you aware of any rules or regulations specific to your city and state.

Any contract is a powerful document. Consequently, some investors become paralyzed by the formality of submitting offers, which can prevent them from closing deals. But if you think of the contract as a moneymaking tool instead of a legal abyss, you'll feel more comfortable with it. As such, this next section demystifies the contract by walking through it step-by-step.

Part 1: Parties Involved

The section shown in Figure 8.1 records the vital information for the parties involved. Though you should fill in your information in, fill in the seller's ahead of time—since you want to get it from the seller's direction to ensure it's correct.

This section will ask for the following:

- Seller information
  - Seller's name.
  - Seller's address.
  - Seller's social security number (this section is optional).
- Buyer's name (or entity if you are buying with an LLC, Trust, or Corp.). In this section, you should also put "and/or assigns," after the name of the buyer. Explain that you may close in an LLC trust or bring in a money partner for the transaction. This also sets up your ability to later assign the contract.
- Buyer's address.
- Buyer's social security number or tax ID.

Real Estate Purchase and Sale Agreement

NOTICE: This is a legal and binding Agreement for the purchase and sale of property. It is appropriate for most BUT NOT ALL such transactions. If this form does not appear to either Buyer or Seller to be appropriate for a particular transaction, you are urged to discuss the purchase or sale with an attorney BEFORE YOU SIGN. Most, but not all, provisions of this Agreement are subject to negotiation prior to execution.

1. THIS Agreement to buy and sell real property is made between:

SELLER: _____
(Names of Sellers)   **hereinafter referred to as "Seller"**   SS/Tax ID (Optional)

ADDRESS: _____
(Address of Sellers)   Town/City   State   ZIP

BUYER: _____
(Names of Buyers)   **hereinafter referred to as "Buyer"**   SS/Tax ID (Optional)

ADDRESS: _____
(Address of Buyers)   Town/City   State   ZIP

FIGURE 8.1   Seller and Buyer Information

Part 2: Description of Real Estate

The section shown in Figure 8.2 simply describes the real property that is being sold and bought. It includes:

a. Street Address.
b. City/Town, State/ZIP.
c. Property Description: For example, single-family dwelling; two-family residence; parcel ID.

Seller agrees to sell and Buyer agrees to buy for the purchase price and upon the terms and conditions stated herein the real property with all buildings and other improvements thereon and all appurtenances thereto, in the same condition as they were on the date of Buyer's signature, reasonable wear and tear excepted.

2. REAL PROPERTY TO BE PURCHASED:

   a) Street Address: _____

   b) City/Town: _____ STATE _____ ZIP _____

   c) Described as: _____

FIGURE 8.2   Description of Real Estate

Part 3: Included in Sale Price

The third section, shown in Figure 8.3, describes what is included in the property. A standard contract generally lists all the main and usual items you want to take possession of with a house.

There is also a section for additional personal property. This is where you include any additional appliances or furniture that you would like the seller to include in the property. It

---

3. INCLUDED IN SALE PRICE: The Real Property shall include all items permanently attached to the property on the date Buyer signed this Agreement and: all screens, storm windows, TV antenna, awnings, security, fire and smoke alarms, garage door openers with controls, venetian blinds, curtain/drapery rods, wall-to-wall carpet, plumbing and heating fixtures (except portable heaters or rented water heaters), light fixtures, shrubbery, and plants. Unless mentioned below, all personal property is excluded.

ADDITIONAL PERSONAL PROPERTY, if any, to be included:
_____
_____

There is no leased personal property except:
_____

FIGURE 8.3   Included in the Sale Price

is generally something you use when the end buyer is a retail buyer or a landlord investor. If it's a wholesale rehab property, it's best to ask the seller what they would like to take with them and if there are any items that would be easier to leave. In addition, there is a section here that allows for describing any terms related to the tenants currently residing in the property.

Part 4: Purchase Price

The section shown in Figure 8.4 deals with a crucial aspect of the contract: the purchase price. The first line includes the total agreed-upon purchase price. This is also where you will write the earnest money deposit that you will be committing to the property. In other words, it gives the seller good faith that you will purchase the home. Failing to purchase puts you at risk of losing your initial deposit.

Include the amount of any additional earnest money being submitted once the contract is accepted. Do not give the deposit directly to the seller. In the event that the seller is represented, the deposit check will be written out to his/her attorney's name as a trustee. If the seller is unrepresented, write the check to your attorney by putting: "Deposit to be held by attorney's name, attorney's phone number." In some states, title companies are used instead of attorneys. In this instance, the deposit check will be written to the title company doing the closing.

You should complete this section when obtaining financing. This section should generally be kept blank when you are a cash buyer. This is important, because it justifies your lower bidding price.

In this section, fill in the type of financing that the buyer will be getting to close the loan and the balance of proceeds that will be coming at the closing. In order to get this number, take the purchase price minus any proceeds listed in lines *a* through *d*.

4. PURCHASE PRICE $ _____, payable as follows:

a) By initial Deposit submitted herewith receipt of which is hereby acknowledged.................................$_____

b) By additional Deposit due upon Seller's Acceptance...$_____

c) By Proceeds of: Financing as specified in paragraph 6 below...$_____

d) By_____...$_____

e) Balance to be paid by certified check or bank check at Closing..$_____

TOTAL PRICE TO BE PAID (Must equal Purchase Price)... $_____

FIGURE 8.4   Purchase Price

The last line adds up all the items above and covers the full purchase price agreed upon with the seller.

Part 5: Deposits

This section in Figure 8.5 simply outlines the rights of the buyer and seller in respect to the deposits given. It also tends to be unique to each state, so check with your attorney to make sure they comply with local regulations.

---

5. DEPOSITS: The Deposit(s) specified above shall be made at the stated times. All Deposits shall be made by check, payable to the Listing Broker or the attorney/title company conducting the closing. All checks are subject to collection and failure of collection shall constitute a default. Except at time of closing, when the deposit shall be delivered to Seller or Seller's designee, the Listing Broker shall not pay the Deposit to anyone without the written consent of all parties to this Agreement. In the event any deposit funds payable pursuant to this Agreement are not paid by Buyer, Seller may give written notice of such failure to Buyer. If such notice is given and a period of 3 (three) days pass without Buyer paying the Deposit owed, Seller may declare Buyer in default and shall have the remedies set forth in Paragraph 14.

FIGURE 8.5   Deposits

Part 6: Financing Contingency

Figure 8.6 shows the section that will outline any financing details if the proceeds are to be financed by a conventional or hard moneylender. Generally, as an investor/buyer, you will simply cross this section out or check off the other box and write in, "cash." Once again, this is to make your offer stronger in the eyes of the seller.

---

6. FINANCING CONTINGENCY:
a) Amount $_____;   b) Maximum Initial Interest Rate _____%
c) Term: _____ years; d) Commitment Date:_____

e) Type: ____Conventional Fixed ____Variable ____FHA ____VA ____CHFA ____Other_____

Buyer's obligation is contingent upon Buyer obtaining financing as specified in this paragraph. Buyer agrees to apply for such financing immediately and diligently pursue a written mortgage commitment on or before the Commitment Date.

f). If Buyer is unable to obtain a written commitment and notifies Seller in writing by 5:00 PM on said Commitment Date, this Agreement shall be null and void and any Deposits shall be immediately returned to Buyer. Otherwise, the Financing Contingency shall be deemed satisfied and this Agreement shall continue in full force and effect.

FIGURE 8.6   Financing Contingency

Part 7: Condition of Premises

Figure 8.7 shows Section 7, which simply states that you have viewed the property in its current condition and have made an onsite inspection. This is mainly a liability release clause.

7. **CONDITION OF PREMISES:** Buyer represents that Buyer has examined the property and is satisfied with the physical condition subject to the Inspection Contingency if applicable. Neither Seller nor any representative of the Seller or Buyer has made any representation or promise other than those expressly stated herein which Buyer has replied upon in making this Agreement.

FIGURE 8.7 Condition of Premises

Part 8: Inspection Contingency

Figure 8.8 shows the section relating to any inspection contingencies and is used when you want your partners, contractors, engineers, or other individuals to inspect the property prior to making a decision. You may also use this clause to gauge the demand for the property and determine whether you can make any money by getting it under contract. This clause allows you to renegotiate the contract after you have a contractor or a partner walkthrough the property.

8. **INSPECTION CONTINGENCY:**
(a) Inspections shall be completed and results reported to Seller on or before 5:00 P.M. on:_____
(b) Seller agrees to permit Buyer's designees to inspect the real property during the period from Seller's acceptance until the date set forth in (a) above. If Buyer is not satisfied with the physical condition of the real property, and so notifies Seller in writing prior to the date specified in (a) above, then Buyer may at Buyer's option terminate this Agreement. Buyer may give Seller the option to correct the conditions that are unsatisfactory to the Buyer. Should Buyer elect to terminate this Agreement or Seller is unwilling to correct any unsatisfactory conditions the Buyer shall notify Seller on or before 5:00P.M. on:_____ of Buyer's election to terminate this Agreement and if terminated this Agreement shall be null and void and any deposit monies paid hereunder shall be returned immediately to Buyer and neither Buyer nor Seller shall have any claims against each other under the terms of this Agreement. If Buyer fails to notify Seller as provided herein, this contingency shall be deemed satisfied and this Agreement shall continue in full force and effect.
(c) If initiated below, Buyer does NOT choose to have any inspections performed and WAIVES any rights to object to any defects in the property that would have been disclosed by a full and complete inspection.

FIGURE 8.8 Inspection Contingency

Part 9: Statement RE: Lead-Based Paint

Figure 8.9 shows the section containing a federally required point discussing disclosures related to lead-based paint. Some states have a completely separate addendum for this line item.

9. **STATEMENT RE: LEAD-BASED PAINT:** The parties acknowledge that dwelling units constructed prior to 1978 are likely to contain lead-based paint which could create a health hazard. In the event that the real property which is the subject of this Agreement consists of or contains a residential unit built prior to 1978, the parties agree that each party has received, reviewed, signed and annexed hereto a completed Disclosure and acknowledgment Form re: Lead-Based Paint as required by federal HUD/EPA disclosure regulations.

FIGURE 8.9 Lead-Based Paint

Part 10: Occupancy, Possession, and Closing Date

Figure 8.10 shows the section that determines the closing date. Depending on the situation, give yourself at least two weeks to close on the property and tell the seller that you'll be closing as soon as possible. Explain that title issues or other attorney requests may hold up the closing, and therefore it is company policy to put down a date at least two weeks away. If the deal is tight and you know that you'll have to work hard to either wholesale it or obtain funding to buy, push for a closing that is at least a month away.

Section 10 should always be dictated by an exit strategy, the quality of the deal and the seller's situation. Remember, as long as you can close within a reasonable time (a couple of days to a week) of this date, you are within the lawful standards for performing on the contract.

---

10. OCCUPANCY, POSSESSION, AND CLOSING DATE: _____
Unless otherwise stated herein, Buyer shall receive exclusive possession and occupancy with keys on Closing Date. The Real Property shall be maintained by Seller until time of Closing and shall be transferred in broom-clean condition, free of debris. Buyer shall have the right to a walk-through inspection of the Property within 48 hours prior to the Closing Date. Closing shall be held at an office to be determined by Buyer's attorney in the county where the property is located or at such place as designated by Buyer's mortgage lender.

FIGURE 8.10   Occupancy, Possession, and Closing Date

Part 11: Warranty Deed

Figure 8.11 shows the section that states that the seller will be conveying the property by virtue of a Warranty Deed, which means that they will warrant the title. The seller warrants that he or she disclosed any known encumbrances on the property.

---

11. WARRANTY DEED: Seller agrees to convey fee simple title of the Real Property to Buyer by a good and sufficient Warranty Deed subject only to any and all provisions of any ordinance, municipal regulation, public or private law, restrictions and easements as appear of record, if any, provided they do not affect marketability of title, current real estate taxes, water and sewer charges, and current water and sewer assessment balance, if any; except in those cases where a fiduciary's Deed or other form of court-ordered deed may be required to pass title. Seller warrants that Seller has no notice of any outstanding violations from any town, city or State agency relating to the property.

FIGURE 8.11   Warranty Deed

Part 12: Marketable Title

Figure 8.12 shows the section that gives you the option to reject the purchase and regain your deposit in the event that the seller is unable to pass clear title to you or you are unable to obtain

12. MARKETABLE TITLE: Title to be conveyed by Seller shall be marketable as determined by the Standards of Title of the "YOUR STATE" Bar Association now in force. Seller further agrees to execute such documents as may be reasonably required by Buyer's title insurance company or by Buyer's mortgage lender. Should Seller be unable to convey Marketable Title as defined herein, Buyer may accept such Title as Seller can convey, or may reject the Unmarketable Title, receive back all Deposit money, and declare this Agreement null and void. Upon such rejection and repayment to Buyer of all sums paid on account hereof, together with the reasonable fees for the examination of title, this Agreement shall terminate and the Parties hereto shall be released from all further claims against each other.

FIGURE 8.12   Marketable Title

title insurance due to a lien or encumbrance that comes up in a title search. This section is an extension of Part 11.

Part 13: Adjustments

Figure 8.13 shows the section that covers any adjustments that will be made at closing. In many states, this includes taxes, water and sewer charges, estimated oil adjustments, and other similar adjustments. Keep in mind that these may vary in your state, so refer to your local contract to make these adjustments in the verbiage of this contract.

13. ADJUSTMENTS: Real Estate Taxes will be adjusted as of the Closing Date. All other adjustments, including Association fees, fuel oil, water and sewer usage, interest on sewer or water assessments, utilities, rent, if any, and issues regarding funds at closing and unavailability of releases at closing and like matters shall be adjusted pro rata as of the Closing Date in accordance with the Residential Real Estate Closing Customs of "YOUR STATE", as adopted by the "YOUR STATE" Bar Association, now in force. Rent security deposits, if any, shall be credited to Buyer by Seller on the Closing Date and shall include any interest accrued to the tenant.

FIGURE 8.13   Adjustments

Part 14: Buyer's Default

The clause in Figure 8.14 restates the seller's rights in the case of a buyer's default on the terms agreed upon in the contract. While this clause can be softened, most sellers' attorneys will require that you have some language outlining your obligations to act upon the terms of the contract.

14. BUYER'S DEFAULT: If Buyer fails to comply with any Terms of this Agreement by the time set forth for compliance and Seller is not in default, Seller shall be entitled to all initial and additional deposit funds provided for in section 4, whether or not Buyer has paid the same, as liquidated damages and both parties shall be relieved of further liability under this Agreement. If legal action is brought to enforce any provision of this Agreement, the prevailing party shall be entitled to reasonable attorney's fees.

FIGURE 8.14   Buyer's Default

Part 15: Risk of Loss, Damage

The clause in Figure 8.15 protects your interest in the event of damage to the property while you have it under contract. It also grants you the option to exercise your right to purchase the property in the event of a fire or other significant damage and receive insurance proceeds for such damage.

15. **RISK OF LOSS, DAMAGE:** All risk of loss or damage to said property by fire, theft or other casualty until delivery of Deed shall be upon the Seller. In the event of loss or damage independently appraised at more than $5,000.00, Buyer shall have the option to receive any insurance payment on account of said damage and take Title, or rescind this Agreement and receive back all Deposit money paid. In such case all rights and obligations of the parties under this Agreement shall terminate.

FIGURE 8.15   Risk of Loss, Damage

Part 16: Common Interest Community

Section 16 is related to purchases of condominiums or co-ops and is standard in many states.

16. **COMMON INTEREST COMMUNITY:** If the property is a unit in a condominium or other common interest community, Seller will deliver the resale documents in accordance with the local statutes and customs.

FIGURE 8.16   Common Interest Community

Part 17: Listing Broker

The section shown in Figure 8.17 covers details about any real estate agents involved, their contact information and commission splits on the transaction.

17. LISTING BROKER: _____ PH# _____
_____ Dual Agent—If the Listing Agent is acting as a Dual Agent, a CONSENT FOR DUAL AGENCY FORM SHALL BE ATTACHED to this Agreement.

COOPERATING BROKER_____ PH#_____ ___ Buyer Agent ___ Sub Agent

FIGURE 8.17   Listing Broker

Part 18: Property Condition Report

The clause in Figure 8.18 covers the property condition report and related statutes will vary from state to state. Note that some states may not have any relevant statutes.

18. PROPERTY CONDITION REPORT: Seller and Buyer acknowledge that if a written residential property condition report is required by statute and Seller has not provided Buyer with the required report, Seller will credit Buyer with the statutory fee at closing.

FIGURE 8.18   Property Condition Report

Part 19: Equal Housing Rights

Once again, this is a clause typical in many states. Most states have similar language due to federally imposed antidiscrimination laws.

19. EQUAL HOUSING RIGHTS: This Agreement is Subject to all local statutory laws prohibiting discrimination in commercial and residential real estate transactions.

FIGURE 8.19   Equal Housing Rights

Part 20: Addendum

This part covers any addendums and common disclosures included with the contract. For example, the multi-family rider includes information about any tenants, leases, or deposits. This section also covers disclosures from the seller related to the condition of the property. Finally, it includes provisions for additional addendums unique to the sale.

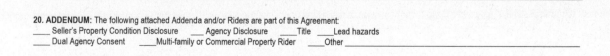

20. ADDENDUM: The following attached Addenda and/or Riders are part of this Agreement:
____ Seller's Property Condition Disclosure   ____ Agency Disclosure   ____Title ____Lead hazards
____ Dual Agency Consent   ____Multi-family or Commercial Property Rider   ____Other _____

FIGURE 8.20   Addendum

Part 21: Additional Terms and Conditions

Use the section shown in Figure 8.21 to include any situational obligations that the seller may ask for when negotiating the terms of the contract. These terms are usually the ones that cover the special needs of a particular seller.

21. ADDITIONAL TERMS AND CONDITIONS: _____

FIGURE 8.21   Additional Terms and Conditions

Part 22: Fax Transmission

This is legal language covering transmissions via fax as well as email. Submission using either method will be legally binding.

22. **FAX TRANSMISSION:** The parties acknowledge that this Agreement and any addenda or modification and/or any notices due hereunder may be transmitted between them by facsimile machine, e-FAX, or via email and the parties intend that a faxed document containing either the original and/or copies of the parties' signatures shall be binding and of full effect.

FIGURE 8.22   Fax Transmission

Part 23: Complete Agreement

Once again, this is legal terminology stating that there are no agreements outside of this contract and if any changes are made to the agreement they need to be signed and dated by both the buyer and seller.

23. **COMPLETE AGREEMENT:** This Agreement contains the entire agreement between Buyer and Seller concerning this transaction and supersedes any and all previous written or oral agreements concerning the Property. Any extensions or modifications of this Agreement shall be in writing signed by the parties.

FIGURE 8.23   Complete Agreement

Part 24: Notice

This section reiterates that any changes to this agreement must be in writing to be legally binding. Remember, this applies to both parties. A verbal agreement between you and the seller (i.e., price adjustments, closing time frame, etc.) is not sufficient. You should always get everything in writing.

24. NOTICE: Any notice required or permitted under the Terms of this Agreement by Buyer or Seller shall be in writing addressed to the Party concerned using the address stated in Paragraph 1 of this Agreement or to such party's attorney or to the party's Listing Broker or Cooperating Broker designated in paragraph 17.

FIGURE 8.24   Notice

Part 25: Buyer and Seller

Section 25 states that it is the obligation of the seller and the buyer to request a copy of the contract at the time of signing.

25. BUYER AND SELLER acknowledge receipt of a copy of this Agreement upon their signing same.

FIGURE 8.25   Buyer and Seller

Part 26: Time to Accept

This section simply dictates how long the seller has to accept the offer. You should generally try to cross through this item. This means the seller accepts it upon signing. However, in instances when the seller refuses to sign the contract, wants to talk it over with a spouse, insists upon a review by an attorney, or simply wants a day to think it over, you can grant a 24-hour window to accept the contract. Do your best to persuade the seller to sign without any acceptance contingencies. However, if he or she is unwilling to execute the contract, it is better to have them take action and partially commit to the contract than to walk away empty handed.

26. TIME TO ACCEPT: Seller shall have until _____ to accept this Agreement.

FIGURE 8.26   Time to Accept

Remember, purchase and sale agreements come in all shapes and sizes, and you may adjust some for certain situations. It is in your best interest to always have the supervision of an attorney or title company in your area. Doing so ensures that you will always be on top of all the rules and regulations specific to your area.

To get a copy of this boilerplate *purchase and sale agreement*, visit www.RehabInvesting Bible.com/resources.

Make sure to contact an attorney in your area and obtain a local contract that is legally binding in your state or have them review any contract you use.

As you become more and more skilled at crunching numbers and filling out contracts, you'll find that it is an integral task to presenting your best offer. On the other hand, real estate is all about understanding people. Each situation you enter will be different, and you'll grow more comfortable as you get more practice. Conversations will vary with the circumstances and the seller. Embrace each potential deal as an opportunity to improve your abilities. When a seller doesn't accept an offer—and trust me, there will be plenty that don't—consider yourself wiser for the experience, and then move on to the next deal. When in doubt, stick to your MAO, and don't let your emotions get the best of you. When you know your numbers and have built a trusting relationship with the seller, your offers should be stronger and your success greater.

CHAPTER 9

Estimating Repairs on Properties

Proficient rehabbers must hone their skills for estimating repairs on properties. Even more important is to categorize what is needed and what is not in a timely and efficient manner on your first physical walkthrough. Ultimately, your goal should be to estimate repairs in an hour or less while at the house, and determine what absolutely needs to be fixed or renovated to achieve the after-repair value (ARV), sell the property, and capture the profit on the back end.

The first time I estimated repairs, with no construction background or experience, I was not good. What I realized is that I did not have to be a construction expert to estimate repairs. Learning, practicing, and leveraging a system is the key for every new investor to accelerate their learning curve on estimating repairs.

At my four-day rehab boot camp with my students we take one day and physically walk-through my rehab properties in three different stages. The first house we visit using our repair estimate sheet and practice using the system and knowledge we have coached on at this point. All of my students practice on their own for 15 to 20 minutes estimating repairs on the subject house. New students with no construction experience who use our repair estimate sheet get within 30 to 35 percent of the correct estimate of the rehab. Then we visit the second house; the students take 10 to 15 minutes to estimate repairs. By the second house our students, having practiced only once, get within 20 to 25 percent of the correct estimate on the rehab. By the third house we visit, it only takes our students about 10 minutes to estimate repairs on the house. The best part is everyone ends up around 10 percent or so of the actual cost. After each house we take the time to explain the cost and actual improvement numbers so they can learn at each house. By investing a day of their time, getting the proper coaching, and leveraging a system, a new investor accelerates their learning curve and sets up their next rehab for success.

You do not have to be in construction to master estimating repairs. You simply have to leverage the knowledge I am going to share, follow a proven path, and execute.

Estimating repairs quickly allows you to answer questions and properly handle any objections you may encounter. If you can't answer a seller's questions about how much work is needed on the house you are buying and how long you estimate the rehab to take, you'll start to lose the momentum and confidence for getting the deal done. Answering the renovation questions your potential seller asks vastly increases your chances of acquiring your next deal.

THE GOAL OF YOUR PROPERTY WALKTHROUGH

Taking longer than 30 minutes to estimate repairs is likely a waste of time and energy. A good deal lasts 24 hours, at best. If you can't determine a deal within that timeframe, someone else will—and you will end up losing out. Your goal is to spend only 20 minutes to an hour and get within a few thousand dollars of the actual repairs.

In order to write a good offer, you need to effectively estimate three critical numbers:

1. The after-repair value (ARV) of the property.
2. The estimate of repairs.
3. The price to acquire the property.

We already know that making offers is the process of backing into our acquisition price. So we will need to know what price the house will sell for once it is fixed up, minus the profit potential and minus the rehab cost.

Using our maximum allowable offer (MAO) formula, we can quickly and safely get to a offer price that puts us in a position to make a profit as the rehab buyer.

MAO = (ARV × 70 percent) − Repairs

Illustration:

After-repair value (ARV)	$ 200,000
Multiply by desired margin	× 70 percent
	$ 140,000
Estimated repairs	−$ 30,000
Maximum allowable offer	**$110,000**

OUR SYSTEM: THE REPAIR ESTIMATE SHEET

The system my company uses to estimate repairs on a property has helped hundreds of thousands of new and experienced investors master the process in writing offers and getting deals under contract. Our Repair Estimate Sheet System, shown in Figure 9.1, is a short, one-page system we use to streamline the process of estimating repairs quickly and accurately. It keeps us

Property Repair Estimate Sheet

- Street Address:_____   Date:____/_____/_____   Inspected By:_____
  City:_____   Bedrooms:_____ Bathrooms:_____ Sq.Ft:_____ Vacant:____

Inspection Checklist	Yes	# Units	No	Repair Cost Calculations	Repair Cost
1. Roof and Gutters?				Architectural Shingle (rip & Re Shingle): Roll Over Existing: Gutters *Tile Roof: Get it inspected*	
2. Exterior Paint/Siding/ Stucco?				Paint: Siding Stucco: All New Stucco:	
3. Windows?				Vinyl replacement: Wood casing: Bay Window: Sliders:	
4. Garage Need Repair?				1 Garage Door: w/Opener Installed: 1 Car Paint: 2 Car Paint: Roof New: (Adjust up on for size) Build New: (depending on size)	
5. Yard/Landscaping/Pool?				Clean Yard (Easy): Clean Yard (Hard): POOL: Plaster only Landscape (Easy): Landscape (Hard): Pool Complete w/Equip	
6. Heating/ AC / need replacing?				Replace 1 Hot Air Furnace or Boiler: depending on size Replace 1 Wall Heater: New Duct Work: AC and Heat (install new):	
7. Plumbing Need Repair?				Plumbing: per wet location Replace 1 H2O Heater: Tankless: **Septic Inspection Needed**: Yes No	
8. Electrical Need Repair?				New Panel: (Aluminum Wiring Y/N) (Federal Pacific, Zinsco, other_____ Y/N) House, Rewire, New service w/New Panel: Fixtures:	
9. Basement Need Repair? 10. Foundation Need Repair?				New Support Beam: Seal Basement: Replace Stairs: **Engineer/Contract Quote Needed: Yes/No _____** Foundation Replace: minimum **Concrete Rules of thumb:** Patio Grade: (L x W x standard 4" depth) Demo: Foundation Grade: Stem Wall: linear/ft	
11. Interior Paint?				Interior Paint: Single Family: Add $ for additional prep if needed	
12. House Need Carpet? 13. House Need Tile/Vinyl? 14. Floors Need to be Sanded?				Quick Rule: Carpet: Ceramic Tile: Sheet Vinyl: Hardwood Install: Sand & Refinish:	
15. Kitchen Need Repair?				Single Family Rental: Single Family Low End: Single Family Nice: Single Family High End:	
16. Kitchen Need Appliances?				Standard: Higher End: Super High End:	
17. Bathroom (Fixtures)				1 Complete Full Bath: 1 Complete Half Bath:	
18. Sheetrock need Replacing?				Acoustical ceiling removal: Single Family Patch:	
19. Dumpsters?_____ **20. Decks?**_____ **21. Pergola?**_____ **22. Termite Damage?**_____ **23. Fence?**_____ **24. Doors and Trim?**_____ **25. Other:**_____				 Other:_____	
26. Permits/Planner/Architect 27. Miscellaneous				City: County: Permit Addition: **(Research Your Area)** Repair Cost _____ x 10-15% = _____ Other: _____	
ARV:				**Total**	

Professional Quotes Needed: Buried Oil Tank: Y/N   FOUNDATION/ENGINEER: Y/N   Mold Remediation: Y/N
ARV Features: Outside: Street: + – Curb Appeal: + – Neighbors: + – Backyard: + – Usable Lot: + –
Inside: Layout: + –(Fixable Y N) Kitchen: + – Bedrooms: + – Bathrooms: + – Master Suite: Y / N
Notes:_____

FIGURE 9.1   Property Repair Estimate Sheet System

focused on what we need to know before we make an offer, and is designed to walk from the outside to the inside, going line by line as a plug and chug to estimate repairs in a quick, efficient manner.

Keep in mind that this is only an estimate of repairs needed. Before we start the rehab, we will fill out a scope of work, which will explain in detail *exactly* what needs to be done (and which we will discuss thoroughly in Chapter 11).

EXTERIOR

Roof

This is one major area of the house that most new investors seem to get wrong. Usually, they estimate it incorrectly because of fear or simple inability to understand the estimated cost to repair or replace a roof. To start, roofers estimate a roofing job by how many squares the roof needs. A square for roofs is a 10×10 area or 100 square feet.

Here is what you should look for when deciding whether or not to replace the roof, repair it, or leave it alone:

You should *replace* the roof when:

- It has more than two layers of shingles. Many building codes do not allow more than two layers due to weight and safety.
- The shingles are cupping or curling. If you stand back from the house and see actual shingles that are not lying flat, that is telltale sign that the roof is nearing its useful life.
- It looks so bad from the exterior that anyone buying would absolutely determine that they couldn't live with the current roof. In the case of the roof being visually worse than its function, it is very important to realize that your retail buyer when the house is completed will have to deal with this obstacle and will compensate by making an offer on your finished house with a requested repair credit or request a new roof before they close on your finished rehab property.

This is a very important concept I call *Pay now or pay later*. Just because the roof is not leaking does not mean you should not replace it in order to help you successfully market and sell your finished product. A new buyer who is going to live in the house will negotiate the retail price or cost of a new roof before they buy the house. Remember, this retail buyer will estimate the repair higher than you will actually be able to get the work done for when they ask for a credit. So you are always better off estimating this repair and doing the work so you actually have a house you can sell when it is complete.

What to look for:

- Under the eaves for rotten starter board. This tells you the roof is leaking or has leaked in the past.
- Shingles that are a different color. This tells you the roof has been repaired in the past.
- Look for leaks in the interior.

For your quick estimate:

- A 1,500-square-foot house costs roughly $6,000 to rip the old roof off and add new plywood, sheathing, and shingles.
- A 1,500-square-foot house costs roughly $3,000 for adding a layer of shingles. We call this a "rollover," since we simply roll the new shingles over the old ones on the existing roof.
- Budget more for two-story houses ($500 to $1,000 depending on size) because the higher the roofer has to climb, the more expensive it gets.
- If you are looking at a 3,000-square-foot house, then double this rough estimate to $12,000 to rip the old roof off and add new plywood, sheathing, and shingles.

Gutters

Gutters can have a *huge* long-term impact on a home's longevity. Most people do not realize that on most houses, bad foundations, damp basements, and water issues typically start from bad water management. Gutters help catch and push water away from the house. All of this makes it very important to identify gutters as a repair or not for you as a residential redeveloper. Adding gutters and redirecting water away from the house will start the process in solving foundation issues and water problems.

What to look for:

- Are there gutters?
- If so, are they seamless (gutters from big-box retailers have seams, typically leak, and are not installed by a professional)?
- Does the entire house have gutters or are they just where people enter and exit the house?
- Are they damaged or rusted?
- Do they divert water 24 inches away from the house?

For your quick estimate:

- Seamless rain gutters for a 1,500-square-foot house should cost less than $1,000.
- Seamless rain gutters for a 3,000-square-foot house should be estimated at $2,000.

Siding/Stucco

Replacing or painting the siding or stucco is a great opportunity to really change a house's appearance. You can replace, repair, or just paint the existing material. Siding in many areas is also an allowable form of encapsulation for lead-based paint.

What to look for:

- Condition or type of siding or stucco.
- Stucco that comes in contact with the ground (dirt) will bubble and flake away over time.
- Look for the type of siding (older houses can have asbestos siding).

    With asbestos siding, you are typically better encapsulating with new siding or painting when it comes to a cost perspective. Asbestos is only harmful as dust particles when it is being removed.

For your quick estimate:

- Vinyl siding for a single family 1,500 square-foot house costs around $7,000.
- Stucco over existing with minimal patchwork is $2,500 per floor (if you have a two-family: $2,500 × 2 = Estimated cost of $5,000).
- All-new stucco costs $5,000 per floor.

Windows

This is an area that we always like to budget for improvement for a few important reasons:

- New dual-pane, insulated windows can be considered a selling feature as they reduce heat and cooling bills while keeping out the elements.
- Landlord buyers cannot get subsidized or Section 8 or government-sponsored rentals approved unless they have fully functional and operable windows that are not peeling or cracking.

What to look for:

- What types of window do the neighbors have? If most are newer dual-pane windows, then replace with these.
- Open and close a few windows and see how they operate.
- Make sure all windows and sliding glass doors have screens (people like to open windows in the summer months without bugs coming in).

For your quick estimate:

- Windows are measured in united inches, which means the price of the window does not vary that greatly until they get into odd sizes.
- Vinyl replacement windows cost approximately $200 a window for the material and labor to install.
- Screen replacements typically cost $30 for a new screen and frame.
- Add $50 to $75 per window depending on the amount of exterior patch and repair work necessary around the window if damaged on replacement.

Paint

What an amazing miracle a coat of paint can be to *any* eyesore! Paint is certainly one of those home improvements that can help any house go from trash to cash. Painting an exterior and interior is an expense that pays for itself in spades.

What to look for:

- Neutral color. Is the house a shade like white, tan, or beige, or did the previous owner paint it their favorite shade of pink?
- You can plan on having to paint the house inside and out about 95 percent of the time.

For your quick estimate:

- $1.8 to $2 for exterior paint per square foot (if the house is 1,500 square-feet, then 1,500 square-feet × $2 = estimated cost of $3,000).
- $1.10 to $1.50 for interior paint per square foot.
- Add $.50 for interior wall prep if needed (i.e., wallpaper removal).

Garage Repair

Repairing a garage is typically a project of just cleaning and whiting it out. You are generally best served to just factor in a repair cost that would cover a simple clean out, repair, and a new coat of white paint. The only time I would suggest otherwise would be if you are estimating repairs on a high-end property or if the garage is a very large selling feature.

If the property has a detached garage that is practically falling over, you might even consider demolishing it. You will definitely want to look at the value of having a detached garage before rebuilding. It may not make sense in many areas of the country to rebuild a detached garage if the house is in a lower-end area. In these scenarios, the recent sales and comparables should determine whether or not you rebuild the structure or abandon it.

Confirm whether the other houses that are selling in the area have garages. If so, what is the price differential between the houses that do and do not have garages? Once you have this information, you'll need to compare that to the cost of rebuilding the garage. For example, if all the sales and comparable houses with garages are selling for $20,000 more than average, and your garage needs a complete rebuild that will cost $10,000, then you should move forward with building the garage. However, if the cost for rebuilding the garage is $20,000 and the increased sale price is $20,000, then you have some further considerations. If your property will sell sooner or it is what someone needs to see to make an offer on your property at that price, then you need to look at the work and cost as a feature needed to liquidate and sell the house quickly. Even if the cost of rebuilding the garage was $20,000 and it only added $20,000 of value, you would still need to rebuild the garage as your sales and comparables are proving that it will be hard to sell the subject property at your estimated ARV without a garage.

What to look for:

- Does the house have a swing-up garage door or a roll-up garage door?
- Does the door have an opener?
- Bad electrical wiring can be a nightmare in a garage (always budget $200 to clean it up).

For your quick estimate:

- $800 for a single-car garage door.
- $1,000 for a double-car garage door.
- $250 per motor.
- New-build cost for a one-car garage is $7,000.

Landscaping

Landscaping has such a dramatic effect on how your house shows, its curb appeal, and the emotional impact on potential buyers. The best thing is it can be very affordable and, depending on what needs to be done, most jobs take only 10 to 12 hours to complete. It's amazing what some mulch, new bushes, and laying some new grass or sod can do to the appearance of the front of your house.

What to look for:

- Keep it clean and green.
- Simple, basic landscaping is just fine.
  - New sod and grass
  - New mulch
  - New shrubs
- Use planter boxes around the home's perimeter (it is always important to keep vegetation away from the house, as it provides a clean and manicured look).
- Bark planters and mulch around trees gives a more finished look. Colored mulch, like a black mulch, can add a selling feature and appeal for many buyers

For your quick estimate:

- A good budget for full landscaping in the front and backyard of an average 6,000-square-foot lot with 1,500-square-foot house is $2,000, including the removal of existing irrigation and installing new irrigation.

Pools

I have repaired pools, filled in pools, and of course, swam in pools. Like other aspects of the home, having or keeping a pool will depend on the cost to repair versus the value conveyed by sales and comparables. It will also depend on what area you live in. When I was renovating properties in the Northeast, pools were a 50–50 amenity. Some potential buyers avoided houses with pools due to the maintenance and upkeep during the winter. When I renovated properties on the West Coast, most buyers viewed pools as a positive and I considered it an additional selling feature. Of course, the neighborhood and comparables dictate ultimately what you should do here. Once you have made that decision, it becomes a matter of cost and repair. Having a good pool company to rely on for a quick estimate and/or repair will serve you well.

What to look for:

- Look closely at a pool that is filled with water, and look for patches of plaster missing.
- If the pool equipment looks really scary (old and falling apart, etc.), you'll probably need to replace it.
- If the pool is empty, walk in and look for cracking in the plaster (if this is present, the pool will need major repair).
- An empty pool will need to be replastered.

For your quick estimate:

- Replastering an average pool is $5,000.
- New standard coping tile is $1,700.
- New decorative (basic) tile is $1,500.
- New pool pump is $1,500.
- New pool/spa heater is $3,000.
- Pools can be very costly, so having an expert who can get out there quickly is a must.

Fence

You should not overlook or downplay the quintessential white picket fence. I have installed probably over 100 white picket fences on our rehab properties over the years. A white picket fence in the front yard conveys the American dream of home ownership. Installing a white picket fence will convey the emotion of home ownership, which in turn helps sell our houses. It is also a great way to create privacy between neighbors' yards. Repairing a fence is typically an affordable activity, as it involves both common material and common skill set for most carpenters.

What to look for:

- The easiest fix. Just because the fence is leaning or falling over doesn't mean it needs to be completely replaced. A few new posts and paint can make an old fence look brand new.

For your quick estimate:

- Basic six-foot dog-eared fence from the big-box stores is roughly $15 per linear foot. If you want to install an 8-foot white picket fence, the cost would be 8 feet × $15 per linear foot = $120 cost.

Deck

I love to add decks when at all possible—to the front of the house, back of the house, or off the master bedroom. When done correctly, decks do a lot to increase a home's selling value and appeal. Installing a new deck simply requires pouring footings and framing up the deck you want. You will have to decide on what type of material and what style of railing you prefer, but always keep in mind that the right deck will help to move the property.

Repairing a deck can become a slippery slope if you don't know what you're doing. Unless the deck is structurally sound and you are just applying some new paint, varnish, or replacing a few boards, then typically most old decks are easier to demolish and rebuild new.

What to look for:

- The height of a deck can add significant costs.
- Having too much deck can be a bad thing. It shouldn't dominate the entire yard.
- A good deck will extend the interior living space to the exterior.
- Unless the house is very high end, use paint-grade wood. Paint the deck surface two shades lighter than the body color of the house and paint the railing the same color as the trim color of the house.

For your quick estimate:

- A 15 × 12-foot deck, roughly 30 inches or less off the ground, costs $2,000 (for paint-grade wood).

INTERIOR

Kitchen

Typically, a kitchen is the most important area of a house and your renovation. As a residential redeveloper, this is your opportunity to identify the current shortcomings of the existing kitchen in the property, then decide what you'll need to replace and what you can repair. Layout and condition are the two approaches I take to breaking down kitchens:

Layout

Ask yourself these questions:

- Is the existing layout optimized in terms of form and function?
  - Are the cooking area, fridge, and sink in a good layout to function?
  - Is there ample seating and work space?
  - Is the space open and airy?

- Is there a non-load-bearing wall that can be removed to create more open space?
- Can you easily alter the current configuration to create a better showing experience once completed, and a better user experience once lived in?
- How do we know what trends are popular or hot in new homes?

We can answer that last one by seeing what new-construction builders are installing and implementing for today's new buyers. For example, the great room is what new buyers expect in today's living space. This is when the kitchen, living room, and oftentimes dining room flow as one large open space. Most people like to be in the kitchen and see the TV or their guests, so they can participate with their company or family. Most older homes were built to have a separate kitchen, a separate dining room, a separate living room, and so on. Some of these old layouts often feel like a claustrophobic mouse maze, and tend to make the house feel smaller. You've got to identify this as an immediate opportunity to add value and get the house sold at top dollar upon the completion of your rehab.

Condition

Ask yourself these questions:

- What is the condition of the existing cabinets?
- How is the current countertop?
- What can I save and what do I absolutely have to replace?

Here are some tips when deciding what to keep, what to repair, and what to replace:

- Check the comparables and make a list of what materials, condition, and amenities are in the other properties' kitchens that are currently selling.
- Next, check your subject property and determine what it needs to make it competitive at your suggested sales price to match and beat the amenities of the other houses for sale. Add this to your scope of work.
- Only reuse and keep cabinets, appliances, and countertops if they can compete with the condition and quality of the current houses for sale. When done incorrectly, painting old cabinets ultimately just looks like painted cabinets. The proper preparation and improvement of the kitchen is vital to anything you keep for rework and reuse.

What to look for:

- Can you keep the cabinets? (A good litmus test is to look under the sink. This cabinet has the most wear and tear—so if it looks good, the rest should be fine.)

- Painting the cabinets and adding new hardware can make old cabinets look new. Make sure your painting professional properly preps, removes, and applies a professional paint job if you do choose to paint cabinets.
- When changing the kitchen's layout, remember to keep the cook top, refrigerator, and sink in a triangle.
- Don't overthink it. If the kitchen is ugly, gut it.

For your quick estimate:

- New cabinets, countertops, and backsplash for an average size kitchen are $5,000+ (remember that in the repair sheet paint, flooring, plumbing, electrical, and appliances are each separate numbers).

Kitchen Appliances

In some markets, houses are listed and sold *without appliances*. However, you should always budget for a new fridge, stove, and dishwasher—this always helps to show the house well and get it sold faster. Finishing a kitchen or house rehab and leaving old or used appliances is just not smart. At the same time, you don't want to put extremely high-quality appliances in a neighborhood that does not need them to get the house sold. Be smart. Replace old appliances with new ones that match or beat the competition currently for sale at your price point and in your neighborhood. In today's competitive market of appliances, stainless steel appliances have become very affordable. To be clear: I *always* suggest buying and installing new appliances versus keeping and reusing old or existing appliances.

What to look for:

- Appliances that can't be cleaned and show well need to be replaced.
- Appliances that are not fully working need to be replaced.
- Is there a water line to the fridge for an icemaker or water station?
- Are you at a price point that demands that the microwave should be a built-in?
- Is there enough counter space for a microwave or should you design and install an overhead microwave for the oven and range?

For your quick estimate:

- Appliances (range/oven, dishwasher, microwave hood, and refrigerator in stainless steel) for a basic, median-price home should cost about $1,800.

Bath

Some argue that bathrooms are more important than kitchens when showing and selling a house. Some buyers will purchase a house just because it has a Jacuzzi tub or a fancy rain showerhead (which, by the way, is very affordable to install!). Most bathrooms can be pulled apart and put back together at a fairly low cost. For this reason, I typically like to budget for renovating the bathroom, especially the master bathroom, if they are outdated or unsightly. Remember the master bathroom can be the decision maker for someone who is determined to put an offer on the house. Repairing the master bathroom will directly affect how easy and fast you get an offer and sell your finished rehab. So don't be afraid to completely gut old and outdated bathrooms, especially the master if your budget and sales price allow it. Be very picky about what you keep in the existing bathrooms when estimating repairs. (The best-looking item in an outdated bathroom, or in a room for that matter, will look bad in a completely rehabbed house.)

What to look for:

- Dated and old tubs.
- Dated faucets and fixtures that show the age of the house and the bathroom.
- Peeling and cracking tubs or sink vanities.
- Old and ugly bathroom countertops.
- Water damage near the base of the toilet and shower perimeter.
- Tile from the 1970s (you know, the pink and teal tile in your grandparents' house).

If you see any of these items, you need to remove and replace them.

For your quick estimate:

- A full bathroom remodeling costs $2,500 to $3,000.
- $1,500 for a half bath.
- Master baths with two vanities, a separate shower, and tub cost $4,500 (remember that in the repair sheet, paint, flooring, plumbing, and electrical are in separate numbers).

Flooring

I have found the flooring combination that shows and sells best in most houses is:

- Carpet in the bedrooms.
- Tile in the bathrooms.
- Hardwood in the kitchen and living areas.

However, you do not want too many different materials breaking up the common areas when rehabbing a small house, because it will make the house feel even smaller. For example, if you have a small kitchen next to the dining room and you put hardwood in the dining room and tile in the kitchen, then these two materials are going to accentuate the break and how small the two spaces actually are; therefore shrinking the space by making it feel smaller. When you're dealing with smaller spaces, keep the material the same between adjoining rooms. I would choose tile or hardwood to apply in both the kitchen and dining room in small spaces. This gives you continuous flooring material in two spaces that are small, however, the continuous use of one material will make the space and house feel bigger.

What to look for:

- What can you keep? In most houses built prior to 1960, you can sand and refinish the existing hardwood floors. I've found that buyers often like the charm and character of sanding and refinishing existing hardwood that is not completely perfect.
- Determine a flooring plan. (Where are you going to put what type of flooring?)

For your quick estimate:

- An average bedroom size is 120 square feet.
- Sanding and refinishing an existing wood floor costs $2.25 per square foot.
- Installing new-engineered hardwood costs $6 per square foot (with labor and material).
- Installing new laminate wood flooring costs $3 per square foot (labor and material).
- Carpet costs $12 per square yard (9 square feet = 1 square yard).
- Tile costs $10 per square foot (labor and material).

Sheetrock/Drywall

This is an area where most new investors get nervous because they typically do not have experience with this installation, the cost required, or the material needed. Below is all you need to know about sheetrock and drywall.

- **Rock**— This is screwing the board into the studs. "Rocking" is easier than taping, which lowers your labor cost on that portion of the activity.
- **Tape**— This is an art form of taping and sanding the seams by applying compound and finishing them as if the wall is made of one continuous board when completed. To test for a good tape job, you should put your hand on the wall, shut your eyes, and drag your hands

over the seam (where two boards meet against each other). If you can't feel the seam at all where the taping and compound occurred, then your taper did a good job.

What to look for:

- Always budget for drywall, because there will always be patching.

For your quick estimate:

- An 8 × 4 foot sheet of drywall is 32 square feet. You should budget $45 per sheet for labor and material.
- A full gutting of a house that needs new drywall costs $4 per square foot, including new texture. For example, a 1,500-square-foot house × $4 per square foot = $6,000.

Mechanicals

A property's mechanical repairs can make or break the success of a rehab project. Budgeting properly and estimating these repairs or potential replacements will ultimately put you as a rehab buyer in the best position to close deals. These components are ultimately what prevent buyers from buying a house, especially if they do not look new or up-to-date with a long, useful life ahead of them. We always want to inspect these different mechanicals in the house with a keen eye and a precise thought process. As discussed earlier in the chapter, you must also apply the "pay now or pay later" concept for mechanicals. This is one of the areas of the house that will either scare away potential buyers or offers, or they will only make an offer with a repair credit or request on your finished rehab.

Plumbing

This is an important part of every house and rehab. Our repair estimate sheet is designed to budget the plumbing to include both the kitchen and the bathroom plumbing. Obvious plumbing fixes will be the issues that are not working. Discretionary plumbing can be something like improving the drain lines in the kitchen from two to three inches for better long-term drainage and usage.

In cold-weather states, your plumber often plays a dual role of plumbing and heating installation. Many plumbers can work on heating systems such as hot water baseboard heating units, as well as their plumbing expertise. This is good to know; it can help save cost and time on your job and allow you to negotiate with one tradesman for both plumbing and heating.

What to look for:

- Know that you will always spend money on plumbing. You will be changing out wax rings on toilets, angle stops, supply lines, and ABS drain lines. These are easy things to see.
- Check the water heater and make sure it is working and has a long, useful life remaining. If the water heater has corrosion or leaking that is occurring, it is typically coming to the end of its useful life and needs to be replaced.
- If the house has major plumbing problems, you will usually be able to tell (walls are opened up and the copper has been removed).
  - Leaking faucets, toilets, sinks, and tubs.
  - Water damage around the bathroom and kitchen flooring near the plumbing.
  - Moisture or mold showing from leaking pipes or fixtures.

For your quick estimate:

- A basic kitchen and bathroom remodeling cost is $500 per wet location (for example, for a three-bed, two-bath house, you would budget a minimum $1,500 for plumbing).
- If you walk a house and you see there is a significant amount of copper missing and you think the house needs to be replumbed, including the drain lines, budget $6,000 for a 1,500-square foot house.
- A 50-gallon hot water heater (tank) costs $600 with labor and materials.
- A tankless water heater costs $1,500 with labor and materials.

Electrical

Lighting is one of the improvements that can have a huge emotional impact above and beyond its cost to install. Adding lights to a bedroom, the kitchen, landscape, and outdoors can *completely* enhance the mood and feel. I love to install under-cabinet lighting in nearly all my kitchens. Low-voltage lighting with dimmers is also a great touch to help show and sell houses. Recessed lighting throughout is a nice selling feature and upgrade. Just like plumbing, the electrical numbers on the repair sheet include the kitchen lighting and bathroom lighting.

What to look for:

- Again, know that you will *always* spend money on electrical. At a bare minimum, you should budget to change all the outlets, switches, faceplates, and lighting fixtures.

- Look at the main service panel. If the disconnect is less than 100 amps, you should budget to do a service panel upgrade to 200 amps.
- Just because the house is not grounded doesn't mean you need to rewire it.

For your quick estimate:

- A minimum budget on electrical if nothing is wrong is $1,500 for new fixtures, new outlets, new switches, and new faceplates.
- A new service panel upgrade costs $2,000.
- A complete rewiring of a 1,500-square-foot house with a service panel upgrade is $7,000.

HVAC

Heating, ventilation, and air conditioning (HVAC) is the technology of blowing hot air through sheet metal or ducts to heat a house. The focus here is to always have a clean or up-to-date system. If you don't, then you need to budget for it.

What to look for:

- If the forced-air unit (FAU) or air conditioner condenser is ugly or old, *replace it*. These items are not very expensive to replace but can scare a buyer away fast!

For your quick estimate:

- An FAU without new ductwork for a 1,500-square-foot house costs $1,500 with labor and materials.
- An air conditioner condenser for a 1,500-square-foot house costs $2,500.

Other

Permits

One of the most important things for you to convey and establish as a residential redeveloper is that you are *pro* permits. We will discuss this more in future chapters, but rehab investors who do not pull permits will eventually either lose business or be stigmatized as an investor who cuts corners. Pulling permits is a necessary part of ensuring that your business thrives, improves neighborhoods and, of course, is profitable. As professional residential redevelopers, we always work with our building departments and have licensed and professional contractors who pull the proper permits for every job.

Permit costs vary across municipalities, since building codes and costs vary drastically depending on what part of the country you live in. This is why it's imperative to familiarize yourself with the process and costs for pulling and paying for permits. This way, you'll have an answer the next time a potential buyer asks you a question on this topic.

Termites

Termites are a problem predominantly in warmer climates, such as central and southern California. Specifically in California, most houses require termite work when they change hands. A typical cost of tenting a house for termites is $1,200 for a 1,500-square-foot house.

Demolition and Dumpsters

Our job as rehabbers is often to transform the worst house on the block into the nicest. This process tends to automatically turn us into waste management experts. You inevitably will, and should, develop relationships with waste management vendors as a reliable source for dropping and picking up dumpsters. I have always found it very valuable to have at least one good waste management service/vendor to call on when I need to do a quick "trash out" on a potential deal.

The other cost to factor when estimating a house that requires a lot of demolition is how much debris and trash is created once you start removing walls, ceilings, and other fixtures in a house. The cost of dumpsters can add up quickly.

What to look for:

- Remember that trash does not remove itself for free; walls don't just fall down and walk into the dumpster by themselves. Budget for the labor of the demolition.
- The more trash or demolition, the greater the cost to you.

For your quick estimate:

- The average 30-yard dumpster (the largest) is roughly $500 per four to five tons. Each additional ton costs about $75.
- Budget $500 per dumpster for the labor cost to fill the dumpster.
- This is not an exact science, so budget accordingly.

Miscellaneous

Finally, you must always factor in a miscellaneous cost for unexpected repairs.

What to look for:

- The older the house, there are more unknown elements.
- The more complicated the rehab, there are more unknown elements.

- The larger the scope of work (SOW) and the higher the ARV, there are more unknown elements.
- Miscellaneous is the "oops" factor … so use it.

   For your quick estimate:

- At a minimum, use 10 percent of your estimated repairs as extra money you can't think of now, but will end up spending on the rehab. Adjust up as needed (15, 20, and 25 percent) for bigger projects or more unknowns at the time you are estimating repairs on the subject property.

QUICK TIPS TO LOOK FOR THAT ADD VALUE TO A RESIDENTIAL HOME

One of the most important aspects of being a successful rehabber is to identify and determine the improvements that can be made to a property to increase its value and improve its appeal to more potential buyers. Here are some of my favorite areas and techniques to improve a house that have a dramatic effect on its resale and value.

- **Open up space to create great rooms.** Look for ways to make the house more open and airy. Open space is what most buyers typically want. Open the kitchen to create a great room.
- **Create more usable space.** Maximize storage by installing shelving and closet systems. Adding closets and built-ins to create open space is a great selling feature.
- **Eliminate unpleasant views.** Often houses look out onto eyesores. If your house has an alley view or looks into a neighbor's house, then look to see how you can eliminate that view with your upcoming rehab and repairs. Some houses have amazing landscapes, mountain views, ocean views, or canyon views that aren't captured due to current window placement. Changing the location of the window can sometimes be an option. Glazing a window to make it opaque in the bathroom can also prevent outsiders from getting a view you don't want them to have! Planting shrubbery or adding a fence are also options to turn an unpleasant view into a pleasant one.
- **Eliminate noise.** Adding insulation, caulking, trees, shrubs, and dual pane windows or even soundproof windows can reduce and eliminate noise in a house. Having peace and quiet in a house is certainly a selling feature and something that people look and pay for.
- **Bring in more natural light.** Take advantage of opportunities to add more natural light—they only add value. You can achieve this by adding enlarged windows, changing

solid doors to glass doors, and adding skylights, where possible. This is especially cost-effective if you are installing new siding or stucco on the exterior. Because the exterior is going to be patched and repaired, you can strategically add windows or enlarge windows.

- **White is good.** Using a lighter color palette will visually open up spaces and make them feel larger. Oftentimes painting dark trim or old wood trim white has a huge visual impact on a room and space that helps show and sell the house.

COMMON MISTAKES WHEN ESTIMATING REPAIRS

The most common mistakes new rehabbers make when estimating repairs on their first deals is allowing fear to hold them back from getting started and practicing their first potential deal. In order to become a pro, you need to follow the outline I've shared and continually practice. Your first Property Repair Sheet is not going to be exact; however, this is the practice you need to improve your skill at estimating repairs.

Another mistake often made is *to make decisions in a bubble*. In order to be successful at estimating repairs properly and get the necessary rehab done to sell your house, you have to study and understand the comparables. Be aware of your subject property's condition to make the correct estimating decisions on the front end, so you can sell at your suggested after-repair value.

Finally, the biggest mistake I see people make is assuming something works or does not need repair and not budgeting for that cost on their repair sheet. For example, if you are walking through a vacant home and the HVAC looks good but you have no electricity to test it, then you have to assume that the HVAC needs to be replaced. If you budget to repair it and make your offer and find out later that it works fine, then you just saved money. If you can't test the mechanicals for any reason, you cannot assume they work.

The most important reason for understanding the basics of estimating repairs as a rehabber is to increase the speed in which you can evaluate and make offers. Before you can actually close on a property to rehab you have to evaluate the numbers and estimate repairs so you make an appropriate offer that puts you in a positive position to make money once you close on the deal. When you are comfortable with this basic knowledge, are efficient at estimating repairs, and can determine decisions on the potential renovation, you can write better offers and increase profits.

To get a copy of the *property repair estimate sheet* my students and I use, visit www.RehabInvestingBible.com/resources and download it for free.

PART

II

Managing the Rehab

The Seven-Stage Rehab System is the key to my rehabbing formula. I have created and simplified a seven-stage process of the crucial steps that need to be managed and executed so that I or anyone on my team can have success from day one managing and implementing a rehab. When followed, this system will allow you to save time by working with the best contractors, using the correct paperwork and agreements to control the timeline, budget, and quality of the finished product. The net result of following the Seven-Stage Rehab System in Part II is a successfully completed rehab that you will take pride in as you list and market it for sale.

CHAPTER 10

Stage 1: Take Pictures, Measure Everything, and Decide What Needs to Be Done

When done without a system, rehabbing typically requires a great deal of time to master and execute. What's even worse is that most investors start with limited experience, let alone a system to follow. The average investor enters into rehabbing having only done work on their home. My proven Seven-Stage Rehab System will teach you how to start, manage, and complete a rehab project with licensed and insured quality contractors—without getting your own hands dirty. Using my Seven-Stage Rehab System will move you from being a do-it-yourself rehabber to residential redeveloper.

Learning how to renovate properties and manage contractors requires you to commit and adhere to a system with a proven track record. If you are willing to dedicate the time to master, train, and implement the Seven-Stage Rehab System, you will get the chance to cash in on some of the biggest checks in the real estate business.

I always recommend that your first project be a cosmetic renovation. Focus your attention on less intimidating tasks such as paint, carpet, and other purely aesthetic elements. As your project experience grows, you can take on larger, more involved projects. Start small and build your experience gradually to keep from getting in over your head. The more rehabs you do, the more experience you will achieve—and the less costly mistakes you'll make. Most importantly, it will drastically increase your chances of achieving early success in your investing endeavors.

The most important actions in growing your rehab business are learning, understanding, and mastering the entire rehab process and system—which means that you won't be spending all of your time on the jobsite. Throughout the process, you will also start to develop relationships with contractors and subcontractors. Good contractors are the most critical team members for building and growing your residential redevelopment business.

I have talked a lot about contractors thus far. I want to be very clear how valuable and important contractors are to this business. My best relationships over the years are from awesome contractors who share the same level of professionalism, character, and respect as I have in doing a job the right way. One of the first contractors I worked with did over 100 properties for my team and me. In that relationship both the contractor and I helped each other grow and improve our businesses. Contractors are as much our customers as we are their customers when it comes to renovating properties—don't forget that.

Preparation is the key to stay on schedule and within budget for a rehab. You need to develop a clear idea of what renovations and improvements you want to undertake *prior to involving a contractor*. You should also have a clear idea of your budget so that you can develop a realistic scope of work.

Part I of this book focused on getting started, marketing for deals, evaluating deals, and estimating deals so we can get them under contract. Part II assumes we own the property and need to execute the details to start and complete a successful rehab. In Chapter 9 we estimated repairs with a focus on getting our offer in and the subject deal under contract. Now we will focus on the exact steps for executing and managing the rehab itself, using my system.

PREPARE FOR YOUR REHAB

This will be your first visit to the property once you actually own the deal. The goal is, in one visit, to gather all the information and necessary details to put together the scope of work that will be used to bid and hire contractors to do the work. On this visit you must accomplish these three tasks:

1. Take pictures of everything and anything you think will need improvement.
2. Make necessary measurements to any rooms that you may change the layout of.
3. Start making final decisions on exactly what you need to do on the rehab to get your subject property sold.

One of your most important tasks to complete during this first walkthrough after you close on the property is to identify the items you need to fix, as well as the things that will help sell the house when complete. For example, should you remove a nonload-bearing wall between the kitchen and living room or add a window to take advantage of a good view? Should you add a skylight to add brightness to a dark room? These are just a sample of the decisions that now need to be finalized *before* you start the rehab with your identified contractor team—not in the middle or after.

The following is a list of the items to take with you that will help you prepare an accurate scope of work.

☐ **Camera.** Take pictures of problem areas so you can refer to them as you prepare your scope of work. This will also give you "before" pictures to illustrate the improvements that you have made. It's rewarding to see the end results of your labor, so keep photo records of each project.

☐ **Flashlight.** Whether there is no power turned on at the property or you need to investigate dark nooks and crannies, a flashlight is always necessary. You don't want to waste a trip and not be able to complete the walkthrough.

☐ **Graph Paper and Tape Measure.** You'll need to make a to-scale sketch of the property, specifically of the areas you plan to repair. This allows you to develop quantities for your scope of work.

☐ **Lockbox with Spare Key.** This will prevent you from having to meet your contractor at the property to grant access, and allow you to send contractors to the property to prepare their bids.

☐ **Marketing Materials.** You can generate motivated buyer leads with "We Buy Houses" or "For Sale" signs to build your buyers' list. However, even if you put up a "For Sale" sign, don't let potential buyers view the house until renovations are complete.

PROPERTY WALKTHROUGH

Break your walkthrough down into the same sections that you will use for your scope of work based on the property repair estimate sheet: exterior, interior, and mechanicals. This will keep the walkthrough systematic and prevent you from overlooking areas that need attention.

Start by approaching the home's exterior as a potential buyer would. Notice everything that gives you a negative impression. Bad landscaping, peeling paint, and decrepit fencing are just some of the things that can turn off interested buyers before they ever walk in the door. Also look for items such as an outdoor seating area or new sod that can be added to increase the home's value. Make sure all exterior lights work and test automatic garage door openers and irrigation systems if they are present.

Begin the process again on the house's interior. Pay attention to the first thing you notice and feel when you walk in the home. How can you improve a bad impression or enhance a good impression? Go through each room and take note of every detail imaginable to get an accurate idea of exactly how much work needs to be done a second time with the property repair estimate sheet, but with much greater detail. You will need this information when preparing your scope of work.

Measure and sketch areas of the property where you may want to change the layout, such as the bathrooms or kitchens, and include any specific problem areas. Note the location of mechanical system items such as the water heater and the furnace.

Stage 1 of the Seven-Stage Rehab System is your first visit to the subject house after you have closed on it. You do not want to take multiple trips to gather this information. If you do take multiple trips, you are wasting time, and we have established that for residential redevelopers, time is … everything! During this stage you are adding to the details of your original property repair estimate sheet and looking for any and all other details that need to be addressed or improved. Now let's get to stage 2 and start the scope of work back at the home office.

CHAPTER 11

Stage 2: Your Most Important Job—Creating a Detailed Scope of Work

The scope of work, or the SOW, serves as the foundation of your rehab. It's an agreement between you and your contractor that outlines the exact details of the project and materials you are requesting the contractors to execute—a detailed to-do list. A SOW minimizes miscommunications between parties and holds the contractor accountable to the agreed-upon terms and exactly what you want and need done.

For example, let's say that you've decided to modernize the kitchen, fix up the bathrooms, and redo the floors. While *you* may have a clear idea of what those three things entail, it would be impossible for a contractor to bid the work based on that scope—much less actually complete any work that you would approve.

Your idea of a new kitchen renovation and a contractor's idea of a new kitchen can be two drastically different outcomes. When you do not have a written SOW, you run the risk of getting the kitchen the contractor wants and not what you want. This is where arguments and meltdowns occur between contractors and investors. Do not fall into this trap. Always complete a SOW before you hire and enroll a contractor.

As my brother says, the best analogy for a SOW is "a scope of work is to a rehab as a screenplay is to a movie." You need to spell out every detail—down to paint color, faucet fixture, kitchen cabinets, appliances, and much more. Without a clearly defined and well-thought-out SOW, it is very easy for project costs to spiral out of control and break your budget.

Developing a detailed SOW is your most important task as the residential redeveloper. Once the job starts, you should be out looking for the next deal and raising money for future investment activities—not supervising work at your rehab. The SOW keeps you from being an onsite project manager and allows you to be a true residential redeveloper. Your highest and best use is finding deals, raising money, and making high-level development decisions … not babysitting on the jobsite to make sure work gets done. The SOW system makes you more money and makes the professional contractors you hire very happy; it allows the contractors to do what they do best and keeps you out of their hair.

HOW TO DEVELOP A SCOPE OF WORK

To get started on your SOW, you begin with the property repair estimate sheet you completed while reviewing the digital pictures you took on-site on your first visit to make final decisions on the items that need to be completed.

Once you have a rough SOW that is within your budget, go back through and add more detail. This is when you decide what modernizing the kitchen means *specifically*: Are you going to take it all out and start from scratch, or simply replace the harvest gold appliances with stainless steel and update the cabinet hardware? You'll obviously need to repair anything that is broken, but you may be able to salvage items for reuse.

Be as thorough and detailed as possible when developing your SOW. One of the major causes of going over budget or getting behind schedule in any type of construction project is a lack of proper planning, definition, and detail at the project's beginning. You need to be decisive and have a clear vision of what you want the end product to look like. If you don't know what you want, there's no way your contractor can have success with you and your project.

I use something I've deemed the Four Question Test to keep me on track when developing my SOW; it prevents me from getting stuck on any single rehabbing decision. If you are in doubt about whether or not to include a particular improvement in your rehab, answering these four questions should give you a clear direction:

1. Will it add value?
2. Will it help sell the property?
3. Is it cost-effective?
4. Is it needed?

Let's look at a brief example that illustrates the Four Question Test at work:

Scenario: You have a single-family rehab with a SOW that includes a new kitchen, a new roof, paint, and flooring.

Question in debate: Should you add a skylight in the kitchen?

Answers:

1. Will it add value? *Yes*.
2. Will it help sell the property? *Yes*.

3. Is it cost-effective? *Yes*.

4. Is it needed? *No*.

In this scenario, we have three yes answers and one no. So we should add the skylight. The swing question in this scenario was, "Is it cost-effective?" to which we answered yes based on the fact that we are already adding a new roof. Therefore, the additional material cost of $150 to $300 for a skylight and a professional to install it is extremely minimal compared to installing the skylight *without* replacing the roof.

Using the Four Question Test will keep you from spending too much time worrying about one decision. Remember, time is everything. Your main goal is to keep the project moving along smoothly so you can have a finished product to market and sell. If you are spending a week to decide between the light green carpet versus the hunter green carpet, you can rest assured that you won't be successful in buying, rehabbing, and selling properties.

SOW KITCHEN EXAMPLE

Let's review the system that my company and coaching students use and leverage to help them successfully put together the detail of improvements using a kitchen renovation. In our scope of work we want to specifically decide and identify the exact finishing material with item numbers and SKU numbers that the contractor will be purchasing and installing. By showing the contractor that we know the material costs, this keeps them honest and stops them from marking up material costs so they can make additional profits.

The goal is to turn the dated kitchen shown in Figure 11.1 into an awesome renovated kitchen that will help get our house sold and earn us a profit. By providing a detail of our request to our contractor, we make their job easier and allow them to have success with us on our first of many jobs.

Step 1: Description of Improvement

Here is the description of work on this kitchen to be included in the SOW:

> Demo entire kitchen and remove appliances. Remove flooring and light fixtures. Install new cabinets, appliances, backsplash, and countertops. Install under-mount sink with new garbage disposal and single-hole faucet. Run electrical for recessed can lighting. Lay new laminate flooring and paint entire kitchen. Replace all outlets and switches.

FIGURE 11.1   Dated Kitchen

What is missing from this description are the exact materials and layout choices that we have to identify as the rehabber so we get the exact kitchen we want. Let's move to the next step to start this process.

Step 2: Desired Layout

The next thing you want to decide before having the contractor give a bid is to detail the layout changes you want or need for the kitchen. Figure 11.2 shows a layout we provided before work started on this kitchen.

Step 3: Material Breakdown and Cost

This is where you decide, pick, and identify the exact finishing material you want the contractor to put into the kitchen. You do not have to get item numbers or SKU numbers on items such as nails or 2 × 4 lumber. Your job is to pick out the finishing material so the contractor can do the work to bring your vision to life.

Figure 11.3 shows a breakdown of the materials needed for this kitchen renovation by item, with costs and links for the contractor to see where to purchase them.

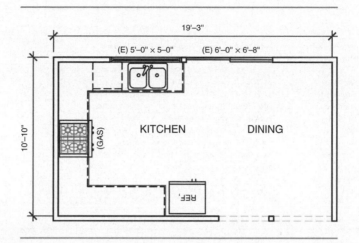

FIGURE 11.2   Desired Kitchen Layout

Fixture / Item	Price	Unit	Width	Length	Height	Link to Store Website
Cabinets **	$23.45	varies	-	-	-	http://thd.co/1e6Mr6v
Lighting	$9.83	each	7.5	3.25	4	http://thd.co/1mZlU3m
Range	$629.00	each	29.875	47	28.5	http://thd.co/1mZlGsP
Freezer/Refigerator	$759.00	each	30	66.625	32.625	http://thd.co/1mZlKJ8
Microwave	$259.00	each	29-7/8	16-13/32	15-1/32	http://thd.co/1lo5DEz
Dishwasher	$369.00	each	24	35	25	http://thd.co/1jEfkeU
Sink	$168.28	each	32.188	9	20.5	http://thd.co/1o9yXLM
Faucet	$184.61	each	2	9.25	10	http://thd.co/1e6MK16
Garbage Disposal	$74.96	each	6.312	11.375	6.12	http://thd.co/1mZlSsg
Countertops ***	$11.25	per 3"	5	8	7	http://thd.co/1erL9Xt
Backsplash ***	$1.65	sq ft	6	3	-	http://bit.ly/1blXr72
Flooring ***	$1.99	sq ft	5	47.75	0.315	http://thd.co/1e6MSgU
Paint ***	$116.00	per 5 gal	-	-	-	http://thd.co/1n3GRes

FIGURE 11.3   Kitchen Material Breakdown and Cost

Figure 11.4 shows the breakdown of exactly how many of each item and total cost of materials needed for this kitchen renovation with SKU number.

Once you have executed those three steps and put in the scope of work, the contractor now has all the information they need to properly bid and quote your project—in this case, the kitchen. When you execute this system with the level of detail presented here, your outcome

Fixture / Item	Brand	Description	Color	Qty	Material Cost	Retail SKU
Cabinets **	Hampton Bay	Wood Cabinets; Base and Wall	White Satin	113	$2,649.85	multiple
Lighting	Halo	Recessed Can Light	White	6	$58.98	556219
Range	Frigidaire	Freestanding Gas Range	Stainless Steel	1	$629.00	* 249116
Freezer/Refigerator	Frigidaire	21 CF Top Freezer Refrigerator	Stainless Steel	1	$759.00	1000002771
Microwave	Frigidaire	1.6 CF 1000 Watt OTR Microwave	Stainless Steel	1	$259.00	533383
Dishwasher	Frigidaire	Built-in Electric Dishwasher	Stainless Steel	1	$369.00	166512
Sink	HOUZER	Eston Undermount Double Bowl	Stainless Steel	1	$168.28	STC-2200SR-1
Faucet	KOHLER	Coralais 1-Hole, 1-Handle, Low-Arc	Brushed Nickel	1	$184.61	856835
Garbage Disposal	Badger	Garbage Disposal w/ Air Gap Switch	Black	1	$74.96	100036481
Countertops ***	Stonemark	New Venetian Gold Granite	New Venetian Gold	78	$877.50	DT-G215
Backsplash ***	Arizona Tile	Skylights Glass SL-Kiwi Stag Joint	Kiwi Stag (Green)	59	$97.35	SL-Kiwi
Flooring ***	Hampton Bay	Laminate Flooring	Brown	105	$208.95	183410
Paint ***	Behr	Flat Finish (R-234 | G-223 | B-201)	Light Beige	1	$116.00	custom
			Total Material Cost		**$6,452.48**	

FIGURE 11.4   Kitchen Material Breakdown and Cost with SKU#

of a beautiful kitchen and house that will sell very easily is just a formality. Figure 11.5 shows the finished kitchen and final product.

That's right—that is the same kitchen that we started with. Figure 11.6 has a side-by-side view to illustrate the system at work.

FIGURE 11.5   Finished Kitchen

FIGURE 11.6   Before and After Kitchen Photos

In Figure 11.7, you can see the tool that we can now put together and stamp out this template multiple times for many rehabs to come.

This example and illustration are to show you the details of the system that will get you the desired outcomes you want as long as you do the work before the contractors set foot in your house. This should drive home the point that the most work we will do on the rehab is at the scope-of-work stage. This is where we make all the high-level decisions as a residential redeveloper.

I have included two of our white kitchen templates and stamps that my team and our coaching students use to execute and fill in our SOWs. To download these kitchen templates and stamps, go to www.RehabInvestingBible.com/resources.

SOW BATHROOM EXAMPLE

Let's do another example on how to organize and detail our SOW, this time with the bathroom. My system has different bathroom templates and stamps that we use for different price-point homes. The reason for this is I don't waste time designing every new bathroom remodel we are going to take on; I simply pick from our conveyer belt system and choose one of the 10 bathroom template and stamps I already completed. This is leveraging a system so you save time and make more money. Better yet, this is how you rehab without ever lifting a paintbrush!

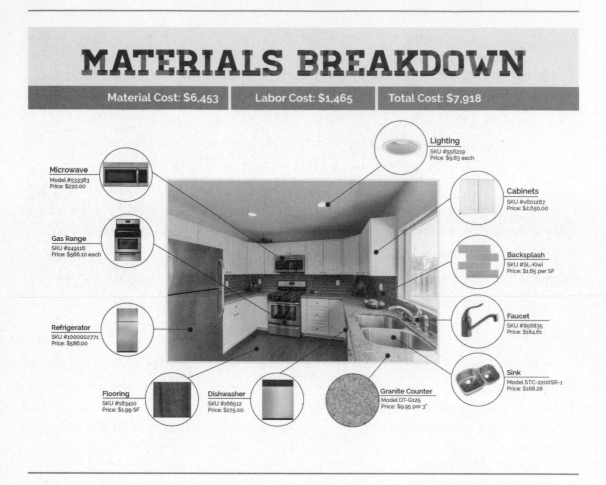

MATERIALS BREAKDOWN

| Material Cost: $6,453 | Labor Cost: $1,465 | Total Cost: $7,918 |

Lighting
SKU #556219
Price: $9.83 each

Microwave
Model #533383
Price: $220.00

Cabinets
SKU #v601287
Price: $2,650.00

Gas Range
SKU #249116
Price: $566.10 each

Backsplash
SKU #SL-Kiwi
Price: $1.65 per SF

Faucet
SKU #856835
Price: $184.61

Refrigerator
SKU #1000002771
Price: $586.00

Sink
Model STC-2200SR-1
Price: $168.28

Flooring
SKU #183410
Price: $1.99 SF

Dishwasher
SKU #166512
Price: $275.00

Granite Counter
Model DT-G125
Price: $9.95 per 3"

FIGURE 11.7 Materials Breakdown

This particular bathroom is tight and cramped. It has an actual wall between the sink and the shower/toilet room. Figure 11.8 shows two views of the subject bathroom.

Step 1: Description of Improvement

Here is the description of work on this bathroom to be included in the SOW.

> Demo entire bathroom and wall between toilet/shower and sink. Remove wallpaper, flooring, outlets, and switches. Install new vanity with corresponding countertop, sink, and faucet. Install new toilet and bathtub with shower valve and trim kit.

FIGURE 11.8   Two Views of Bathroom

Install shower field tile (straight set) with complementary accent tile. Install tile flooring (subway style) and grout accordingly. Hang a new mirror above the sink and install bathroom accessory kit. Install vanity light fixtures on the wall above the sink. Install new ceiling fan. Paint according to the color scheme and replace switches and outlets. Install new baseboard throughout the bathroom.

Step 2: Desired Layout

Again, the second step is to clearly convey the new layout with a drawing or sketch, as shown in Figure 11.9.

Step 3: Material Breakdown and Costs

Figure 11.10 shows a breakdown of the materials needed for this bathroom renovation by item, with costs and links to show the contractor where to purchase.

Figure 11.11 shows a breakdown of exactly how many of each item and total cost of materials needed for this bathroom renovation with SKU numbers.

Figure 11.12 shows the finished bathroom and final product from this SOW bathroom example.

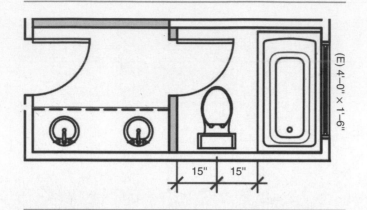

FIGURE 11.9   Desired Layout of Bathroom

Fixture / Item	Price	Unit	Width	Length	Height	Link to Store Website
Toilet	$98.00	each	17.25"	31.62"	29.63"	http://thd.co/1mZUV8X
Lighting	$59.97	each	18"	8.375"	5"	http://thd.co/1e71eOx
Vanity	$279.00	each	36"	33.5"	21"	http://thd.co/1nkn3np
Mirror	$99.00	each	32"	24"	-	http://thd.co/1nkFgkB
Countertop	$61.00	sq ft	-	-	-	http://thd.co/1nkngHg
Sink	$140.00	each	15.62"	9.62"	21.62"	http://thd.co/1bKe8pY
Faucet	$84.70	each	6.3"	2.75"	15"	http://thd.co/1fwJDp2
Bathtub	$347.70	each	32"	20"	60"	http://thd.co/1esN3TW
Tub & Shower Valve	$76.45	each	6"	5"	5"	http://thd.co/1mZV5x3
Bath & Shower Fixtures	$95.70	each	-	-	-	http://thd.co/1esN4aA
Exhaust Fan	$59.47	each	10.25	10.5	5.75	http://thd.co/MsbSYx
Towel Bar	$24.98	each	4.5	24	3.25	http://thd.co/1esEp7Y
Towel Ring	$16.98	each			-	http://thd.co/1nkxUO3
Tub Enclosure **	$2.98	sq ft	12"	24"	3/8"	http://bit.ly/1cJtOP3
Tub Enclosure Accent **	$3.98	sq ft	12"	12"	3/8"	http://bit.ly/1cJu3i5
Flooring **	$6.38	sq ft	20"	20"	3/8"	http://thd.co/1esMQAo
Paint **	$116.00	5 gallons	-	-	-	http://thd.co/1n3GRes
Grout	$14.97	25 lbs bag	-	-	-	http://thd.co/1n3GRes

FIGURE 11.10   Bathroom Material Breakdown and Cost

And finally, Figure 11.13 shows a side-by-side view to illustrate the system's results in this bathroom remodel.

In Figure 11.14, you see the tool that we can now put together and stamp out this template multiple times for many rehabs to come.

Fixture / Item	Brand	Description	Color	Qty	Material Cost	Retail SKU
Toilet	Glacier Bay	2-piece 1 GPF Flush Saver Elongated	White	1	$98.00	173239
Lighting	Hampton Bay	3-Light Vanity Wall Fixture	Stainless Steel	1	$59.97	292995
Vanity	Glacier Bay	Vanity Cabinet	Java Oak	1	$279.00	997390
Mirror	Glacier Bay	Glacier Bay Hampton Framed Mirror	Brown	1	$99.00	598716
Countertop	LG Hausys	Viatera 2 in. Quartz Countertop	Ultra White	5	$305.00	LG-Q5125-VT
Sink	American Standard	Studio Rectangular Undermount Sink	White	1	$140.00	344024
Faucet	GROHE	Eurostyle Cosmopolitan 1-Hole 1-Handle	Chrome	1	$84.70	23042002
Bathtub	Sterling Plumbing	Ensemble 5 ft. Right Drain Bathtub	White	1	$347.70	71121120-0
Tub & Shower Valve	GROHE	Pbv Rough-in Valve in Chrome	Chrome	1	$76.45	172387
Bath & Shower Fixtures	GROHE	Bauloop Shower Combination	Starlight Chrome	1	$95.70	27547000
Exhaust Fan	NuTone	NuTone 110 CFM Exhaust Fan	White	1	$59.47	672R
Towel Bar	Delta	Kaya Towel Bar	Polished Chrome	1	$24.98	229219
Towel Ring	Delta	Kaya Towel Ring	Polished Chrome	1	$16.98	232565
Tub Enclosure **	Arizona Tile	Fibra Series	Linen	54	$160.92	36300
Tub Enclosure Accent **	Arizona Tile	Skylights Glass SL-Spa Melange	SL-Spa Mélange	9	$35.82	SL-SPA
Flooring **	DalTile	Veranda Pearl Porcelain Tile	Pearl	40	$255.20	200068
Paint **	Behr	Semi Gloss (R-234 | G-223 | B-201)	Light Beige	1	$116.00	-
Grout	Custom Building Product	Polyblend #382 Sanded Grout	Bone Color	1	$14.97	123852
			Total Material Cost		$2,269.86	

FIGURE 11.11   Bathroom Material Breakdown and Cost with SKUs

FIGURE 11.12   Finished Bathroom

FIGURE 11.13   Before and After Bathroom

I have included two of our bathroom kitchen templates and stamps that my team and our coaching students use to execute and fill in our SOWs. To download these bathroom templates and stamps, go to www.RehabInvestingBible.com/resources.

THE SOW LAYOUT

Here are the areas of the house and work that should be spelled out, in order, on your scope of work for your rehab.

- Property Address
- Exterior
  - Demo details
  - General details
    - Paint
    - Front door
    - Exterior lighting
    - Front Door
  - Roof details
  - Landscaping
  - Windows

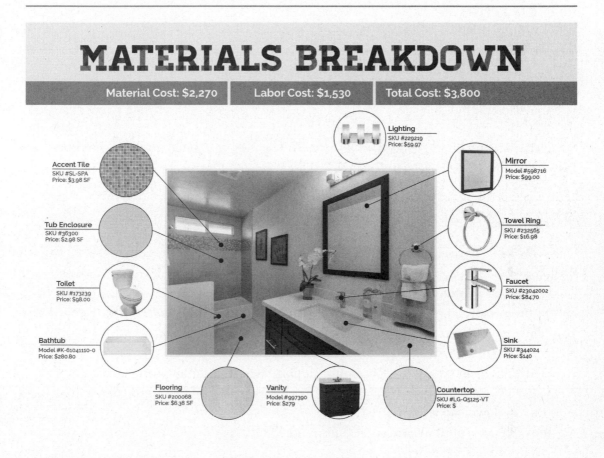

FIGURE 11.14 Materials Breakdown for Bathroom

- Interior
  - Demo details
  - General details
    - Hardware for doors
    - Carpet
    - Baseboard and trim
    - Paint
    - Drywall

- Kitchen details
- Bathrooms details
- Plumbing details
- Electrical details
- HVAC
- Garage and outbuildings

To get a copy of an example *scope of work* from one of my completed properties, visit www.RehabInvestingBible.com/resources and download it for free to copy and emulate.

CREATE YOUR BID PACKAGE

Once you have completed the SOW, you start putting together the bid package that will be left at the house so you can send qualified contractors to bid your job and work. Contractors will need to see the SOW to understand the detail involved in the work. For contractors to actually bid on the project, they will need to use the SOW to fill in your *Quote Itemization Form*. This allows you to compare apples to apples among multiple contractors instead of apples to oranges—because they are not bidding on a uniform system.

Figure 11.15 shows an example of our simple Quote Itemization Form.

To get a copy of the *quote itemization form*, visit www.RehabInvestingBible.com/resources and you can download it for free.

Your bid package you leave at the house should include the following items:

- Bidding instructions (how you want contractors to prepare and format the bid, and when it is due back to you).
- Final scope of work.
- Quote itemization form.
- Contractor credibility packet. (The next chapter provides details on this.)

Once you've assembled your bid package, you should print at least 10 copies to leave at the project site. You then drive to the house for the *second time* after you have closed on and own the property to drop them off. Once you undergo the contractor prescreening process (which the next chapter will cover), you'll send potential contractors to the site with the lockbox code to pick up a bid package and examine the property for bidding. Inform them of the deadline for their quote so you can review and award the winning bid to start work. This process saves you

QUOTE ITEMIZATION FORM

PROPERTY ADDRESS: _____

CONTRACTOR: _____

Time needed to complete project: _____

**Fill in all appropriate blanks pertinent to this scope of work:

EXTERIOR:

- ➤ Demolition/Dumpsters $_____
- ➤ Landscaping $_____
- ➤ Driveway/walkway $_____
- ➤ Roof $_____
- ➤ Paint/Siding $_____
- ➤ Windows $_____
- ➤ Doors $_____
- ➤ Misc.
    - ○ Explain _____ $_____
    - ○ Explain _____ $_____

INTERIOR:

- ➤ Demolition/Dumpsters $_____
- ➤ HVAC $_____
- ➤ Plumbing $_____
- ➤ Electrical/Lighting $_____
- ➤ Framing $_____
- ➤ Sheetrock/Taping $_____
- ➤ Paint $_____
- ➤ Doors/Trim $_____
- ➤ Flooring (Carpet) $_____
- ➤ Flooring (Hardwood) $_____
- ➤ Flooring (Tile) $_____
- ➤ Appliances $_____
- ➤ Kitchen Misc. (fixtures, countertops, etc.) $_____
- ➤ Bathroom(s) Misc. (fixtures, vanity, etc.) $_____
- ➤ Misc.
    - ○ Explain _____ $_____
    - ○ Explain _____ $_____
    - ○ Explain _____ $_____
- ➤ **Total Project Cost** $_____

FIGURE 11.15   Quote Itemization Form

hours and hours of time that would otherwise be spent driving, waiting at houses, and walking multiple contractors through the job. When we talk about rehabbing properties without lifting a paintbrush, you can see it is all about leveraging a system and valuing your time at each step of the process. Again, at stage 2 you should have visited the subject property only two times—first for the initial walkthrough and information gathering, and the second visit is after you complete your SOW and return to drop it off with copies of your bid package.

DO YOUR COMPARABLES MATCH YOUR AFTER-REPAIR VALUE? DOUBLE-CHECK YOUR SOW

One of the biggest concerns when doing a rehab is keeping the home's post-renovation value in line with the comparables in the neighborhood. Before you start thinking of all of the work you want to do to the house, look at recent comparable sales in the area to make sure they are in line with the price you want to resell it for.

For example, let's say you purchased a property for $130,000; you would like to put $30,000 in renovations into it, and resell for $190,000. However, recent comparable sales in that neighborhood are averaging $160,000. Based on your renovation amount, your sales price would put you $30,000 over the comparables in the area. Even though you made the house look fantastic, you would have a hard time selling it for $30,000 more than other homes in the area. Not only would buyers prefer the less expensive houses, they would also have difficulty getting a loan for more than the appraised value of the home, which is largely determined by sales comparables.

Use your scope of work as a tool to define the project and make sure that the new after-repair value stays within reasonable limits. Keep the comparables you use to get an initial ballpark figure and continue to update comparables throughout the project. At the end of the project, you will have an up-to-date packet that, along with the scope of work, your potential buyers can present to their bank to support the purchase price.

The scope of work is where you make all the executive decisions on exactly what you want to go into your finished rehab. It is the most important stage for setting up your rehab on a successful platform and increasing the success of any contractor you hire to deliver the finished product you want. You should stay focused and identify the details in the scope of work—your contractors and future profits will thank you for it.

CHAPTER 12

Stage 3: A System for Hiring the Perfect Contractor

Once you have finalized your scope of work and put together your bid package, you are ready to interview and invite contractors the opportunity to bid on the project.

The success of your rehabs will depend on two things: having a good, solid system in place like the Seven-Stage Rehab System, and hiring a quality contractor to work within that system. In order to attract these kinds of contractors, you have to sell them on the opportunities that you provide. You can do this by using a contractor elevator pitch as your introduction to a new contractor, whether in person, through a document such as a contractor credibility packet, or over the phone. You should design your elevator pitch with a specific outcome in mind.

The following questions will help start the thought process on how you develop and deliver a powerful pitch.

- What is a problem in your industry for contractors—and how does your company solve it?
- What credibility do you bring to the table to share with a contractor?
- What is your niche, target customer, or target market?
- What type of contractors and professionals do you want to meet?
- How or why are you different from your competition?
- What are the benefits of working and creating a relationship with you and your company?
- Will you be able to refer business and keep them busy throughout the year?

CONTRACTOR CREDIBILITY PACKET

As mentioned above, you will want to prepare a contractor credibility packet to market for contractors. This is especially important if you are inviting contractors who are unfamiliar with you or your organization to bid on your project. Your contractor credibility packet is *not* job specific—so once you have one developed, it will only need minor updating from time to time.

Since your end goal is to establish a trusting relationship with your contractor, you will want to put some effort into creating a professional looking document. A contractor credibility packet template is available for all of our coaching students and allows them to hit the ground running. The bulleted list below summarizes the main items you want to cover.

- **Background about your company.** This is your introduction to potential contractors, so it's crucial to make a good first impression and let them know that you are serious.
- **Your short- and long-term goals.** Potential contractors may be concerned about whether or not you will be able to bring in consistent work. Use this section to illustrate where your company is going.
- **Why you are good to work with.** Again, you are impressing your contractor to establish a good working relationship—so you will have to establish trust by laying out how you respect contractors and deal with them fairly. Let your potential contractors know that you are an investor with a continuing stream of work for them if you can get good pricing.
- **A sample scope of work.** This will give your potential contractors a good idea of what type of client you will be to work with. An organized SOW typically means an organized client.
- **A list of past projects.** Your past projects speak clearly about the standards you set for your contractors, and will give potential contractors a better understanding of your quality expectations. If you are new, you need to reference the coach or investing community in which you enrolled to learn their system and leverage the experience as you get started.
- **A description of your ideal contractor.** Let your potential contractors know what characteristics and qualities you are looking for in a contracting partnership. Motivate your contractor by mentioning the high potential for repeat business if they follow your standards. Let them know that they can produce a quality product and renovation on time and on budget. You also need to detail any licensing, insurance, and warranty requirements you have—which may serve to immediately eliminate some contractors.
- **Examples of how you administer a project.** You can include a sample contractor agreement, pay schedule, and so on to show potential contractors that you mean business and are a reputable investor or firm.

I have included a sample credibility packet for contractors form to get you started. You can download this *sample credibility packet* for contractor form at www.RehabInvestingBible.com/resources for free.

FINDING QUALITY CONTRACTORS

Marketing for contractors is extremely important—so important, in fact, that I have a specific marketing system and prescreening process (including a full application and interview) that we use before working with them. Remember: 50 percent of the success of your rehab is dependent on the contractors you locate and hire. So finding a quality contractor takes a little more effort than just looking in the Yellow Pages.

Essentially, a quality contractor is professional, competent, licensed, and insured. They will have the highest probability to work within your system and do the best, most efficient, job possible. Here are some of my favorite marketing strategies to identify potential contractors to interview.

Online Websites

There are several websites with contractor databases that you can search. I've listed a few below that I've been successful with. Though all four sites require you to register to search for contractors, Angie's List is the only one that charges an annual fee to use its services. It also varies based on the area you are searching. Bid Clerk works a little differently from the other three sites, acting more like a marketplace where you, as the owner, can post a job for contractors to bid on. Remember, even though you may meet a contractor from one of these sites, we still have to interview and prescreen them before we actually make a decision on hiring them.

- www.thebluebook.com
- www.homeadvisor.com
- www.angieslist.com
- www.bidclerk.com

Local Trade Supply Stores

I love networking at a local supply store and asking the staff for a contractor referral. When a staff member refers a specific contractor, it means a few positive things. For starters, if a contractor is well known at a supply store, that means they have repeat work. If they have repeat work, that means they are making customers happy and doing good-quality work, otherwise they would not continue to get more jobs. And finally, if the supply-store staff member refers them, they pay their bills and are typically financially responsible. These are all positive traits we get in a supply-store referral.

- Electrical supply houses
- Plumbing supply houses

- HVAC supply houses
- Paint supply houses

I will never forget when I asked for a referral from my sales manager at the Sherwin Williams paint supply store—he gave me three. One of them worked out for a small paint job I needed at the time. That same contractor grew with me and we completed over 100 rehabs over the years and made each other a lot of money!

Big-Box Supply Stores

These are great spots to meet a lot of contractors and network with the team and staff at the professionals' desk. Make sure if you are actually going to meet and look for contractors at these stores that you get there early because that is when the good contractors spend time at Lowe's or Home Depot—not in the middle of the day when they should be working and completing jobs.

Building Department

Your local building department sees a lot of contractors and can be a great resource if handled correctly. Finding contractors in this way helps ensure that you are dealing with individuals who are familiar with the permitting process and that they actually pull permits, do quality work, and know the local inspectors.

Because the building department is a municipal department, they won't be able to show preference for one contractor over another. In other words, they can't recommend a contractor for you. You must simply go in to introduce yourself and tell them that you are trying to find local contractors to work on your projects that are licensed and insured. Let the building department know that you will be identifying vacant and dilapidated houses that you plan on revitalizing and putting back on the tax rolls to help the city and bring in tax revenue (this is how they get paid). This gives them an opening to share the contractors they work with on a regular basis without showing prejudice.

Jobsites

Look around your area for contractors doing renovation projects. Stop by and introduce yourself, and be ready with your elevator pitch. Visiting a contractor's jobsite tells you a lot about that contractor without even exchanging words. Assess the worksite's organization and the workers' attitude. If the contractor is present, you have an opportunity to watch him or her in action—and not just when they're on their best behavior. Don't be shy about asking the property owners if they are happy with the work the contractor is doing. Good or bad, you'll definitely get an opinion.

Real Estate Investment Associations (REIAs)

Don't forget, as discussed, that networking is an extremely useful tool, especially when it comes to finding a contractor specializing in rehabs. Make sure that you make contact with your local REIAs and talk to members about contractors working in the area.

Contractor Referrals from Other Good Contractors

Other good contractors are a great source for referrals. Once you find one you like, ask him who *he* likes working with. Contractors who do the same quality of work tend to stick together. Good contractors work with good contractors; this is a great resource.

The One-Minute Contractor Elevator Pitch

Just like you, contractors are in the business to make money—so they want to know how you can help them do that. The one-minute elevator pitch is perfect for grabbing a contractor's attention. This will help ensure they will actually go to your subject house and bid on the project. Develop and practice a pitch that covers these main points:

- **I am not a retail client.** Start by sharing that you are not simply a homeowner doing a onetime kitchen remodel. This lets them know that you will make decisions quickly, and that you don't expect retail prices. You expect wholesale prices.
- **I work with a network of investors.** Explain how this network can keep these contractors busy, meaning you can provide them with job after job after job.
- **I use a proven system with a predetermined scope of work.** Let them know that you have a detailed scope of work, itemized down to the materials and item numbers, so they can focus on what they do best—the work itself.
- **I *love* to pay contractors when work is completed.** Remind them that you do not make any money or gain any benefit until the job is complete. Deliver this line just as I have shared it with you, "I *love* to pay contractors when work is completed." Contractors are not used to hearing the words *love* and *pay* in the same sentence from clients, so this is a huge motivator for them to work with you.

- **Ask, "Would you like to make money in my system?"** End with a question that gives them no choice but to say, "yes." This will leave you in a positive space to share the next steps on how they can move forward with you.

Explain to contractors how your system for completing rehabs will free them up to do what they do best and keep them from having to do their job *and* yours. Let them know that you are an investor and will have a steady stream of projects for the right contractor, so they won't have to worry about where the next job is coming from. Make it clear, as well, that you pay promptly and willingly for completed work.

You also want to take the time to pitch your company principles. Now is the time to explain your zero-tolerance policy for poor quality work or lack of professionalism. Set expectations right up front. Let the contractors know that you believe that good renovations come from good contractors. Make sure you emphasize how critical listening and communication are to the project's success, and foster collaboration among all parties involved.

Contractor Meeting and Prescreening

There are certain criteria you must find in a contractor to ensure a positive experience. The following questions help focus what you should be looking and interviewing for when you meet and prescreen contractors.

How many years have they been on the job?

Everybody has to start somewhere, but for successful rehab projects, you want a contractor who has been in business for a while. I recommend that they have a minimum of three years of trade experience; five or more is better.

Do they own the proper tools for the job?

A contractor should own all the tools necessary to do the job you are hiring them for. Could you imagine hiring a specialist to refinish your hardwood floors who has to rent a sander from Home Depot or Lowe's? When a project isn't finished on time because all of the sanders have already been rented out for the next week, you'll run into a problem and, worse, hear excuses blaming Home Depot or Lowe's. You need to ensure that the contractor you hire owns the proper tools to do the job within the allotted time frame.

How many workers are on their crew and how many jobs are they currently working on?

You also want to make sure that your potential contractor isn't stretched too thin. If you find out that the roofing contractor you're interviewing currently has three employees and three roofing jobs at the same time, you might want to reconsider. You don't need years of rehabbing experience to tell you that someone with that many jobs and that few workers will more than likely be slow, unresponsive, and stressed out.

Do they use subcontractors?

In our system, it is important that we contract directly and pay all contractors. That means the carpenter, plumber, electrician, HVAC, and so on. What we are trying to avoid is paying one person all of our money who then asks someone to do work at your house who never gets paid. This is when you run into the problem of disputes and mechanic's liens. No one cares more about your money and your job more than you. Our independent contractor agreement spells out that they cannot hire any subcontractors without our approval.

Are they licensed and insured? Do they carry the proper liability insurance and provide workers' compensation insurance?

You do *not* want to work with *any* contractor who is not licensed and isn't willing to get the proper permits. You also want to steer clear of anyone who doesn't have insurance, as they will become a liability for you. It's definitely an added layer of protection for you to choose only the licensed contractors who don't cut corners. Remember, any damage or injuries that happen on the jobsite will be your problem if you are unwise enough to work with an uninsured contractor.

Have they ever declared bankruptcy?

You want a contractor who is financially stable enough to be able to front material costs using their supply house lines of credit and isn't pressuring you for money all the time. Contractors who need money all the time are always difficult to work with. Contractors who do not have a proven track record of handling money and running their business are a liability and could be a future problem waiting to happen if you hire them.

Can they provide you with referrals or access to previous jobs they've completed for reference?

Obviously a contractor won't give you references from customers who were dissatisfied with their work, but you will be able to learn a lot about the contractor from their past clients. Don't be reluctant to ask references specific questions about the contractor's work habits, crew, and professionalism. Viewing previous jobs will give you a concrete example of the care and quality this individual puts into their projects. They can talk the talk, but if the workmanship is shoddy, you don't want to work with them.

These questions are all pulled from my contractor meeting interview sheet. This is a two-page sheet with specific questions and processes that my team asks a new contractor to properly prescreen them. To get a copy of the *contractor meeting interview sheet* I use, visit www.RehabInvestingBible.com/resources and download it for free.

You have to have a good system in order to experience a great contractor. Many new investors or those without a system hire good contractors; but even the best contractor will flounder in a bad system or no system at all. The only person to blame in this situation is you, the investor, for not doing your job up front with a detailed scope of work. Realize that a good contractor is worth his weight in gold. Take care of them, grow with them, learn with them, and both parties will make a lot of money.

The key to our contractor system is superior communication. The pricing I have shared thus far is wholesale pricing, not retail pricing. Meaning if you cannot communicate well that you are an investor who can add value, make their job easy with your proven system, and possibly give them future work, they will give you one-off retail pricing. Basically, if you can't sell the contractor on the benefits of working with you, then it will be hard for them to see why they should give you discounted wholesale pricing and preferential treatment over a homeowner doing their one-time kitchen remodel.

Let me illustrate why you, as an investor with a system, should and will get preferential pricing over Sally the homeowner. Realize Sally the homeowner does not give a contractor a detailed scope of work with exactly what they want installed and completed in the house. Sally the homeowner lives in the house, so contractors have to coordinate around the schedule of her work and family, which adds more time to complete the job. If it takes the contractor more time to complete the job, then it also increases the timeline for when they get paid. And finally don't forget that Sally the homeowner is probably going to ask them to repaint her kitchen remodel three times until she is happy with the color she choose. For all these reasons, contractors should charge a retail homeowner more than they will charge you as an investor. As an investor, you have systems that they can work in, complete the job, and get paid!

A very important tip that will save you time and money: before you send a potential contractor to bid, *give them your estimated budget for the project*. If it's unrealistically low, it's your contractor's job to justify and educate you as to why their quote is higher than the budget you originally assumed. However, you should estimate a little bit lower than your allowable budget in case you have overestimated in some areas, and the contractor is able to get the job the done at a lower price.

The following outline is a longer version of how I introduce and sell our residential redevelopment company CT Homes, LLC, to contractors at a prescreening meeting, whether in person or over the phone. Knowing what you are going to say in detail and not just winging it conveys your professionalism. It allows you to state your rules up front and reassure the contractor that you have clear expectations that you expect to be met. Because the contractor will also be interviewing you, you need to sell him or her on why you are great to work with and how a long-term partnership will benefit you both.

Sample Introductory Contractor Meeting Outline

1. Introduction to our company (3 minutes).
   a. Description of our company.
      i. We are a residential redevelopment house-buying company.
      ii. We purchased x homes last year; goal to purchase x homes this year.
      iii. Typical rehab costs range from $5,000 to $50,000.
      iv. An average renovation cost is $30,000.
   b. Company goals.
      i. Our primary goal is to renovate and sell a quality product to the marketplace.
      ii. We run our company as efficiently as possible to earn profits.
      iii. We increase homeownership opportunities in the community.
      iv. We improve the neighborhoods where we invest.
      v. We help affiliated businesses like them succeed.
2. Benefits for their company (5 minutes).
   a. Consistent work for contractor.
      i. Allows them to keep best team members on their crew.
      ii. Little to no marketing expenses for company owner.
      iii. Takes the risk and uneasiness out of the business.
      iv. Increases income for their company.
   b. Business building assistance we provide:
      i. Regular business-building meetings to help them improve.
      ii. Help them set up their company correctly and avoid liability.
      iii. Help them grow their company correctly.
3. The benefits of working with CT Homes, LLC, as a residential redeveloper. Our goal is to make the rehab as hassle free as possible (3 minutes).
   a. We do this via constant communication. Without it, projects are delayed.
   b. We are continually improving our rehab systems. We want to make their business more efficient and increase profit margins, because it will do the same for us.

(continued)

(Continued)

   c. We systemize the rehab business.
      i. Scope of work is detailed with exact materials.
      ii. Takes the guesswork out of construction and their work.

4. Pictures and scope of work for past jobs (3 minutes).
   a. Photo examples of four of our past jobs.
   b. Scope of work for four jobs, without prices.
   c. Timeline of work for four jobs.

5. How we expect to conduct business (5 minutes).
   a. Scope of work completed.
   b. Bids must be obtained from the scope of work.
   c. Walkthrough with contractor.
   d. Material selection and ordering.
   e. Independent contractor agreement signed.
      i. Payment scheduled signed.
      ii. Schedule of work signed.
   f. W9, proof of insurance, proof of workers' comp provided.
   g. Building permits obtained.
   h. Work schedule is monitored.
   i. How we handle change orders.
   j. Change order form.
   k. Punch list is signed and finished.
   l. Waiver of lien is signed.

6. How our company handles problems (5 minutes).
   a. Consistent communication solves 90 percent of problems. We have avoided many past problems when both parties communicate.
   b. Quality of work problems.
      i. This is of the utmost importance to us. Our work is our reputation.
      ii. Their reputation is also on the line.
     iii. We have had contractors who skimp and are short-term thinkers; they don't last in this system.
     iv. Problem solved by contractor taking care of the details.
   c. Job scheduling.
      i. We have someone from the office check on the job daily and weekly to make sure we are on schedule.

> ii. If contractor does not show up when scheduled, it needs to be commu-
> nicated. If not, there is a warning, then we release (fire) them from the
> job.
> 7. Next potential jobs to bids on with CT Homes (3 minutes)
>   a. Scope of work provided.
>   b. Timeline for acceptance of bids.

Once you have prescreened a number of qualified, licensed, and insured contractors to quote your house, you are in the home stretch. These carefully prescreened contractors then get the opportunity to bid on your current project. Make sure you communicate to all contractors the timeline for sending back the quote itemization form so you can review all bids and award the job. By following stage 1 and putting a lockbox with a key on the house, we do not have to coordinate or meet the contractors at the house for them to bid on the property. This will save you an enormous amount of time. You should obtain at least three bids for every area of the house to make sure you are getting the best pricing.

Do *not* accept a flat rate of one lump sum bid for the project. Make sure to tell contractors to itemize their bids as detailed by the quote itemization form. This will show you exactly what the contractor is charging you for and in what area.

When you have received all your bids, you need to evaluate them. At a minimum, each should meet the following requirements:

- Quantities should reasonably match the quantities you estimated when preparing your scope of work.
- Every area from your scope of work/quote itemization form needs to be present in the bid.
- No additional items have been added.
- License and insurance information is confirmed and up-to-date.
- Professional references have been confirmed.

Evaluate each bid for professionalism, accuracy, and overall feel. If you have any questions on an item that a contractor has included in his or her bid, don't hesitate to ask for clarification and education. The lowest bid is not the automatic answer to whom we choose to work with. Once you have followed the prescreening system and have a group of quality contractors submitting bids, it is okay to follow your instinct and gut about who you believe will be the best working partner and team member to start and complete your rehab.

My final piece of advice for choosing your final contractor comes down to respect and whether you like him or her. If through this process you and the contractor do not have mutual respect, then I would not move forward with that individual. Once you have mutual respect, it finally comes down to who you like and believe you will get along with the best, moving forward.

CHAPTER 13

Stage 4: The Six Critical Documents

Must-Haves for Your Rehab

You've selected a contractor and are anxious to get started on the project—but not so fast. You need to establish rules and introduce the contractor to your rehab-management system. You also need to walk him or her through the six critical documents that he or she has to sign before starting the project and stepping foot on the job site.

VERIFY CONTRACTOR LICENSE AND INSURANCE

Every contractor you work with should provide copies and verify the following before you hire them for your job. He or she will need to provide:

1. **Contractor's license.** State and local licenses are required for their individual trade.
2. **Proof of liability insurance.** Get the insurance company contact and information and call to confirm that their insurance is paid and current.
3. **Proof of workers' compensation insurance.** This only applies if they employ crewmembers.

THE SIX CRITICAL DOCUMENTS TO PROVIDE AND EXECUTE

It is crucial that you have all of the appropriate paperwork ready for the contractor to sign *before the job starts*. No work should be done on the project until the binding agreements have been signed; this protects you both. It is your job to have and provide paperwork that looks after your interest and protects you as the residential redeveloper and investor. If you sign the contractor's paperwork that will more favorably protect them and not have the rules we need to motivate them to complete a quality job within the budget and timeline.

Here are the six critical documents we sign on every job with every contractor that we pay directly:

1. Independent contractor agreement
2. Final scope of work
3. Payment schedule
4. Insurance indemnification form
5. W-9
6. Final and unconditional lien waiver

Let's go into detail on each.

Independent Contractor Agreement (ICA)

The ICA is the Holy Grail—the main binding contract between you and the contractor. This document specifically states who is responsible for pulling permits, buying materials, and scheduling Building Department inspections—all of which are the contractor's job. The independent contractor agreement is the contractor's reference document for how things will be done, the start and end dates, and covers many other aspects of the project. If a contractor knows what is expected of them and it is clearly communicated and spelled out, you have drastically increased the probability that both you and the contractor will have a successful project and relationship moving forward. This is why our six critical documents are so important. These documents directly affect the behavior, timeline, budget, and quality of the job.

This document should cover the following:

- **Independent contractor status.** This document clearly spells out the contractor is not our employee. This is very important for liability and tax purposes. We are hiring them for services one job at a time. This makes them responsible for their own insurance and taxes.
- **Materials.** Detail who is responsible for selecting (the investor) and buying (the contractor) the materials to be used in the rehab.
- **Services provided.** Points to the final scope of work as the exact services the contractor will provide in this contract.
- **Taxes and building department.** Points out that pulling permits, paying all taxes and fees related to the work, labor, and material are the responsibility of the contractor being hired.

- **Inspection.** Defines that the contractor is responsible for coordinating, completing, and passing all inspections required and needed by the Building Department.
- **Cleanup.** Let the contractor know your expectations for his or her behavior on the project site. It should specifically state that the contractor is responsible for cleaning up the job site at the end of *every day*. This is crucial, because you want to be able to walkthrough the property with potential private lenders after work or on the weekends. If it looks messy—trash and materials everywhere—it will not leave a very good impression.
- **Client Approval.** Points out that you, as the client, will approve contractor services based on:
  - All governing building codes have been meet
  - All required building permit inspections have been completed and passed
  - The services and punch-list work is completed and to your satisfaction
- **Completion Schedule.** State specific milestone completion dates as well as a final project completion date, and the penalty for not completing the work on time.
- **Penalties.** Clearly states the start and end dates of the project. I always ask the contractor how much time they need to complete the job. Once they give me an answer I always add a week and put it in the contract. Then if they go past that date, they will incur a financial penalty every day the job is not completed. This makes it crystal clear to the contractor that as an investor you need the house completed on time so you can market and sell it to get your money back.
- **Change Orders.** Clearly outlines how to handle unforeseen work and additional payment for that work. We then introduce our simple change order that the contractor will need to use if they expect any additional payment for work. When both parties agree on this, it will eliminate headaches and shouting matches at the end of the job. To view and get a copy of the *change order form* I use, visit www.RehabInvestingBible.com/resources and you can download it for free.
- **Insurance.** Detail the specific insurance and workers' compensation requirements that the contractor will need to have in place for the project. Liability coverage of $500,000 from the contractor's insurance is good; we prefer $1,000,000 of liability coverage since the cost is not much more for the contractor to increase it from $500,000 to $1,000,000.
- **Subcontractors.** State that no subcontractors are to be hired without your approval. It should also specify that subcontractors are to be paid by the owner and that each subcontractor will also sign a lien waiver as applicable.
- **Cancellation.** Gives you the right to cancel the services and contract at any time without further obligation or penalty.

- **Warranties.** I require all contractors to warranty their work for a period of time after the house is compete. I require a one-year warranty on the contractor's work. We do not make them responsible for any material defects.
- **Arbitration.** Detail how any disputes will be handled.

Final Scope of Work

As discussed in Chapter 11, the SOW is the agreement between you and your contractor as to what work will be completed on the property being renovated. It contains detailed instructions and calls out item numbers, SKU numbers, paint colors, and specific materials. Having a detailed SOW allows your contractor to work much more efficiently, which is passed on to you as wholesale pricing and preferential treatment.

Take the time to walkthrough the project with your contractor before signing off on the final scope of work. Your contractor will see the project with a different eye and may have some good feedback for additional work that you did not think of.

When my students and I do our job as the residential redeveloper, and complete and hand off the SOW to a contractor, we are always seen in a very professional light and earn more respect from our contractor. Most contractors are not used to such a detailed and organized system to work in that makes their job easier and allows them to get paid faster. Basically, you have spelled out everything you want done on the property—and everything they need to do to get paid! When you do this, the contractors always fall in love with you and sing your praises.

Payment Schedule

The payment schedule sets milestones that your contractor needs to reach (based on the SOW) before getting paid for work completed on your renovation. As an example, the first payment is made after the demo and trash removal is complete; the second payment is made after the new kitchen frame out and roof is completed, and so on. The reason we do not pay every week is because if a contractor knows they are going to get paid every week, they won't focus on the job at hand; they'll just think that payday is coming Friday. You don't want to end up in a situation where you have paid out 80 percent of the fee with only 30 percent of the work completed. Then before you know it, you are behind on work and ahead on payments. If there is one thing I can have you remember when it comes to payments and work completed at your job, it is this rule:

> The only leverage you have with a contractor is the money you have not paid them yet.

If a contractor tells you that he or she will not start the job without a payment, then you should tell them, "I'm sorry, but we don't know each other quite yet, and we're just starting to establish a working relationship. So the only way to get started is if I make smaller, more frequent payments as work begins. This will allow both of us to establish trust and a good track record to move forward with."

It may be a bit of a red flag if they try to talk you into putting money down up front to get the project started. If a contractor cannot do the demolition, set up, and initial material ordering to start your project, they may have some adverse financial situations that are keeping them from establishing credit accounts with suppliers (for example, a prior bankruptcy that has hampered their credit). Of course, he or she might just be cautious about working with you for the first time. This is why it is critical that you pay contractors promptly upon completion of milestones. You may be thinking that no contractor will start work without payment or even a large payment. Well, if you have found a good contractor, they will have credit accounts at supply houses. The only out-of-pocket work we are asking them to do is to set up at the jobsite (so we know they are actually going to work) and the initial demo. This step does not require the contractor to come out of pocket with money. They are just fronting time and labor. Immediately after the first week or so we make the first payment and move the relationship and the job along. Remember, "The only motivation you have with a contractor is the money you have not paid them yet." If you pay them too much money ahead of work completed, you will find yourself in bad situation. There is nothing worse than paying out money and not having work to show for it.

You must set up the payment schedule so a contractor can reach the first payment milestone relatively soon after the project starts. Here is a rule of thumb and an example for making payments at each milestone. You should start with the smallest payment at the beginning and save the largest payment of the job be to be paid upon completion. Here is what a payment schedule for your contractor may look like using this rule of thumb.

1st payment for demo and frame out = 15 percent.

2nd payment for insulation, Sheetrock, doors, and trim = 20 percent.

3rd payment for installing kitchen and bath cabinets = 20 percent.

4th payment for countertops and flooring = 20 percent.

Final payment for punch-list and final closeout = 25 percent.

The key takeaway here is that your first payment is the smallest percentage of the payment and the last payment is the largest percentage of the payment. If you make your last payment a measly 5 percent of the payment, and there is 20 percent of the work needed to complete the job, there is a good chance your contractor will not be motivated to do 20 percent of the work for the final 5 percent of the final contractor payment.

Insurance Indemnification Form

This is a stand-alone document that clearly states the insurance you require the contractor to carry—which should include both liability and workers' compensation. Even though this is also spelled out in the independent contractor agreement, it is prudent to have the contractor acknowledge multiple times in writing that he or she will meet your insurance requirements and keep their insurance current for the duration of the job. On your end, you need to make sure the requirements in both documents match identically. Any contractor you hire should carry a minimum of $1 million in liability insurance as discussed. In addition to the insurance indemnification agreement, the contractor will also need to supply the following three documents before they begin work:

1. Proof of liability insurance.
2. Proof of workers' compensation insurance.
3. A certificate of insurance from their carrier adding you as additional insured with the project address.

Insurance *You* Need for Residential Redevelopment Projects

You need two specialized types of high-risk insurance for your rehab properties:

1. **Builder's risk and vacant dwelling insurance** insures against the property and its replacement cost should anything happen to it, such as the electrician accidentally starting a fire and burning the house down. Having this type of policy in place ensures that you are compensated for the replacement cost of the structure.
2. **Liability insurance** protects you against lawsuits filed by someone who gets hurt on the property; for example, a curious neighbor who trips over a pile of lumber and sprains his ankle while peeking in the window. Even though you require your contractors to also carry insurance, you also need to have this insurance in place to stay protected.

Since both types of insurance pose a higher risk to the insuring agency, you will need to purchase them through an insurance broker rather than your regular agent. The premiums and cost will also be higher than traditional insurance coverage due the additional risk the insurer takes on with your rehabbed property. This insurance is provided through the excess surplus markets. These policies are typically paid up front with a minimum coverage period. Depending on the policy, a portion of the purchase may be refundable if you sell the house before the term of the insurance has expired. For instance, if you bought a six-month builder's risk/vacant dwelling policy for $1,200 that had a 50 percent minimum earned stipulation, the most you could get refunded would be $600 (three months), regardless of how soon you sold the property.

I have only found one insurance carrier that issues these types of insurance on a month-to-month payment basis. It took me many years to track them down, and I've included them as a resource for you to use. Go to www.RehabInvestingBible.com/resources to get access to this valuable insurance referral. They insure throughout North America.

W-9

The IRS requires real estate investors and business owners to issue a 1099 form to every independent contractor we pay more than $600 to in a calendar year. To be able to issue the 1099, you need to have the contractor fill out and sign a W-9 form. I have my independent contractors sign a new W-9 for each year I work with them.

To make it easy, I have downloaded and saved the most recent IRS Form W-9 and provided it for you to download at www.RehabInvestingBible.com/resources.

There are two major reasons why it is important to have this form completed at the *beginning* of the project. One is so that you don't have to try to track down the contractor when your CPA or accountant is in a crunch come tax season, and the second is because this is the time when you are on the best terms with the contractor. Nothing has gone wrong yet, and no one is disenchanted with one another. The truth is that you are not going to be best friends with every contractor you work with. You're apt to have some disputes and may even fire some contractors, as you do projects. Imagine calling a contractor you fired at the end of the year and requesting their information so that they are responsible for paying the taxes on the income you paid them. Not a pleasant thought, is it? Do yourself a favor and have each contractor sign their W-9 once a year while you are on good terms.

Final and Unconditional Lien Waiver

This is the one document that won't be signed until the end of the project. It is very important, however, to explain this form up front. We want all of our contractors to know that in order to receive their final payment, they will be required to sign this final and unconditional lien waiver confirming they have been paid if full. The lien waiver basically states that the contractor has been paid in full for the agreed-upon work and has no right to a mechanic's lien on the property for any reason whatsoever.

Every city, county, and state has different laws on how someone can attach a mechanic's lien to your property. A mechanic's lien is attached to a property when someone, such as a contractor, claims that he or she provided work and services at the subject property but did not get paid in full for said work and services. The mechanic's lien clouds and encumbers the title to the property, making it impossible for you to sell until the dispute is resolved. To clear the title and be able to sell the house, you will need to pay off, fight, or negotiate with the contractor to release the lien.

You can prevent this by becoming intimately familiar with the mechanics lien law in your area and getting a final and unconditional lien waiver signed before you make the final payment. This waiver states that all work and services at the subject property have been completed and that the contractor has been paid in full for said work and services. Have the check ready to go so that the contractor knows the payment will be made. You must *never* make a final payment until you get the final and unconditional lien waiver signed.

THE TIMELINE AND ORDER OF EXECUTING THE SIX CRITICAL DOCUMENTS

The timing of these documents is also critical. You must have the first five documents signed *before* you start construction, but *after* you have closed on the property. The last document, the final and unconditional waiver of lien, should not be signed under any circumstances until the contractor has finished work on the project.

Here is a timeline for when the documents should be signed.

1. Once you close and actually own the house you can sign the:
   a. Independent contractor agreement
   b. Final scope of work
   c. Payment schedule
   d. Insurance indemnification form
   e. W-9
2. No work should be started on the house until your contractor pulls a building permit and makes a copy for your records.

3. Once all of the work is completed and you have the final sign-off from Building Department in writing, the final steps to get the lien waiver signed are to:
    a. Get a copy of the final approval from the Building Department on the closed permit.
    b. Sign the final and unconditional lien waiver.
    c. Issue and deliver the final check.

HOW TO GET PAINLESS PERMITS: WHY YOU WILL LOVE THE BUILDING DEPARTMENT

Before you can get started on any job you and your contracting team are responsible for pulling permits. Specifically, your contractors are the actual team members who go down to pull permits and pay for them as dictated in your independent contractor agreement. In some municipalities, you will need to provide additional paperwork for contractors to pull permits for the property you own.

I have listened to too many investors, real estate groups, or investor forums complain that pulling permits slows them down or creates more problems for their rehab. Worse, I hear some investors giving the advice to *not* pull permits—to me that is a cardinal sin. As a residential redeveloper, we pull permits. As a residential redeveloper, we create jobs by pulling permits. As a residential redeveloper, we improve neighborhoods one house at a time by pulling permits. As a residential redeveloper, we generate tax revenue by pulling permits. It's simple: as a residential redeveloper of one property or a dozen properties, we must pull permits.

The city will typically require a building permit for constructing, enlarging, moving, demolishing, or changing the occupancy of a structure, as well as for making major changes to electrical, gas, mechanical, or plumbing systems.

My rule of thumb is to always direct the contractor to pull permits on any scope of work. If a contractor says that the work needed does not require a permit, you can let him or her know that the Building Department will determine that *after* the contractor explains the scope of work they will be doing at the subject property. It's always best to have the Building Department on your side. A building inspector can make your life a complete nightmare if they catch one of your jobs being done without a permit. They will fine you, penalize you, and typically make you wait a long period of time before you can resume the job.

Why are pulling permits so important?

For starters, enrolling the Building Department and your local inspector to approve and oversee your hired contractors' work adds another set of eyes that your contractors are doing the job correctly. This is of great benefit to you as the owner of the project; someone else is double-checking the work done by the contractors on your project.

Second, pulling permits protects us from a long list of liabilities such as future claims, lawsuits, or issues that may arise from the house or the people living in it.

Finally, pulling permits and making friends with your local Building Department is what residential redevelopers do. If you think of yourself as a small-time do-it-yourselfer trying to fly under the radar screen with a couple of deals a year . . . well, then you are thinking small and irresponsibly.

One of the biggest benefits of being a residential redeveloper is creating jobs. The byproduct of following the Seven-Stage Rehab System outlined in this book is that you save time and increase your profit potential whether you do two deals or two hundred deals in a year. The Building Department will love you more and more if you show respect by following the code and pulling permits, because following this process puts vacant, dilapidated homes back on the tax rolls, thereby generating tax revenue for the city that pays the very people who work at the Building Department.

You may worry that pulling permits will add time to your job, but it doesn't have to. The key is to enroll the Building Department to root for your success. You do this by creating and practicing a building inspector elevator pitch to inform and educate your building official when you visit the Building Department for the first time. Here is an example.

"Hello Mr. Building Inspector, my name is _____. I want to introduce myself because my company is currently identifying and buying dilapidated, vacant, homes in need of repair that are not currently on the tax rolls. My team and I will be investing large amounts of money, time, and resources to redevelop these properties and place new families and homeowners in these homes. We are very excited about helping to improve our city and adding homeowners to the tax rolls. We know this will create revenue for this department and other municipalities. I want to make sure to have my contractors apply and pull all proper permits on every job to be compliant with the Building Department. The faster we can pull permits to start and finish a job, the faster we can get to the next property and continue working on the goal of helping our city grow by improving properties. What can my contractors and I do to ensure we get you everything you need to effectively and efficiently issue us the needed building permits to start work? How can we pull permits and seek approvals throughout our jobs in a timely and efficient manner?"

When you enroll the Building Department and let them know you are not going to cut corners and that your primary goal is to improve properties by listening to their feedback, they will help to make the permit process efficient. Getting the Building Department on board will help make the permit process as painless as possible. In return, they will actually fall in love with you and your company for doing the right thing and helping to improve the city.

Do not skip the crucial step of walking through the paperwork and contract with your contractors. This is what will save you management headaches and time once the job starts, by clearly defining and setting the necessary expectations. The time you take to walkthrough, explain, and share what you expect from them by using the six critical documents—and what they should expect from you—is what guarantees a professional and respectful working relationship.

CHAPTER 14

Stage 5: Managing the Rehab

Getting the Work Done On Time and On Budget

This is the stage of your rehab where all of the work that you did in the previous four stages begins to pay off. At this point all your heavy lifting is behind you as a residential redeveloper. It is now time for the licensed and insured professionals that you hired to execute and rehab a beautiful property to perfection. As spelled out by the six critical documents, you have minimal obligations on the day-to-day activities once the rehab actually starts. Thanks to your executed paperwork and system, you have clearly defined the lines of communication, roles, and responsibilities for every member of the rehab team to move forward successfully. You can now stand back and let the professionals do their work.

CONTRACTOR KICKOFF MEETING AND COMMUNICATION

Once all contractors have signed and executed the six critical documents, it's time to set up a project kickoff meeting on the site or as a conference call. This is when you'll introduce the contractor and all subcontractors, share a phone list, establish the go-to contact person on site as the lead carpenter, and that your role as the project manager is to oversee the progress and release payments based on the payment schedule.

This meeting allows you and the contractor to verify that you are on the same page regarding the rehab. It's also your chance to ensure the contractor understands your expectations for the project scope, budget, and timeline one last time. Now is a good time to remind them again that they are responsible for action items such as pulling permits, purchasing and installing materials, and coordinating any ongoing building inspections.

If your kickoff meeting is onsite, you have another chance to walkthrough the project with the contractor team to make sure that nothing essential was left out of the scope of work. As the owner, you are the project's director and manager; but you want to take advantage of your contractor's experience and expertise. He or she may be able to see more economical or efficient ways to achieve the same end results and share them just before you get started.

At this stage, you can let your contractor know that while you will be involved in the project as the project manager, you will not be micromanaging or running errands for the job. It's important to remind them that you need to spend your time marketing to find other deals, raising money to finance those deals, and negotiating and putting them together. If you need to, use an example to explain this at the kickoff meeting. Let them know that what they may think is just a simple call to you in the middle of the day to pick up a bucket of paint actually takes an hour and a half away from your day that you needed to put the next rehab deal under contract. That means they just missed out on another $20–$30,000 job. When you communicate to team members how their requests affect the cash in their pocket, they always seem to understand your points more clearly and without hesitation.

REHAB MILESTONES THAT HELP YOU STAY ORGANIZED

I have broken down the rehab into five distinct stages for new rehabbers. Keep in mind that the workflow of the rehab is critical. As residential redevelopers, we always want the exterior to be the first thing fixed up and looking good so the neighbors can start talking. This will also generate interest from those just passing by (and therefore more potential buyers). I call this "working from the outside in." This approach also prevents doing interior work that can be damaged later if you do not properly address the roof, windows, and doors at the start. The beginning is an ideal time to complete exterior work such as roofing, siding, or replacing windows—which just happen to be milestones that typically align with the permit-pulling process. Since the payment schedule is tied to these milestones and provides benchmarks for the job, this ensures that we stay ahead on work and behind on payments.

Here are the milestones and coinciding building inspections; these will vary slightly by area:

1. **Demo and cleanout**—The initial permit is pulled before demo starts.
2. **Frame out**—The first onsite building inspection by the building inspector.
3. **Rough in**—The second onsite building inspection by the building inspector.
4. **Insulation**—The third onsite building inspection by the building inspector.
5. **Finishing**—The fourth and final inspection completion by the building inspector; can't get a certificate of occupancy without the final inspection.

Milestone 1 Demolition and Cleanout

"Out with the old, in with the new" is the theme of this phase. And it's exactly what it sounds like: demolishing everything that is coming out and cleaning up the property so that you can start with a clean slate. This stage is also when you are most likely to discover unpleasant surprises. You will be tearing out flooring, removing fixtures, and knocking down walls, finding anything from rotten floorboards to oddly placed piping. Depending on how much demo and trash is at the house, your team may need multiple dumpsters. It is always good to walkthrough the property after the demo and cleanout as you may have new ideas or a different feel for the space after it is wide open. If you are going to make any changes to the layout and your original scope of work, now is the best time to do so.

Milestone 2—Frame Out

Framing out the house creates the space's skeletal structure. Your team will be framing any new spaces like bathrooms, kitchens, additions, and so on. Carpenters will frame any new walls and mark the location of new utilities, appliances, and lighting. Once the frame out is complete, other trades can come in and get started on the rough out.

Milestone 3—Rough In

After the carpenters are finished, the electrical, plumbing, and HVAC (heating, ventilation, and air conditioning) subcontractors will come through and work their magic. Critical building inspections take place at this time and will need to happen at the end of the rough-in phase before the insulation and walls are closed up. Get the electrical, plumbing, and HVAC work signed off on before scheduling the final rough inspection.

Milestone 4—Insulation

After you've passed all of the inspections, insulation can be placed in the walls and around the new utility work. Insulation will obscure wiring, piping, and ducting, so make sure it goes in *after* the inspections. In some municipalities, the building inspector needs to make one more visual sign-off on the house after the insulation is complete and before you can close up the walls.

Milestone 5—Finishing

This is the fun part of the rehab! At this point you are starting to see the finished product you designed from your scope of work turn into reality. If you are doing major work and opened up a lot of spaces, sheetrock and taping will take the most time at this stage. Next, contractors will install the door trim, window trim, baseboard, and crown molding. Then, the painting should commence. At this point, it is a race to the finish. The electrician is installing electrical fixtures, light switches, plugs, and plates. The plumber is installing fixtures, faucets, toilets, and shower trim. The HVAC contractor is installing the heating registers, thermostat and final cosmetic touches. Finally, the carpenter is completing all big and small finishes such as cabinets, counter installation, tile work, touch-up painting, flooring, and so on to deliver a finished product that matches your original scope of work. You are watching your vision become a reality.

Although this stage has the most physical work done by the contractors, you as the investor are actually on the downhill coast to the finish line. At stage 5, our primary job was preparing and completing stages 1 through 4. It takes practice at the rehab stage not to get involved and do work on the house itself. However, when you do this, you are actually rehabbing without ever lifting a paintbrush!

CHAPTER 15

Stage 6: Contract Closeout and Final Payment

When the last milestone has been completed on the rehab, you are ready to start closing out the project.

Here are the final things to confirm and closeout before you issue the final payment:

- Final certificate of occupancy (if needed)
- Final punch list
- Final lien waiver executed
- Final payment to contractor

No matter how good your contractor is, they will inevitably miss a few details. Before you do a thorough walkthrough of the project with the contractor to develop punch-list items that need to be addressed, have the contractor use a job completion checklist. This checklist helps the contractor confirm everything is completed and in good working order before you come out to the house to create the final punch list.

I have a very detailed job completion checklist that we use at CT Homes, LLC. This checklist is given to the contractor to do a final walkthrough of the project before they request us to come out to the finished project. This system allows our contractors to catch any small or big details that need to be buttoned up and, most importantly, saves us time from coming to a house that is not yet completed.

To download the *job completion checklist*, go to www.RehabInvestingBible.com/resources; this will save you hours of time and frustration when you actually do your final walkthrough to make the final payment.

FINAL CERTIFICATE OF OCCUPANCY

This is also often referred to as the final CO (certificate of occupancy). This documentation is needed to close out and sign off on all of your pulled building permits. You do not want to make the final payment until you have a copy of the final, signed-off permits or another form of proof that the building permit is now closed with the building department to their satisfaction. Don't rely on a call to the building department; if you don't actually have something physically signed from the Building Department, this could come back to you bite you.

FINAL PUNCH LIST

This is a list that you as the owner and investor make upon final walkthrough to catch small or big things that were missed or still need to be fixed before you pay the contractor in full. You don't want to make multiple trips to the property with your contractor to go over final punch-list items. I recommend purchasing a roll of blue painter's tape and marking off any areas throughout the home that need touch-up work so they do not get missed.

FINAL LIEN WAIVER EXECUTED

Once the permits have been signed and the punch list completed, and you are happy with the completed project, have the contractor sign the final and unconditional waiver of lien before issuing the final payment for the job. This document indicates that both you and the contractor agree that the project is complete per the contract, and that the contractor does not have any grounds to make a claim or file a mechanic's lien against the project. The amount of the final payment should be included with the waiver of lien and is acknowledged as payment in full.

FINAL PAYMENT TO CONTRACTOR

The first three items need to be done before you sign off on the work and issue the final payment. If you do not have physical proof that the building permits are closed to the satisfaction of the building official and department, do not issue the final payment. If you still have items on your punch list that are not fixed or completed, do not issue the final payment. If the contractor has not physically signed the final lien waiver, absolutely do not issue final payment.

It is very important to complete these final steps *in this order*. Do not, under any circumstances, make the final payment to the contractor until you have received the certificate of occupancy from the Building Department upon final walkthrough, and until the contractor has completed the final punch list. Once those steps are completed, the contractor signs the final and unconditional lien waiver, at which time you may issue the final check and thank the contractor for a job well done.

CHAPTER 16

Stage 7: Final Touches and Home Staging

The Secret to Getting Your House under Contract and Sold

This is the final stage of the rehab process before you start marketing and selling your finished rehab. At this point the property should be professionally cleaned and staged to make it look its best. The most important mindset you are now approaching your finished house with is the eye of a potential buyer. Take your owner hat off and put on the potential-buyer hat. From the time you pull up to the property, is the landscaping perfect? Is the exterior house clean and showing flawless? When you open the front door does it stick or open with ease? Inside is the house clean, staged, and showing immaculately? You have put a lot of work into rehabbing your property, so go the extra mile at this point and put some effort into making sure it is perfect for the first initial showings so it will sell immediately.

Here are the final steps to close out stage 7 of the rehab system:

- Get the house professionally cleaned.
- Get the house staged.
- The power of professional pictures.
- Your final walkthrough with your buyer hat on to prepare to sell.

GET THE HOUSE PROFESSIONALLY CLEANED

Now is not the time to get cheap. Spend money and send a professional cleaning crew to make your finished rehab spotless. No one will want to buy a dirty house. The last thing you want a potential buyer to be adversely affected by in making an offer is they felt the property was too dirty and did not show well. A clean house equals a clean sale!

THE ART OF STAGING

Staging your newly completed rehab is an *extremely* important detail that could determine the speed of your sale. An unstaged property spends an average of about five times longer on the market than a professionally staged home. Staging helps to turn an ordinary space into an extraordinary home by highlighting it's best features. An empty house can call attention to imperfections, which prevents buyers from being able to see the home's true potential.

However, that doesn't mean that you need to spend a ton of money or fully furnish the house. The goal is to give potential buyers an idea of how they might use the space and provide a lived-in feel. In general, it's enough to stage the main living area, the kitchen, the dining area, the master bedroom, and a bathroom. A lot of people aren't too great at visualizing, and may only see four walls and a window. Placing furniture can help the buyer determine the scale in the room. Once a buyer falls in love with the place, the next thing they're going to want to do is make sure they can logically fit their belongings. A bed in the bedroom can serve as a way for the buyer to compare how their bed will fit. They may look at how you placed a loveseat and think, "I have a couch that would go great there too!" The more your buyer envisions themselves living there, the more emotionally attached they will become to the property.

I remember finishing a great rehab on a pretty straightforward project in New Haven, Connecticut. Because the rehab itself went so smoothly, I just assumed the property would sell with the same ease. I listed the property and must have had two dozen showings in the first two weeks. Well, after two and a half months, I still had not sold the property or even received an offer. This house had an unconventional layout for the family and dining room in relation to the kitchen. I finally decided after two and a half months that I had to do everything possible to help get the property sold. I brought in one of my professional stagers. By placing furniture and showing potential homebuyers exactly how the space was functional and could be used, I was able to get an offer and sell the house. The moral of the story is to start by leveraging every competitive advantage to get your house sold from day one.

You want your buyers to notice all of the hard work you put into your remodeled space, so why not let it shine? When you make your house feel more like a home, you are bringing in a higher volume of buyers and increasing the likelihood of receiving multiple offers.

Whether you hire a professional or you decide to get things done yourself, here are some general do's and don'ts to be aware of during the staging process.

The Do's of Staging

- **Do** make the entrance and landscaping as inviting as the house itself. Remember, that first impression goes a long way. You want freshly cut grass, trimmed hedges, clean and polished door handles. Add a new mailbox, nice-looking house numbers, potted plants, and a welcome mat to greet the potential buyers at the door.
- **Do** find a way to highlight the most attractive feature in each room. For example, call attention to the living room fireplace by putting a mirror or painting on the mantel with some candles and a few logs in the fireplace.
- **Do** use lighting to your benefit. Allow the sun to shine through your windows and open the shades. Lighting can make the space seem larger and more inviting. Increase the wattage in your light bulbs so that you get 100 watts for every 50 square feet.
- **Do clean** all the little nooks, crannies, and window sills. A rehabbed house should be clean from all debris, inside and out.
- **Do** pay attention to the two main spaces that sell a home: the kitchen and the bathroom. If there's a breakfast bar, stage it with plates. Use decorative soaps in the bathroom. Buy a matching set of bath mat and towels.
- **Do** stage the awkward little corners or spaces that you may have in a home. This helps interested buyers see the function of the area and the possibilities of what you can do. Try using things like bookshelves or cocktail cabinets.

The Don'ts of Staging

- **Don't** *over*stage your home. Too much stuff can make a house feel cluttered. You also run the risk of dictating a space in a way that the buyer wouldn't want to see and actually turn them off from the property.
- **Don't** make the common mistake of pushing the furniture against the walls. Instead, position furniture in a cozy way that lends itself to a conversational manner. You also want to avoid using furniture that is too big for the space, since this can make the space look small.
- **Don't** skimp on the details. Yes, the couch and coffee table look nice; but a bare coffee table doesn't maximize the benefits of staging. Go out and purchase the little trinkets and decorations that complete the look. Buy fresh flowers or collect them from the area and bring in that touch of nature. Strategically applied pieces can distinguish your home from others. A short list of trinkets or decoration possibilities are:
  - Fake fruit to put in a bowl in the kitchen.
  - Kitchen hand towel.

- Kitchen utensils or cutting boards.
- Potpourri in the bathroom.
- Rubber ducky for the tub (so they can envision giving their kids a bath).
- Martini glass and shaker to stage the bar.
- **Don't** stage *every* room. Other than the kitchen and the bathroom, you should stage your master bedroom and a main living area.
- **Don't** use old or outdated items. Using cheap and old-fashioned staging pieces isn't saving you money—and you are actually shooting yourself in the foot. Use newer and more modern décor that will attract the right buyer.

To view an example of staged properties, go to www.RehabInvestingBible.com/resources to download and view.

THE POWER OF PROFESSIONAL PICTURES

When the staging is complete, bring in a professional photographer to take pictures of your new rehab. This will allow you to introduce your buyers to a variety of visually appealing photographs that reflect the house's true character. It is important to include a high-quality picture of *every* feature you are trying to sell—individual photos of the living room, kitchen, dining room, family room, master bedroom, backyard, and any additional feature worth revealing. Showcasing additional assets, such as location, can help as well. Include any views your property may have of the beach, a lake, mountains, a golf course, and any other selling point.

However tempting it may be, do not use smartphone pictures for your listing just to save a little money. It has been proven time and time again that a listing shot with a high-quality camera will get more views and sell for more money than those with a low-quality point and shoot camera. Because so many prospective buyers nowadays have the luxury of doing their shopping online, they will gravitate toward the properties that display the best photos while viewing them online.

Here are points to make sure your professional photographer considers.

- Lighting techniques are one of the most influential aspects of quality photography. You have to consider both the lighting you're bringing in and the outside lighting.
- When taking pictures of the exterior, plan your photography session on a day or night that has a clear sky.
- Eliminate the risk of unwanted elements in your pictures and try to capture the curb appeal as it was intended.

- Consider which direction the house faces when scheduling a time to shoot, remembering that the sun rises in the east and sets in the west. Daytime photos will require you to position the camera between the property and the sun, to prevent harsh light from entering the shot altogether.
- How you position the camera is often determined by environmental factors—for example, unmovable signage, flagpoles, fences, and trees. However, by placing the camera higher and slightly to the side, to suggest a sense of three-dimensionality, photos can be greatly improved.
- Try to do your interior photography during the middle of the day. This will give you more of a color balance as well as a contrast to avoid any excessive direct light. We try to make the best use of natural light when planning our photography. Sunlight helps sell the house!

Once you've determined the appropriate lighting, you want to make sure to establish the home's best features. Remember, you are trying to capture a prospective buyer's attention—so show them something he or she wants to see. I've carved out a few key tips on how you can get the most out of your interior photos.

- Use the room's perspective to your advantage by paying attention to window lines, arches, and stairways.
- Avoid large areas of open space.
- Use tabletops and their settings to lead into the rest of the room.
- Remove clutter from the field of vision.
- Don't photograph the toilet.
- Don't take a picture of a room if you can't tell what it is.
- *Never* use your phone to take your pictures.

The extra time you put into digitally editing a photograph is well worth it. House hunters will appreciate the time and effort you put into marketing your house and it will sell that much faster. Make sure your professional photographer edits and uses Photoshop to enhance all your finished pictures.

YOUR FINAL WALKTHROUGH WITH YOUR BUYER HAT ON TO PREPARE FOR SALE

Once the house has been staged and photographed, the exterior landscaping is spot on, and the interior cleaning has occurred, do a buyer's-eye walkthrough before you list the house.

This means you need to take off your investor-owner hat and think like a buyer from the minute you pull up to the property. Ask yourself questions like:

- Is the landscaping perfect?
- Does the front door stick?
- Is the house clean inside?
- When you go into the kitchen and open the cupboards under the kitchen sink, is it spotless?
- Does the bathroom smell like a typical bathroom or does it smell like potpourri?

This is also a great time to bring a family member or friend who has not been working on the house with you to get a second opinion on what he or she notices, likes, or dislikes on this walkthrough. Because you have spent so much time on this property, a fresh set of eyes can often see things you might miss at this final stage.

The goal of this final stage is to put your best foot forward as of day one. If you list the property and it's not clean, the lawn is overgrown, and the bathrooms smell like they have been used, you're undoing all the hard work you've done rehabbing the property. When a new property is listed on the MLS with a real estate agent, the serious and qualified buyers are the first to walkthrough—so you have to bring your A-game as well.

To view an example of professional pictures, go to www.RehabInvestingBible.com/resources to download and view.

THE THREE BUYING CRITERIA OF EVERY POTENTIAL BUYER

The fact of the matter is, you will always make money rehabbing if you follow my system and understand the three simple buying criteria every buyer has and is prescreened for:

1. Neighborhood.
2. Price.
3. House statistics.

Neighborhood

It's true what they say—location is everything. Homebuyers choose to buy a given house based on the school system they want their kids to attend; or the neighborhood that is closest to their work; or the area near where their friends and family live.

Price

A qualified buyer will have undergone the financial process to be preapproved for a mortgage. Remember, buying a home is typically the biggest purchase an individual will ever make in their lifetime. So to say they are picky is an understatement. They are looking for the perfect house at the perfect price. Your finished house will always beat out the competition.

House Needs (Bedrooms, Baths, and Square Feet)

Homebuyers are seeking a certain number of bedrooms, baths, and square footage. This is simply based on how big their family is, how many kids they have, and the necessities they require as a buyer.

The home buying decision is very important, so buyers are very particular. Often they've had their Realtor show them house after house and still can't decide on one. They are looking for the perfect house. Our goal with our rehab, staging, and pricing of the house is to provide just that. When your finished, single-family home hits the market with a brand new kitchen with the tile backsplash—all new bathrooms with a hot tub and rain showerhead—and beautiful new hardwood and carpet flooring, they realize *this is the house for them*! Think about it: 90 percent of the houses they have walked through and viewed are not fully renovated homes. In fact, most are currently being lived in. When they walked through your competition, they saw another family's pictures on the wall, another child's posters up in the bathroom. When they view the bathrooms in these lived-in houses, they smell like—well, bathrooms.

Your listing has professional pictures of your finished rehab. The house itself is spotless and clean. It is perfectly staged and looks amazing. And the best part is that your finished rehab is the *same price* as the other lived-in houses. When potential buyers compare your house to the others they have viewed, and they realize they are in the same neighborhood, same price, and same number of bedrooms and baths—it's a no-brainer.

This is the wonderful thing about residential redevelopment. Single-family homes are the most resilient part of the real estate market. No matter what the market is like, people are *always* getting married and looking for their first home. People are *always* relocating because of their work. People are *always* growing out of their current home because they had another child. If your home is rehabbed, priced right, and meets the three buying criteria, it will easily become another sold rehab home and rehab profit produced by the Seven-Stage Rehab System.

In closing Part II I provide you with a valuable rehabber's checklist to review, leverage, and use on the rehab process we have covered. The rehabber's checklist has been used successfully by hundreds of my students to achieve a successful rehab and profit, time and time again. Download a copy of the *rehabber's checklist* at www.RehabInvestingBible.com/resources.

Selling the Rehab

Once the property is complete and the rehab is finished, it is time to market and sell it. You can't sell a property if no one knows about it and never sets foot in it. Part III breaks down the most important steps and provides a system to market and sell your finished rehab property. Once sold, the property closeout and postgame analysis via your accounting is imperative to your immediate understanding on how much money you put into the project and how much money you walked away with. More so, this ritual and exercise is how you get better for your next deal as you learn from your just-completed project and metrics.

CHAPTER **17**

The Selling System

One of the most exciting and rewarding aspects of the real estate investing process occurs when you actually sell your property. Although it can be easy to become caught up in the anticipation of the close, it's important to maintain focus. Just as in any other portion of this process, you need to be quick and efficient. You know that the faster you sell, the more profitable you are. The less time your property spends sitting on the market will save you money in holding costs—as well as precious time that you should be spending on your next project. At this point we have a finished rehab that is staged with professional pictures that is ready to market and sell!

Selling a property is an art form. Before we get into the details of the system, remember that buying a house is typically the biggest investment the average American will make in their lifetime. To say that a buyer is anxious throughout the home buying process is an understatement. Part of your role, therefore, is to put the buyer at ease during the walkthrough so they're able to mentally start moving into the house right then and there. I have sold finished rehabs that range in finished prices from $60,000 to $1,450,000, and higher. Following the selling system I have laid out allows you to sell to both high-end and first-time homebuyer price points.

PRESELLING YOUR REHAB

The only thing that feels greater than selling your property is *preselling* the property before you even put it on the market. Preselling occurs when you're able to promote and sell a house before renovations are fully complete. You may assume that you could never sell a home in this condition—run-down, walls half destroyed, yard in grave condition. But this process gives buyers a vested idea of how you're improving the property and how it will look when all is said and done with your scope of work in hand.

The timeline I use to start preselling my properties is about two weeks prior to listing the property on the Multiple Listing Service (MLS). There are six campaigns that I've found work best during the presale phase. Some of these strategies can be considered guerrilla marketing, which is more of an in-your-face style of doing things; but sometimes that's what you need to do in this business.

House banners are a great way to advertise your home while it's still being rehabbed and they draw lots of attention and create a great buzz. Try using things like "We Buy Houses" bandit signs to put outside your property. Bandit signs are advertising signs placed out in visible locations just like political campaigns signs you see throughout town during elections.

Another option is to create a sign with a link to your blog or website so the neighbors can follow your renovation's progress. Not only does this help you generate buyer leads, it also lets your contractors know that people are watching—so they better keep things up to par while working on your project.

Neighbor referrals can be a huge resource when selling your property. The people who live closest to this rehabbed property are often the home's best salespeople. One way to engage neighbors is to use "Choose Your Neighbor" flyers. You—or someone in your office—create a flyer with your name, company, logo, and a brief paragraph explaining how people in the community should choose their next neighbor by referring quality buyers to you. You can also get neighbors involved through door knocking, which is similar to cold calling, but should be more welcomed since you are trying to revitalize the neighborhood. Make sure you reach out to about 5 to 10 local neighbors who are in walking distance. Let them know your goal and maybe even offer a reward for referrals. Show how excited you are about the property and invite them to see it themselves at the open house. Nobody wants a bad neighbor, so the locals love the idea of telling their friends and family who have shown interest in moving into their neighborhood in the past.

Text and phone-automated hotlines are excellent ways to find buyers. If you advertise a phone number on the front of the house, you can promote your renovations and build a buyer's list. You have a choice of services to create an advertisement via a recorded message that describes the home. When a buyer calls, you capture their phone number, allowing you to call them back. We love to use a text-friendly number that ties to our database. This allows interested parties to text us to receive listing and selling information and generates a recorded voice blast with details of the property. We use a mobile marketing platform called Moby within our database that allows us to leverage this amazing piece of technology.

Pocket-listing flyers to agents have always proven to be a great marketing resource. Real estate agents love being able to see something that hasn't hit the market yet. This way, when they meet with buyers, they have an opportunity to show them a property that no one else has access to and hasn't even hit the market yet.

Here's a premarketing checklist I use in my business.

Premarketing Checklist

- ☐ Get a lockbox code.
- ☐ Pull the comps and get a solid list price.
- ☐ Get all the property details organized (such as dimensions, room count).
- ☐ Stage home (covered in Chapter 16).
- ☐ Take professional photos and create a video tour of the house.
- ☐ Go to the property and create a punch list (covered in Chapter 15).
- ☐ Start biweekly landscaping.
- ☐ Make sure all punch-list items are taken care of.
- ☐ Pull up a list of open houses that are being held in the area from the MLS and the newspapers.
- ☐ Schedule a broker's open house and a public open house.
- ☐ Schedule and hire a worker to put out flyers and hang them the day before the public open house.
- ☐ Check Google or the local town website for any local events, such as a flea market, farmer's market, carnival, concerts, parades and so on.
- ☐ Buy directional signs (small, plastic signs that point to your house).
- ☐ Put up all for-sale directional signs three to five days before the open house.
- ☐ Get a list of agents who sold property in the area in the last three months.
- ☐ Input all office names and fax numbers into your database or spreadsheet
- ☐ Create an online folder under contacts with the street name.
- ☐ Input each contact individually under that folder.
- ☐ Print flyers with the open house date and time on them.
- ☐ Print warranties and bring to the house.
- ☐ Print seller flyers to put in the display and on counter.
- ☐ Attach plastic flyer display holder and put flyers inside (bring screws and screwdriver).

MARKETING YOUR PROPERTY ONLINE

The Internet has propelled a fundamental shift in the way that homeowners market their homes for sale, and how buyers search for homes. We've already covered your company website, social media presence, blog, and squeeze pages in prior chapters. A few other tactics and platforms now follow.

- **Online classified websites.** One of the quickest and most efficient ways to build a buyers list is to utilize online classified websites like Craigslist and Backpage. These sites allow you to not only market your properties and services, they also give you the chance to place links to your websites, social media pages, and to use any other of your online marketing tactics. This kind of free marketing provides an open range to try out a variety of different things. Make sure to include lots of professional pictures of your past finished projects to show a potential buyer what this will soon look like. One ad can take only five minutes to make.

- **Contractor sites and agents' websites.** Typically, people in the contractor markets aren't that great at advertising for themselves. By using their website to advertise your rehab project, you are not only helping yourself out, you are also able to broadcast the quality of *their* workmanship. This will also ensure that your contractors do a good job, because they know people are watching their work. Don't forget to also ask your Realtor to advertise a "Coming Soon" post about your property to attract potential buyers. If you renovate consistently, they should be more than willing to.

The most critical part of establishing online marketing tools, as discussed previously, is *to stay on top of it*. Building and sustaining your online presence is the key to success. Keeping things fresh will not only help drive traffic to your business, it'll help it stay there. You will also need to become aware of what is working and what isn't working. Different techniques work for different areas. Trial and error is a huge part of the puzzle.

BUILDING A BUYERS LIST

You never want to be in a situation where you have to scurry around looking for buyers. The only way to ensure that doesn't happen is to have a quality buyers list at your disposal. The bigger and better the buyers list, the faster you will sell your property. The main goal here is to *continually grow* the list of quality buyers, even if you don't have a property to sell at the time. This list should include information like first and last name, email address, phone number, buying criteria, type of funding, and any other important information. Once you've got your arsenal lined up and ready to go, you have to maintain relationships with every person on that list and effectively market your properties to them. Remember to treat your list of buyers like the gold mine it is.

Rehabbing is not a property-centered business; it is a people-centered business. We buy from people, sell to people, and work with many different people during the process to make sure things are done effectively. Every soul you encounter should know what you do and what services you offer. This is especially true when you are starting to build a buyers list. As with any venture, focusing on your own needs will never pay off. You must make your networking efforts all about the other person. The law of reciprocity will always ring true. You will find that the more you do for others, the more they will want to do for you.

Networking

We already touched on the importance of networking in Chapter 3. Whenever you meet anyone remotely interested in real estate of any kind, add him or her to your buyers list. That person may not be ready today, but he or she might just call you up in three years. There are several opportunities that you should take advantage of when looking to network with potential buyers—specifically, networking events.

Email Blasts

Sending mass emails to everyone on your list increases your chance of gaining quality buyers to add to your funnel. You always want to use a professional email broadcast service to do so. Using a database such as Realeflow will allow you the platform for proper email marketing. Another very popular email marketing platform is Constant Contact. Taking these steps will ensure that you are maintaining compliance, getting maximum deliverability of your email, and staying off of blacklists. Also include several links to your websites and squeeze pages when you send these out. Email blasts should be consistently sent to other investors, real estate agents, mortgage brokers, and title agents.

Prescreening Retail Buyers

It is important to effectively communicate and ask the proper questions when screening for your buyer. While it is important to meet with buyers, it's more important to use a systemized approach to prescreening them. The main two components to focus on when analyzing these leads are *financial preparation* and *mental preparation*. Financially, you want to make sure that the buyer is working with and is qualified with a mortgage broker or another financial source to purchase the home. If the buyer hasn't prearranged the financing, it is an indicator that he or she is only in the early stages of looking for a home. If he or she isn't working with a lender, then you want to immediately put that person in touch with your preferred mortgage broker. You don't want to waste time showing homes that are out of the buyer's price range or that they simply are not financially qualified or ready to buy. If you are working with a cash buyer, you will want to verify a proof of funds. You will not typically sell to a cash buyer since you are selling finished retail rehab properties; however, it does occur from time to time.

Even when someone is financially prepared, they may not be *emotionally* ready. If your potential buyer hasn't done the research and the preparation necessary to go through with buying a home, they are likely not going to budge. A lot of retail buyers are in the early stages of looking for a property, and may not be ready to buy a property immediately, but they may be ready in the near future. That's why you must save all prospect information in your database.

Once you have all of the basic information, set a time to show the buyer through the property. Who the buyer meets with will depend on whether or not you have the house listed. If you list your property, then you will want your agent to meet with the buyer. But if you decide to sell it without the MLS, you will need to meet with the buyer yourself. Keep in mind that as your business grows, you can definitely outsource this task to someone in your office.

The Initial Phone Call

There are four main factors you want to remember during your initial call with a potential buyer. If it helps, make a sticky note and keep it with a pad and pen by your phone so that you won't forget these key steps:

1. Get as much information as possible.
2. Find ways to build rapport.
3. Have something to offer them.
4. Ask that they meet with you.

Once your buyer is ready to discuss moving forward, try to find somewhere comfortable to meet in person. You can use your office if you have one; if not, then meet at a neutral location such as a coffee shop, restaurant, or even your attorney's conference room. Just make sure that the location is easy for the both of you. Make sure to schedule distraction-free time and come prepared with all the necessary information you will need.

When you are ready to show the house, you will begin a four-step process to gain commitment to the presale of this property. You will meet with the buyer, give a walkthrough of the house while in construction, sign contracts, and collect a deposit. I've outlined the four steps here:

1. **Meet and greet.** Ask a lot of questions so you can prequalify your potential buyer.
2. **Property walkthrough.** Talk about the deferred maintenance and keep the enthusiasm going throughout the conversation. There may be a lot of construction going on, so make

sure to help paint the picture as much as possible. Pick out the positives and touch on the value of actually seeing the quality of work you're putting in. (This is an advanced strategy; many new buyers aren't able to walkthrough an unfinished rehab and envision the final property.)

3. **Contract write-up.** Have an attorney write up a contract outlining items of the remodel on which you are flexible and those on which you are not. Include deadlines by which the buyer must make decisions and make sure to get a larger deposit if a specific change they wish to make is one that can hurt you. Have the attorney go over the contract with the buyer to answer questions and make them feel safe. Don't forget to have the scope of work (SOW) signed as well.

4. **Deposit collection.** It is important to obtain your good-faith money if you're doing all of these special-design features. Potential buyers may speak with a real estate agent who can talk them out of the deal, so you want to make sure you get commitment up front.

I have included our *retail buyer prequalification form* for you to use when prescreening your next retail buyer at www.RehabInvestingBible.com/resources.

LISTING YOUR PROPERTY

If you were not able to make any moves during the presale phase, the next step is to list your property. You primary goal here is to gain maximum exposure. The more buyers you attract, the more likely it is that you will find that one person who loves and is qualified to buy the property. It is estimated that 97 percent of buyers find the house they want online before they even call the buyer. Whether you use the MLS, syndicated listings, or both, getting your property listed brings you one step closer to finding your buyer. Choose the best Realtor who will implement the marketing campaigns you require and get your finished rehab listing on the MLS. This site gets the most buyer eyeballs of any selling platform.

You'll want to create a checklist to help you prepare for how you're going to sell this home. Documents such as the following example will help you to start a foundation for marketing your properties the right way.

Marketing Checklist

Online Ads
- ☐ List with Realtor on the MLS.
- ☐ Post on Craigslist—repost every Friday and Monday.

- ☐ Syndicate to online marketing portal or software—Realeflow.
- ☐ Make a photo album with a description on Facebook.
- ☐ Create a Facebook Event for the open house.
- ☐ Copy and paste the album link on the wall of the event.
- ☐ Copy and paste the virtual tour link
- ☐ Create and purchase an ad at www.militarybyowner.com (if in a military neighborhood).

Flyers

- ☐ A new listing flyer with the open house date (print 100 to 200) and without (100).
- ☐ MLS flyer—for client's use (print 25 and leave at house).
- ☐ Seller flyer in color (print 25). Put one in the display and others next to it on the counter.
- ☐ Drop off flyers at town events, local businesses, and on neighbor doorsteps.

Email Blasts

- ☐ Email all buyers in our database.
- ☐ Email all agents in our database.
- ☐ Email all agents who have sold something nearby from the MLS.
- ☐ Create a flyer and send it out.

Fax Blasts

- ☐ Fax our entire list of offices that have sold a house recently nearby.

Calls

- ☐ Phone all agents who recently sold homes in the neighborhood. Tell them about the house and its open house.
- ☐ Follow-up with agents who showed the listing.

Signs

- ☐ Put up For Sale sign—the project manager should put this up while construction is going on.
- ☐ Put up For Sale directional signs three to five days before the open house.
- ☐ Put up open house directional signs with balloons the day of open house.

WORKING WITH AGENTS

An agent can help you sell your home on the MLS at the highest price possible, help you negotiate during the process, and close on time while working with escrow or the attorney.

The fact is that rehab investors who understand the power of the relationship with a good Realtor are the most successful investors in the business. Both parties can offer invaluable services to each other, resulting in partnerships that work together for higher paychecks.

While it *is* a smart idea to obtain your real estate license, working with additional agents can only help you and your business grow in the following ways:

- First-time buyers are usually reluctant to work with an amateur seller and may only trust an agent.
- An agent has experience and knowledge in areas like inspections, repairs, and the presentation of your home.
- Good agents are also knowledgeable on current financial and legal issues, which can come in handy during negotiations.
- Local agents can hone in on the highest price that you can get for your property in the area and provide an insider's take on financing and work orders to save you some cash.
- Agents can take care of advertising, promotion, and maybe even the open house.
- Agents take all the calls, follow-up with prospects, screen buyers, and handle the contract close and negotiations. When all of those tasks are done by a professional, they save you time. Don't forget time is *everything*.

When you're ready to start your search for the right agents, make sure to do your homework and ask around among friends and colleagues, as well as former neighbors who may have sold in the past year. This is going to be a long-term relationship, so it's well worth spending the extra time up front to network with the best.

There are plenty of ways to find agents. You can, of course, just walk into an agent's office and introduce yourself, or you can try some of these options.

- **Multiple Listing Service (MLS).** If you want to find agents fast, go straight to the MLS. If your property is listed on the MLS, you will talk to other agents who may be interested in it, so take advantage of those conversations to create new relationships.
- **For Sale signs.** Any time you see a For Sale sign in front of a home, it should catch your eye. Pay attention to the name of the agent on the signs around the neighborhood as well. This is a good way to get an idea of who the big person on campus is.
- **Online search.** Conduct a mainstream online search by going to a website such as Realtor.com, where you can search more for millions of Realtors nationwide. Be sure to cross-reference and check reviews for any Realtors on sites like Yelp, Zillow, and Angie's List.
- **Networking at meetings.** Other ways of finding these top agents would take place in your daily course of business. These include networking meetings and normal daily interactions.

Agents should be reliable, fast, and willing to learn your real estate investing process. A good agent has a great network of buyers and professional relationships that you can tap into.

It's important to build relationships with agents who have knowledge in your location and who list in your area. Their experience marketing within that neighborhood can bring in a lot of traffic. You can research their history by looking at the MLS to find agents with the most sales.

Also consider how well they will promote your property. Who will provide mass exposure? The more people who see the property, the higher the odds are that you will find a qualified buyer.

HOW MUCH DOES IT COST?

Real estate sales commissions are split a variety of ways. Traditionally, a real estate agent who lists a property is paid a percentage of the home's selling price, and the listing agent will typically offer roughly half of that commission to the buyer's agent in the transaction. The average cost and commission is between a 5 to 6 percent listing commission that is shared between a listing broker and a buyer broker for a standard listing.

If you ever decide not to use an agent on a deal, some brokers do offer what is called a flat-fee listing. In this scenario, you agree to pay the buyer's agent and a small fee to a listing broker, but not agreeing to the full listing fee. A flat-fee brokerage will take the services traditionally done by an agent and list the property for sale in the local MLS without requiring the seller to use services such as valuation assistance, negotiation, transaction management, or showing accompaniment.

In my experience, a full-service agent is preferable to a flat-fee service. If your property does not sell, you are always going to wonder if you should have gone with a full-service Realtor instead of being cheap on the listing commission. Remember—you make your money when you buy; but you *realize* your money when you actually sell the property.

HAVING AN OPEN HOUSE

When the time comes to host an open house, the main thing you should focus on is being able to generate lots and lots of traffic. You want as much activity going on as possible to create the energy you need to get things moving. This can be a very timely and cost-effective way to introduce your home to potential buyers. The first step is to decide on the date and time.

Weekends, particularly Sunday afternoons, work best. Take advantage of the time when people are out and about, looking for things to do, and expecting open houses. Check the calendar in your local area to make sure you aren't conflicting with any big events taking place that day. You may even want to check with the local public works department to see if any construction will be going on during the time of your open house that might cause detours.

The next step is to market and advertise your open house in order to get people in the door. As with all of your marketing efforts, pay attention to what works and remember that the little things are what count.

Below is a list of the five senses and why each one is important when hosting an open house and showing your finished rehab. You want to use each one to increase your ability to attract a buyer and sell your rehab.

1. **Sight**
   a. Your finished rehab and all new materials will do the job here.
   b. Your staging helps buyers visually move in as they walkthrough the house.
2. **Hearing**
   a. Make a playlist and always have music playing. Use mellow-feel, good music (jazz, Jack Johnson, and so on)—nothing too harsh and alarming.
   b. Instead of music, you can play the sound of waves crashing, waterfalls, or other natural sounds to calm and relax people.
3. **Smell**
   a. Take some lavender liquid or vanilla extract and dab some on light bulbs throughout the house. The fragrance will emerge when the lights turn on during your showings.
   b. Put cookies in the oven and actually bake them. Baking cookies brings folks back to their childhood memories of making cookies.
4. **Taste**
   a. Always have some food and snacks so people can enjoy themselves during the walk-through.
   b. I love to have chocolates and truffles for people. One of my favorite spots for outstanding chocolates is www.vosgeschocolate.com.
5. **Touch**
   a. Pick a thicker carpet cushion so your potential buyers can experience how soft it is.
   b. Quality finishing materials, like the front door handle being very sturdy, go a long way towards leaving a good first impression. Granite countertops, and other high-quality finishings, also help in this arena.

Spreading the Word

When you are making your open-house plans, have plenty of signs saying "Open House This Weekend" with balloons around the neighborhood. These signs have been around for a long, long time and there's a reason for that—they work! This tool is a simple, low-tech, and inexpensive form of marketing that is extremely effective. Make sure you put these signs out a few days before the event. If you plan on having your open house on Sunday, try and get the signs out by Friday—and always include the event's date and time.

Most MLSs across the country will allow you to post an open house and allow local real estate agents to conduct open house tours. Many of these agents will take their clients on these tours to avoid losing them to another agent. Use Craigslist, Zillow, Trulia, or other online classified websites to create an effective ad that is easy for people to search. Use keywords in your ads to attract your crowd; you want your property to be everywhere your audience is looking.

Social media has become one of the biggest advertising outlets. Once again, if you have a business page and/or a personal page on Facebook, you want to share all the excitement of your open house with your network. Once you tell your Facebook friends that you are selling a property, each of them has the opportunity to share that information with their friends, which will spread the word rapidly. Creating an event on Facebook for your open house is a great way to get additional social media buzz and leverage.

As I discussed earlier, neighbors often want to help pick the next buyer that will be part of their community and may know friends and family members who want to move into the neighborhood. Inform them of how the home's selling price will affect their property values. You can also use neighbor letters if they aren't home in order to effectively advertise your property.

Individuals renting a home in the area could also jump at the opportunity to finally own. One of the most effective direct mail campaigns involves mailing to renters who have a 720 credit score or higher in the chosen areas. If you can, get a list of a renters and contact them about the home you have for sale today, and the ability to buy in the future.

An open house is a great opportunity for you to send out email blasts to your buyers list and fax blasts to other local real estate agents about your open house. When realty offices have their morning meetings, there is often a discussion of the activity in the area. In cases where inventory is low and buyer demand is high, local open houses are likely to be shown at these meetings.

Open House Set Up

While you are marketing for people to attend your open house, make sure that every corner of the property is ready for the spotlight. As I emphasized previously, staging is a pivotal element when selling. A rule of thumb for the cost of hiring a professional stager who has their own furniture and material is .5 to 1 percent of the listing price of your home.

Greeting Potential Buyers

Be prepared when potential buyers walkthrough the door. A great way to keep you on track is by having a sign-in sheet with three major components:

1. Name
2. Phone number
3. Email address

This allows you to obtain information for potential buyers immediately. Even if it's only an email address, that's still one more email address to add to your buyers list. Even better than a sign-in sheet is to bring your tablet or iPad and have a person check in using social media. This alerts their friends, family, and other people online interested in real estate to the fact that they are at your open house.

Following Up with Buyers

Follow-up is essential. You have to constantly try to connect with your potential buyers and make sure that you are always at the forefront of their minds. The most important step is to follow-up and check in with potential interested parties. If someone called, visited, or emailed you about your specific property, follow-up with each lead until your property is sold. You never know where your buyer is going to come from, so be persistent!

As always, stay organized in this process and come up with a system that works. Create a checklist of things that you want to do and keep up with it as you go. I use the following preparation checklist on the day of my open houses.

Open House Checklist

☐ New listing flyer with the open house date left at house.
☐ Warranties for appliances or for the home.

- ☐ Knock on the doors of 50 neighbors to ask questions; see if they're looking to sell, too.
- ☐ Sign-in sheets.
- ☐ Town information packet.
- ☐ "Come on in" sign for front door.
- ☐ Frequently asked questions about the home.
- ☐ Balloons.
- ☐ Open house signs.
- ☐ Open house directional signs.
- ☐ Laptop with a portable printer.
- ☐ List of improvements.
- ☐ Business cards.
- ☐ Drinks, chips, and so on.
- ☐ Purchase and sale contracts.
- ☐ Pens.
- ☐ Signs.
- ☐ Install air fresheners.
- ☐ Bring radio with music for open house.
- ☐ Tape.
- ☐ Bring mop to clean floor.
- ☐ Towels.
- ☐ Bring an iPad to become friends with everyone who shows up.
- ☐ Sponsor brochures/flyers/business cards.
- ☐ Straps.
- ☐ Scissors/razor.
- ☐ Comps.
- ☐ Client-view MLS sheets.

Selling your property is critical; every detail counts. Take the time to leverage as many opportunities to get someone into your finished rehab. What I know is you can't sell a house that you can't get people to view. What I also know is that when we price our finished rehab to sell and actually get people in the door, it will sell itself. I have included a very comprehensive checklist and system for you to use when marketing and selling your rehab. This is our working with buyers and controlling the selling process checklist. This is a step-by-step process on what to do before, during, and after the sale of your property so you do not miss any details. The *working with buyers and controlling the selling process checklist* can be downloaded for free at www.RehabInvestingBible.com/resources.

CHAPTER 18

Common Selling Mistakes

The biggest mistake an investor can make is to *not* learn from other investors' mistakes. I was so pumped about my first rehab project when I first got started—so excited that I jumped right in, head first. You should, of course, be excited about what you do, but don't let that excitement keep you from taking the proper precaution and necessary steps to have a successful project. Too many investors look back on their first projects and kick themselves for falling victim to some of the silly mistakes I specify in this chapter.

Simple missteps, such as installing appliances before the house is complete, putting in flooring before all the tradesman have finished, or just not having a weekly house check-up system in the winter to ensure the pipes don't freeze can all add up to huge headaches. Some of the things I have learned the hard way will help you avoid getting stuck with a property … or even worse, having your own nightmare story to tell.

I'll never forget how excited I was to finish my first rehab. Because I was rushing to get everything completed, I failed to follow the order of operations. I could start to see that my kitchen was looking like a kitchen—and even though my contractors still had work to do throughout the house for another *10 days or so*—I rushed to install the appliances. I really wanted to see the finished kitchen so I could start to envision how awesome my completed rehab was going to look.

Two days after I installed the appliances, I got a call from the neighborhood watch lady across the street. She called to compliment me on my contractors and how dedicated they were to getting the job done. I asked what prompted her to call and tell me this, and she said "last night they were working so late moving appliances in and out of the front door it actually woke me up." That's how I learned that the appliances I just installed a week and a half too early had been stolen. Not by contractors of course, but the neighborhood watch lady could not tell the difference at two in the morning. The thieves broke the window in the back of the house and then were nice enough to unlock the front door and just wheel them out the front. Unless you like buying appliances twice, learn from my lesson: appliances are one of the last things to complete your rehab.

MISTAKE 1—LEAVING THE PROPERTY UNSECURED

Security is a top priority. Since your hands are not the only ones on the project, you'll need to take the proper precautions. We all want to believe that everyone we work with and the neighborhood is trustworthy and safe; however, sometimes it's just not the case.

Leaving a property unsecured is a mistake you don't want to make. Changing the lockbox code, using floodlights, and turning a radio on in the evenings are just a few of the ways you can deter thieves who are looking for an easy score.

Lockboxes

You never know who still has a set of keys when you first purchase a property or what contractor will come back with the existing lockbox code. Change the locks from day one and put a lockbox on the door so that tradesmen can come and go freely. As you near completion, you'll have more and more finished materials and valuables in the house that you need to secure and protect. Once the carpenter, plumber, electrician, and HVAC have installed their fixtures and the renovation has been completed, change the lockbox code again so that only the selling team has access to the house. This diminishes the number of people going in and out who could possibly walk off with any valuables in the property.

Lighting

When you start your project and *certainly* when you finish, one of the best theft prevention systems you can use is lighting. I know it sounds simple, but you'd be surprised—a lot of people just don't think about it. Put dusk-to-dawn floodlights at the back and front of your property. As soon as it gets dark, that property will be lit up like Yankee Stadium. I also like to keep a few of the lights on in the house as well. Typically, we'll place the lights in various rooms throughout and set up timers on them. Doing so makes it unclear to people in the neighborhood whether the property is actually vacant or not. We want passersby to question if someone is actually living on the property.

Radio Noise

Another trick I love to use is the sound of a radio. This works similarly to the interior lighting strategy: it fools outsiders into believing that someone is home. The noise usually deters most thefts and individuals who are just curious to know if the house is vacant. Take one of your painter's or carpenter's radios, plug it in, and let it rock all night.

Alarm Systems

One of the more obvious ways to prevent theft is by installing an alarm system. It doesn't have to be state-of-the-art; you can always install a portable alarm system. There are affordable, introductory prices offered on systems that can provide monthly monitoring. If you want an even more affordable option, you can also display small signs in the window or in the front lawn just to give the appearance that alarm systems are in place.

Faux Cameras

I like to set up fake battery-powered cameras with lights on my properties. Though they do not actually record anything, placing them around the property in plain sight deters would-be thieves.

Beware of Dog

One option is to put up a Beware of Dog sign. However, if you are in a very active neighborhood, you may want to consider allowing someone you know—a friend, your contractor—to leave his dog in the house overnight. Though it goes without saying, you would want a dog with a meaner reputation than a teacup Chihuahua. The sound of their bark should deter all other common thieves looking to pull the copper pipes for cash.

Even if you have every piece of security put in place, you still have to be careful. Let your contractor know they'll need to remove anything they don't want taken from the property at the end of the day. Be wary of your materials (cabinets, appliances, fixtures, etc.). Do not put your appliances in until the very last day before you're going to show your house. Your contractor will need to be conscious of this fact, and never have anything on the jobsite for longer than needed. Don't leave items hanging around loose in the house that can easily grow legs and walk away. Because our Seven-Stage Rehab System requires the contractors to purchase the materials, this typically won't happen on your job site, since a contractor certainly doesn't want to buy the same materials twice.

MISTAKE 2—SKIMPING ON LANDSCAPING

Consider this scenario: It's a perfect, sunny Saturday afternoon, and you and your family decide to take a drive to look for your dream home. You look through the classifieds, browse the Internet, and map out the homes you want to view. You jump in the car and head to your first house. You drive past the first location and see a messy front yard, overgrown grass and bushes, and a cracked walkway to the front door. Next, you pass a house where you find fresh grass, beautifully trimmed hedges, blooming flowers, welcoming decor, and a lovely walkway to the front door. Which house would you prefer to tour?

Of course, you choose the one with the awesome entrance. Landscaping is the most important point of contact with a customer looking for a new home. The front of the house is your advertising poster for the property, so why not approach it with as much care and attention as you do with the rest of the rehab?

You should always have your exit strategy in the forefront of your mind, and be thinking about how you can improve your chances of selling your property. Landscaping is just one example of an inexpensive yet effective means to an end—which is why it should be one of the first items on your agenda. You don't have to turn the front yard of your property into a botanical garden; however, it is amazing to see what a nice, trimmed lawn, a couple of shrubs, and a few accent flowers can do to a property's appearance and marketability. Here are a few quick tips that will help your home's curb appeal:

- Buy sod (grass that is already cut and rolled up) instead of waiting for new grass to grow.
- Work from the outside in. Doing this will allow you to market the property beforehand. If weather permits, you always want to start landscaping from day one.
- Use plants that are indigenous to your area so that they are affordable to purchase and easy to maintain.
- Add pops of color with flats of annuals (they are also relatively inexpensive).
- Apply a fresh layer of mulch in all garden beds to enhance surrounding plants.

Realize that the outside of a house speaks volumes about the inside, and about the owner. Take care of the little things and make sure that you improve your home's entry and make visitors feel welcome. Failing to present a wow factor on the outside prevents potential buyers from walking in the door. Good landscaping can literally transform your home's exterior look and feel. Hire a landscaper to do the job professionally, and see how the results bring people in.

MISTAKE 3—FAILING TO MAINTAIN THE PROPERTY

This next mistake is an especially critical one to avoid. You can complete the best project of your life, but if you don't take care of the property, you're going to have a hard time selling it. A lack of maintenance in the beginning will cause you to miss the most important wave of buyers.

Yard Maintenance

Keeping up on the curb appeal is just as important as creating it. So even if you did a great job on landscaping, remember that grass grows and bushes will always need trimming. It's not a task that you can do once, wipe the dirt off your hands, and move on. Unless you sell the property quickly, you'll have to stay on top of maintenance. If your property is in bad shape from the outside, then it won't look like a professional is taking care of it.

Debris Removal

You should not be the only one worried about how your project looks. Your entire team should share the same desire to always be on their *A* game. A lazy exterior reflects a lazy interior and that's not the image that you want your buyers to have about the home you're selling. Make your expectations clear to your contractors up front. Although this is outlined in your contractor documents, remind them that you are always looking for more projects and if they want to continue to get business from you, they have to clean up their mess and keep the house looking great.

Heating and Power Systems

The yard isn't the only thing you want to maintain. In cold-weather states especially, it is absolutely imperative to check that the heating system and power are working and maintained. You will need a weekly and daily checkup system when the temperatures drop below freezing. The last thing you want to do is walk into your finished rehab in the middle of winter with a waterfall of water cascading from the second floor bathroom and a busted frozen pipe … ask me how I know …. It's no fun rehabbing a property twice.

MISTAKE 4—FORGETTING ABOUT OUTDOOR AND LANDSCAPE LIGHTING

Outdoor lighting is not something you may think of right away when beginning your rehab; however, it all contributes to the very important first impression. A bad first impression may be the only thing a potential buyer needs to avoid looking at a property altogether. Give a buyer who decides to drive by at night something to get excited about. Evening is the most dramatic time to see your landscaping. If properly lit, homes can give off a very warm and inviting feel.

Lighting fixtures also instill an enhanced sense of security. Their presence also illuminates characteristics that you wish to display, further contributing to the overall feel of the property.

If executed to the potential buyer's liking, they will want to immerse themselves in the home's features even further.

Landscape lighting is easy to install and economically friendly. Here are a few options for you to choose from:

- **Path lights** are used to illuminate paths and driveways.
- **Accent lights** are used to draw attention to fountains, sculptures, or trees.
- **Well lights** are designed to be hidden in the ground and illuminate shrubs and trees, or exterior walls from below.
- **Floodlights** illuminate dark areas around windows and doors and can also bring out textures in your landscaping by highlighting trees and bushes
- **Rope lights** create an up-lighting effect by simply outlining landscape bed edging.
- **Underwater lights** are submerged lighting for a water garden to show off fish or plants after dark.

Another great option is to use solar lighting, which is an excellent choice for adding a soft ambiance to the front of the house without using any energy other than the sun. You definitely have to be careful where you place these lights, because they may not be useful if your front yard has too much shade. When installing solar lighting, use flashlights that have a variety of settings to determine where the light would look best. You also want to check for whether or not you will be shining light into your neighbor's house. One of the best tips I can give you for installing outdoor lighting is to install them so that you can see the light, but not the fixture. You lose a lot of the effect when you can see where the light is coming from.

MISTAKE 5—FAILING TO INCORPORATE SIZZLE FEATURES

They say it's the sizzle that sells the steak—and the same holds true in real estate. Sizzle features are the improvements made to a property that are not necessary to live with, but are what put the emotional hooks into your buyers. When people can see themselves living in your home, they're as good as sold.

You must go above and beyond the quality of the competitors product that you are putting out into the marketplace. You have to remember that for a homebuyer, choosing a place to live is, to a large extent, an emotional endeavor. It is about finding that special place that feels *just right* after a long day of work, school, a business trip, or where one safely raises a family. Oftentimes, a property fails to sell because it does not have anything special to separate it from the competition.

Those looking to improve the features of their house would be better suited to focus on specific rooms. As most of you know, kitchens and bathrooms are the essential rooms that ultimately help a house to sell, so investing your time and money primarily into those rooms will yield you the best results. Prospective homebuyers are naturally drawn to these functional areas, especially the master bathroom. Here are some of my favorite sizzle features:

Kitchen

- Undercabinet lighting in the kitchen
- Hard-surface countertops
- Above-counter microwave
- Pot-filler faucet
- Double oven
- Ice maker
- Flat-screen TV mounted on the wall (or simply wiring for one)
- Undercabinet wine fridge
- Skylights in the kitchen
- Custom tile backsplash

Bathrooms

- Jacuzzi tub
- Rain showerhead
- Body spray showerheads
- Steam unit in the shower
- Heated floors in the tile bathroom
- Heated towel racks
- Mini chandelier over the tub in the bathroom
- Subway tiles
- Showerheads that sync with devices via Bluetooth so you can play music in the shower

Outdoors

- Patio
- Fire pit
- Grass
- Outdoor shower
- Barbecue station
- Hot tub

Miscellaneous

- Surround-sound system
- Built-in bookcase
- Drop-stair scuttle into attic
- Skylights

Some of these sizzle features may seem more expensive than others on this list. However, keep in mind that a lot of these items I have listed become pretty easy to install during the renovation process. For instance, adding in extra receptacles for power isn't very difficult when the walls are exposed. If you ask your electrician to wire an extra receptacle where you would have placed a base cabinet in the kitchen, for as little as $200 you could purchase and plug in an undercabinet wine fridge to wow a potential seller. Do whatever you can to make your home shine and differentiate it from the competition.

Education and information is not just sharing what works. Sharing what to avoid is as valuable as what to implement. Learn from my mistakes in this chapter and you will save time and money on your future rehabs.

CHAPTER 19

Postgame Analysis

How to Make Even More Money On Your Next Rehab

Now that you've sold your property, it's time to take a step back and analyze your deal. It's crucial to do this at the end of each real estate transaction so you can figure out what you did right and what you did wrong. It's always a good idea to compare your projected to your actual profit, and discern where things worked and where they didn't. This will keep you from making the same mistake twice.

To be excellent or exceptional at any discipline, you have to consistently work toward mastering your craft. If we just work, work, work nonstop without ever taking a second to analyze what we're doing, we'll never identify where we need to improve. By stopping to review what we're doing and where we are going, we continue to identify improvements and efficiencies that will accelerate our business. Most importantly, the time you take to review a past deal will help you make more money on a future deal. Working without actually analyzing if we are, in fact, improving prevents us from actually getting better and heading in the right direction. It is important that we all take the time to analyze and postgame our efforts and learn from our good and bad application. When we postgame properly we can improve on *every* project we complete.

POSTGAME ANALYSIS

Every rehabber should do what I call a postgame analysis after every project. This procedure entails an effective accounting system and closeout process that can help you track down every penny of your rehab profits and expenses. It will help you to determine whether or not you correctly estimated rehab costs, holding times, and whether or not you made a large enough profit.

Systems are vital to your success and won't be as effective without proper rules. Rules are not hard to set; they're hard to follow. That's why every team member you have and every employee you hire needs to buy in toward the goals in which you're working and the rules you've set. If they don't, you're going to have a hard time managing your team and improving productivity.

Organizing Your Filing System

No matter how much you attempt to do online and how hard you try to operate a paperless business, you will inevitably have to deal with and stay on top of paperwork. Regardless of whether or not you use a paper filing system or operate electronically, it's important to establish a well-organized system. The way we file and organize our documents allows us to be effective and productive. Keeping your filing system organized ensures that everyone on your team can easily organize, identify, and find information and documents when needed.

You should have two separate folders for each property: a *monthly invoice folder* and a *master property folder*.

The monthly invoice folder will have subfolders for invoices, receipts for gas/oil, electric, water, sewer, first mortgage, second mortgage, contracts and invoices, and building permits.

The master property folder will include both buying and selling folders, and should be kept in a locked file cabinet. This file contains private information, such as buyers' Social Security numbers or purchase price. The whole idea is to rehab properties without doing all the work yourself. So when you hire or bring on your first assistant, this is an easy-to-follow system for them to execute and take work off your plate. They only need to access the filing and paying of the monthly bills in the monthly invoice folder for your accounting purposes. This system allows for growth and takes you from technician to business owner a lot sooner and with a scalable system to execute your accounting and filing.

When I started, I got our company's business mail at a post office box. Then I paid all the bills, filed the invoices, and organized the paperwork. As we got more deals, I only had time to do this in the evenings. As we got even *more* deals, I could only do this on the weekends—until I finally did not have any time for this at all. Because I had an easy-to-follow process, I was able to hire another person who could retrieve and open the mail. Then they would log into our accounting system to print checks in tandem with the invoices. Once they printed the check with the invoice, the assistant would place both invoice and checks to be signed on my desk each day. Never assign the responsibility of reviewing and signing checks to someone else. That is the one thing you will always do as residential redeveloper ... write checks and get checks.

At this final stage, all I had to do was review and sign (make sure and give the signed checks and invoices back to your assistant so you do not spend time stuffing the envelope and putting it in the mail. Time is everything!). This system gave me two full working days back into my personal and business life that allowed me to find more deals and make more money.

The monthly and master folders are green hanging folders that go into your filing cabinet. The bullets underneath them are the manila subfolders labeled for each invoice or document type.

Included in the monthly invoice folder

- Gas/Oil bills
- Electric bill
- Water bill
- Sewer bill
- First mortgage
- Second mortgage
- Insurance
- Contracts and invoices
- Building permits

Included in the master property folder

- Buying system checklist (buying)
- Buying financial/comps and exit (buying)
- Purchase and sale (buying)
- Title search (buying)
- Land trust (buying)
- Mortgage info (buying)
- Insurance (buying)
- Closing statement/HUD-1 (buying)
- Deed (Buying)
- Title insurance (buying)
- Short-sale package (buying)
- Disclosures/listing agreement (selling)
- Offers (Selling)
- Purchase and sale (selling)
- Appraisal (selling)

- Closing statement/HUD-1 (selling)
- Seller carryback mortgage note (selling)
- Selling system checklist (selling)

This system has made managing and organizing expenses simple and effective. I can always find something when I need it to cross-reference items. When a team member needs property information, he or she can track it down without a problem. This should be one of the first activities you outsource to a new team member to bring time back into your life.

POST-REHAB ACCOUNTING

You won't find many real estate investors chomping at the bit when it comes time to do book-keeping and accounting. But even if it is not your cup of tea, you need to be aware of every check that comes in and every check that goes out. I've seen many investors get tunnel vision looking only at their properties' purchase prices, sale prices, and rehab costs. Too many ignore the everyday dollar amounts and transactions involved in utilities, financing charges, closing costs, and other holding costs. When you ask them how much profit they made on a rehab deal, they can't give you an answer!

There is no reason that you shouldn't know *every single dollar* spent or made on a deal down to the penny. The last thing you want to happen is to walk away from the closing table thinking that you made $30,000 when you really only made $10,000. You'll never know whether you're running an efficient, effective, profitable business. Worse, you may not know if you're even making a profit. Your business's success depends on the profit of each deal, so you've got to track each transaction down to the penny.

However, before you start using accounting software like QuickBooks, you'll need to under-stand the fundamentals. The basic function of an accounting system is nothing more than organizing financial information and providing accurate reports to track your money. You don't have to be an expert, but you should become familiar with accounting principles and proce-dures. Having a working knowledge of accounting before you hand it off to a bookkeeper allows you to complete your own checks and balances as well.

QuickBooks

For the most part, you can execute your accounting very simply with QuickBooks. Quick-Books Pro or QuickBooks Online are easy-to-use accounting programs designed to help small to medium-sized businesses know exactly where they stand financially and how to be more effective. The tools keep track of customer and vendor information via checks, keeps detailed information for each and every bank account in the business, and allow you to run reports. They also manage any inventory you have (the properties you buy and sell). While there is certainly more than one way to set up and do your accounting for a rehab and flip business, I will share the system I've used for the past decade for tracking and closing out thousands of properties.

In order to keep an accurate account of your funds and where your company stands financially, you'll need to have bookkeeping and accounting systems that are set up for the long haul and that can sustain growth. There are many different kinds of accounting software available; I like to work with and find QuickBooks to be very simple and straightforward.

Chart of Accounts

Setting up your chart of accounts in QuickBooks is the initial step to optimizing your bookkeeping system. This is just a listing of all the accounts you are tracking—cash, inventory, loans, revenues, and expenses, and it is the basis for all of the accounting entries in QuickBooks. You don't want to skip this initial and essential step. Within QuickBooks, there are templates for the chart of accounts; or you can create one from scratch. One tip that makes the accounting process easier is to use account numbers for each item on the chart of accounts. This is an option you can turn on in the QuickBooks setup. I have provided an *example chart of accounts template* for residential redevelopers that you can leverage and use at www.RehabInvestingBible.com/resources. Use it, as it will save you time and headaches in the short and long run.

Once you are using QuickBooks or other software to enter all of your transactions, you will have put into the system the necessary information for it to generate the next two elements for understanding the finances of your business. These are the income statement and balance sheet.

Income Statement/Profit and Loss

The income statement, or profit and loss statement (P&L), summarizes your company's revenues and expenses over a period of time. Many businesses look at a quarterly or annual P&L to view their performance and discern whether they are truly making or losing money. So many real estate investors are unable to answer that question on a week to week, month to month, or even a quarterly basis. A P&L with proper reporting will allow you to do just that by tracking your products' profitability via the revenues and costs associated with the product (namely, the house). Because of the type of product you're selling, your P&L will show large spikes every four to six months when you sell a finished rehab and bring in a $30,000 to $60,000 rehab profit.

Balance Sheet

The balance sheet gives you a picture of the financial assets and liabilities of your business *at one point in time*. It's like taking a picture and capturing that exact moment when you view this report. You will see exactly what is going on with the assets, liabilities, and equities at the moment you pull the report, or for the time point you choose to view. It shows your assets (cash, inventory, properties, deposits), your liabilities (mortgage loans on properties, accounts payable, etc.) and your equity (cumulative net income or loss over time as well as any personal contributions to the business). As you purchase properties, spend money to rehab, and sell properties, you enter each of the transactions in QuickBooks so the program can create these financial reports for you.

Again, I have provided both the income statement and balance sheet accounts as a template for you to use and follow in the *example chart of accounts template*. Download and view it at www.RehabInvestingBible.com/resources.

THREE MAJOR AREAS OF ACCOUNTING FOR A REHAB

Your bookkeeping departments should track three major areas for each property: the purchase, rehab and carrying costs, and the sale. Let's go into detail on each.

Purchase

The costs regarding the purchase of a property will vary and include the amount we purchase the property for and the closing costs associated with that transaction. These costs are all capitalized and put in our asset account within our accounting system. You would set up an asset account (we used fixed asset for this purpose) in your chart of accounts with the property address. You'll also establish a liability or loan account in the chart of accounts with the property address. You should record any borrowed funds (whether new loan or assumed mortgage) as a liability.

Rehab and Carrying Costs (Holding or Maintenance)

Rehab costs are all the costs associated with materials and labor during the rehab. Rehab costs also include all holding costs. Essentially, the rehab costs include anything spent to renovate the property that will stay with the property. When you spend this money, you record it in the asset account you set up when the property was purchased. The rehab funds increase the total value of the asset account and simply add to the cost basis of your original purchase and acquisition price and cost.

Carrying costs are those costs incurred to hold the property. These include any mortgage or loan payments for the property, property taxes, insurance premiums, utility payments (water, electricity, gas, garbage, etc.), lawn care (once the rehab is complete), and so on.

Much like the purchase, these carrying and holding costs are going to be recorded (capitalized) in the asset account as well. Costs can include:

- Utilities
- Inspections
- Advertising
- Landscaping
- Debt service

Keep in mind that all invoices for rehab and carrying costs are filed in the monthly invoice folder.

Sale

Selling costs are all the costs incurred in order to get the property sold—commissions, any closing costs paid on behalf of the buyer, selling closing costs, any mortgage or loan payoffs, and so on. This category also includes items the buyer has required as part of the purchase contract. For example, if the buyer wants you to place a fence around the property in order to close, then you could account for that as part of the selling costs. However, if the buyer requires a specific repair that should have been made as a part of the rehab process, I would include it in the rehab costs.

The sale is when we enter a journal entry to write off the total balances in the asset and liability accounts to record the cost of sales and the proceeds received as revenue. This entry allows the program to calculate your gain or loss, which is shown on the income statement. For instance, let's say you purchase a property for $100,000 and sell it for $180,000 after rehab. The profit would be $80,000 less the costs incurred in acquiring, carrying, and selling the property. Selling costs include:

- Title.
- Attorney/escrow fees.

- Conveyance taxes.
- Real estate commissions.
- Miscellaneous expenses. These expense amounts should be taken off the HUD-1/closing statement.

Following these definitions will help you and your team input and organize every check and dollar spent on buying, carrying, and selling your rehab within your accounting system.

FINANCIAL CLOSEOUT SYSTEM

Next we'll review the property closeout checklist. My bookkeeper must use this system to provide me with a financial closeout package for every property once it's sold. This helps me in my postgame analysis so I can see what works and what doesn't, how much money I made, how many days I owned the property, how much I paid in utility bills, and much more. The package includes these items:

1. **Profit analysis.** This is a summary sheet created in Excel that details the financial aspects of the deal. It includes a summary profit and loss statement detailing the original cost, cost of improvements, carrying costs (utilities, insurance and debt service), selling price and closing costs, and the calculation of gain or loss. It also compares our final costs with our estimated budgets and profit analysis. Furthermore, it includes and compares the number of days the property was held, number of days it was listed for sale, and any other information that will help understand the deal. This one report and view allows me to understand if we improved, stayed the same, or got worse from a financial performance on that individual deal. I will break this down in further detail below and provide a template for you to use and leverage.
2. **Copy of buying HUD-1 Statement.** This is the final closing statement I receive for the property when I purchase it.
3. **Copy of selling HUD-1 Statement.** This is the final closing statement provided at the closing when I resell the property.
4. **Copy of check or wire from sale.** Having a copy of the check or wire confirmation makes it easy to trace the funds back to my bank account. It also allows me to confirm the correct amount when preparing an entry in QuickBooks.
5. **Quick report from QuickBooks.** This report shows every single transaction incurred from the time the property was purchased to the time the sale is recorded. The report assists the bookkeeper in making the correct entries in QuickBooks, as well as to remove the property

from the books and record the gain or loss. I also need this report so I can quickly review all invoices and other payments that were included as costs of the project.

6. **Journal entry from QuickBooks.** The journal entry made by the bookkeeper is how the property is taken off the books and the sales proceeds; the gain or loss gets recorded on the financial statements.

7. **Class income statement/profit and loss statement.** The class (property) income statement is the final QuickBooks statement that summarizes the deal. The net gain or loss on this statement should be the same as shown on the profit analysis. When these two statements agree, I can determine that the bookkeeper captured the correct information in Quick-Books.

Profit Analysis Breakdown

When I view this report, it contains all of the financial information for the project that allows me to quickly get an understanding of my postgame analysis on that deal. I mainly focus my time on the profit analysis that breaks down three categories to review: acquisitions, rehabs, and sales analysis. The following elements are important to view in detail. I always compare the statistics below to what we accomplished on our previous rehab and our annual averages. These tracked metrics display if we are actually improving as residential redevelopers. Figure 19.1 shows a view and a breakdown of the profit analysis using our CT Homes LLC template.

I. Acquisitions Analysis
   a. Holding time in days—Tells us if we are getting more efficient and using our time better.
   b. Profit—Tells us if we made more or less money.
   c. Improvement cost—Shows our final improvement expenditures.
   d. Utilities cost—Shows how much we spend on utilities.
   e. Insurance cost—Illustrates our average insurance cost over time.
   f. Financing cost—Shows the cost of the money we borrow.
   g. Staging cost—Shows our staging expense.
   h. Marketing cost—Shows our marketing expenditures.
II. Rehab Analysis
   a. Rehab start date—The day we actually start the rehab.
   b. Days from close of property to start date—Tells us how soon we started from the day we owned the property to starting the actual rehab itself. (This should be less than a week when you get good.)

			PROPERTY SALE ENTRIES				
			Sample Property Address				
Date:							
x		1	Profit Analysis				
	12/13/13	2	Buying HUD				
	3/28/14	3	Selling HUD				
x		4	Copy of Check from Sale				
x		5	Quick Report				
x		6	Journal Entry				
x		7	Class Income Statement/P&L Statement				
			Profit Analysis				
						Pre-Project	
		1	**Acquisition Analysis**		Actual	Analysis	Annual Average
			Holding time in days		105		119
			Profit	$	27,096.51	$ 20,000.00	$ 39,875.32
			Improvement Cost	$	24,875.51	$ 25,000.00	$ 78,207.81
			Utilities Cost	$	52.41		$ 462.39
			Insurance	$	526.00		$ 1,145.76
			Financing Cost	$	3,999.87		$ 22,145.61
			Staging Costs	$	1,086.00		$ 2,153.47
			Marketing Costs	$	378.00		$ 416.06
		2	**Rehab Analysis**				
			Rehab Start Date		12/26/13		
			Days from close date to start date		13		
			# of days in rehab		63		
			Improvement savings or (overage)	$	124.49		
		3	**Sales Analysis**				
			List Date		2/27/14		
			List Price	$	225,000.00		
			Offer Acceptance Date		2/4/14		
			# of days from listing to contract		5		
			Offer Acceptance Price	$	245,000.00		
			Days in Escrow		24		

FIGURE 19.1   Profit-Analysis Report

c. Number of days to complete the rehab—Illustrates how well we managed our contractors and implemented the rehab system.

d. Improvement savings or overage based on initial estimate and scope of work—Illustrates if our initial estimates on rehabbing our properties at the time of purchase is high so we can adjust and factor this in our next offer.

III. Sales Analysis

    a. List date—The day the property is listed.

    b. List price—The price the property is listed at.

    c. Offer acceptance date—The day your offer got accepted.

    d. Number of days from listing to contract—Illustrates how long it took from listing to offer acceptance (our goal here is within 14 days of listing the property).

    e. Offer acceptance price—Illustrates the offer acceptance compared to list price.

    f. Days in escrow—Illustrates how many days it takes to close the deal once the offer was accepted.

If you consistently complete a postgame analysis on every property, you will improve and make more money.

I end this chapter with an example of my step-by-step process on how to close out a property. You can continue to reference this system as you buy and sell deals.

A STEP-BY-STEP REVIEW OF ACCOUNTING FOR A REHAB

Following is a summary of the accounting procedures for a rehab. I will use the following example transaction:

- Present offer on 15 Red Street paying a deposit check of $5,000.
- Complete purchase of 15 Red Street for a total of $105,000 ($5,000 deposit plus additional $100,000).
- Borrow $80,000 for the purchase. (The remaining balance is personal funds in this example.)
- Closing costs are $1,000 and attorney fees are $325.
- Rehab costs $10,000.
- Utilities—two months at $50 per month.
- Debt service—two months at $300.
- Sell property for $160,000 and pay $5,000 in closing costs.

1. Set Up Your Quickbooks File

1. Enter in company information and preferences.
2. Under the company tab, select preferences. Turn on class tracking and account numbers
3. Set up your chart of accounts. (Download the *example chart of accounts template* at www.RehabInvestingBible.com/resources.)

4. The accounts needed for a rehab property are:
   a. Primary property account (account type—asset).
   b. Primary property subaccounts (account type—asset) that include improvements, debt service, utilities, insurance, accumulated depreciation, and any other costs you want to track separately.
   c. Property liability account (account type—other current liability).
   d. Gross proceeds account (account type—other income).
   e. Cost of property sold (account type—other income). Although this is an expense, setting up the account type as other income allows for the gross proceeds and costs of property sold accounts to appear together on the income statement. The costs of property sold account will appear as a negative other income amount when the entries are completed.

2. Record the Acquisition of the Property

1. You need to have the amount of any checks you wrote for deposits and the closing HUD.
2. In Quickbooks, under the company tab, select journal entry. You will enter all transactions here.
3. Record the $5,000 deposit paid with the offer (entry 1).
4. Record closing costs, such as points and miscellaneous fees, $80,000 mortgage and $20,000 cash (entry 2).

Entry #	Account #	Account Name	Memo	Debit	Credit	Class
1.	1500	15 Red St	Deposit paid—15 Red St	5,000		15 Red St
	1000	Checking Acct	Deposit paid—15 Red St		5,000	15 Red St
2.	1500	15 Red St	Purchase 15 Red St	100,000		15 Red St
	1500	15 Red St	Points	1,000		15 Red St
	1500	15 Red St	Attorney and other fee	325		15 Red St
	2100	Liability new loan	15 Red St		80,000	15 Red St
	1000	15 Red St	Funds to close		21,325	15 Red St

3. Record the Rehab Costs and the Carrying Costs

You can record costs in QuickBooks using either a journal entry or a check. The example journal entries are below.

Entry #	Account #	Account Name	Memo	Debit	Credit	Class
1.	1500-1	Improvements	contractor payment	4,000		15 Red St
	1000	Checking Acct			4,000	15 Red St
2.	1500-2	Utilities	Electric Bill— month 1	50		15 Red St
	1000	Checking Acct			50	15 Red St
3.	1500-3	Debt Service	loan payment	300		15 Red St
	1000	Checking Acct			300	15 Red St
4.	1500-1	Improvements	contractor payment #2	6,000		15 Red St
	1000	Checking Acct			6,000	15 Red St
5.	1500-2	Utilities	Electric—month 2	50		15 Red St
	1000	Checking Acct			50	15 Red St
6.	1500-3	Debt Service	loan payment	300		15 Red St
	1000	Checking Acct			300	15 Red St

When you enter a check in QuickBooks, the screen looks like an actual check. You will enter the date, payee, amount, and memo in the provided fields. In the bottom section of the check you will enter the account number, the amount, the description, and the class. In this example, when entering a check, you would use the account numbers shown in the journal entries.

4. Record the Sale of the Rehab Property

Entry #	Account #	Account Name	Memo	Debit	Credit	Class
1.	1500-1	Improvements	Record sale		10,000	15 Red St
	9900-2	Cost of Property Sold	Record sale	10,000		15 Red St
2.	1500-2	Utilities	Record sale		100	15 Red St
	9900-2	Cost of Property Sold	Record sale	100		15 Red St
3.	1500-3	Debt Service	Record sale		600	15 Red St
	9900-2	Cost of Property Sold	Record sale	600		15 Red St
4.	1500	15 Red St	Record sale		106,325	15 Red St
	9900-2	Cost of Property Sold	Record sale	106,325		15 Red St
5.	9900-1	Gross Sales Proceeds	Record sale		160,000	15 Red St
	2100	Liability—15 Red Street	Record sale— payoff loan	80,000		15 Red St
	9900-2	Cost of Property Sold	Sale closing costs	5,000		15 Red St
	1000	Checking Acct		75,000		15 Red St

The results of all the transactions on your cash and income statement can be summarized next:

Cost of Property Sold (Cash out):

Deposit for purchase	$5,000
Funds to complete purchase	$21,325
Improvement Costs	$10,000
Holding costs and debt service	$700
Pay loan	$80,000
Sale closing costs	$5,000
Total Cost of property sold	**$122,025**
Sales Proceeds (Cash In):	**$160,000**
Total Gain	**$37,975**

Using this example, you can see the deal profit is $37,975. This does not include your business overhead like your cell phone bill, office rent, and so on. This example and illustration can be used step by step so you do your financial accounting on your first rehab flawlessly.

I have invested in and improved this system over many years and many deals. You will save time, energy, and money if you implement this postgame analysis on every deal you complete. This is how to improve and set up your business for long-term success. Following this system will directly impact how much profit you make on your next deal and reduce the time you spend on it.

PART IV

Owning and Growing a Business of Rehabs

True residential redevelopers do not do every job in the business. In fact, they are very good at replacing themselves and enrolling, outsourcing, or hiring someone who can do it better when put in a proper system. Part IV shares the steps to properly outsource and train others. Part IV also shares the entity choices a real estate investor has, as well as the very important job of keeping as much money as possible within their business and wealth structure following the law and tax code provided for business owners.

CHAPTER 20

How to Fire Yourself

What Every Entrepreneur Must Learn

The ultimate goal of every entrepreneur and business owner is to repeatedly fire themselves from every task and job they have in their own business by teaching others to do these tasks for them. You can get to this point by following these steps:

Step 1. Do the job yourself and get good at it.

Step 2. Create a system so another team member can do the same job successfully.

Step 3. Create the training system for that job and task that will make your new team member successful.

Step 4. Fire yourself from that job and activity and work on the next higher-level job, project, or goal within your business.

THE TRAINING PROCESS

If you would prefer sipping on a fruity drink at the beach while your business runs itself, follow these steps to build an automated learning system for your next team members or managers to train with.

- Acquire a screen capture and recording software to record your training presentations. I like to use the software called Camtasia.
- Create a training outline with a PowerPoint/Keynote presentation. (This is like a training syllabus about what your team members need to know to excel at their jobs.)
- Record and deliver your training.
- Set up a file, database, or online platform to post or upload your recorded trainings.
- Make sure your new hire watches your training presentation to learn your system.

- While your new team member is learning from your recorded training, you are free to work on more important things, spend time with your family, or, of course, go to a beach and drink fruity drinks.

These steps will help you create and design your own online training platform for your business. Essentially, you can hire as many team members as you want without allocating all of your personal time to actually train them. Camtasia software captures the images on your screen and your audio so you don't have to take time out of your busy schedule to reteach new staff members and managers the same topics you have already trained and taught. In removing yourself from the training equation, you can concentrate on higher-level growth-building activities such as higher-level marketing ideas, raising more money, or prospecting the next great deal.

BUILDING A TEAM

Leverage is the key to doing more, growing more, and earning more. You do not necessarily have to hire employees in order to build a great real estate team when first starting out. It is critical to understand, however, that hiring or paying independent contractors to run certain areas of your business can result in more deals and bring in more profit.

You want your team of professionals to include a selling real estate agent, a real estate transaction attorney or escrow company (depending on the state in which you work, you must close deals with attorneys or escrow companies), a mortgage broker, a property manager, an insurance agent and insurance broker, a hard-money and private lender, and a title company. All of these professionals receive compensation as a result of each profitable deal. All of these key relationships will make you more successful, allow you to move faster, and bring in more money when you take the time to prescreen, interview, and enroll the best. There are also a few other people you'll want to bring on board to help your team function as seamlessly as possible.

Your first hire should be an *assistant* who can help you with marketing, take leads, analyze deals, and complete tasks like running errands and doing some administrative duties. Essentially, your first hire has to be a team player who will take work off of your desk and give you time to acquire more deals. The second person you should hire is an *acquisitions and marketing manager*. This individual's major priority will be to focus on implementing marketing and identifying deals to put under contract. Your third hire needs to be a *rehab project manager* who follows the rehab systems explained in this book, and continues to find and manage quality contractors while completing rehab projects. The fourth person you should hire is the *liquidation and sales marketing manager*, whose main job should be focused on selling all of your rehabs and wholesale deals. If you would rather not have this position in-house, enrolling an *A+* listing agent on your team can fill it.

OUTSOURCING AND AUTOMATING

When your business starts to grow, your time is best spent locating deals, money, or buyers. Eventually, as your business becomes more automated, you want to be able to recruit quality talent into your company, manage those individuals, and motivate them to accomplish great things within your organization.

That's where outsourcing comes into play. Every successful business ultimately becomes a people business—so the better you become at finding, motivating, training, and managing quality people, the more successful your business will become.

The goal of outsourcing to team members, employees, or service providers is to delegate work that must be done in order for the business to maintain itself. If you have systems in place and established a competent team, you are already in a perfect position to outsource the majority of your vital daily activities.

Up to this point, I have talked about following a system, building a team, and outsourcing. The final step is to *automate*, which you can do via any number of systems, checklists, and technologies. Executing this final step ensures that you own a business that works for you instead of owning a business that you work for.

I have seen countless individuals go into business for themselves because they are overworked and hate their jobs, only to work longer hours and sometimes even make *less* money. If you execute the first three steps I've discussed (establishing and using systems, team building, and outsourcing), you should avoid a similar fate. Conversely, if you can truly leverage the systems, technology, and automated business systems discussed throughout this book, then you will start to enjoy the money and lifestyle that very few achieve.

The most important task you have is to implement systems and provide a structure where other people can succeed in your business. When other team members, employees, or independent contractors have success in your business system, you will have more time back in your life. The toughest thing to do is to fire yourself from a task and hand it off to another team member. Practice this process and do it repeatedly. Eventually you will fire yourself out of all the jobs in your business so you can truly have a business that works for you instead of you working for it.

CHAPTER 21

A Roadmap to Keeping and Growing Your Wealth

The only thing that gets me more excited than rehabbing real estate is growing and managing the money we make from rehabbing real estate. To that end, this chapter focuses on sharing the tools of wealth. People who have more money are using more of the tax code to save and keep more of their money. The information contained in this book isn't just about how you to *make* more money, but to *keep* the money that you make.

ENTITY STRUCTURE

Picking and identifying an entity to do business is a very important decision. You can buy and sell real estate as a sole proprietor, of course. However, when you do volume and multiple transactions, there are a lot of benefits to establishing a proper entity and asset-protection plan sooner rather than later. Here are a just few primary reasons:

1. Identity protection and privacy (depending on what state you domicile your entity).
2. Asset protection.
3. Accounting benefits and efficiencies.
4. Tax benefits and efficiencies.

Here are some choices when picking an entity:

1. **Limited Liability Company.** Better known as an LLC, this is the most versatile entity for a majority of business owners.
2. **S-Corp.** This flows to your personal tax return so you do not have double taxation at the corporate level.
3. **C-Corp.** This gets taxed at the corporate level and then dividends are distributed to you personally, which get taxed again, resulting in double taxation.

There are more selections available for forming a business entity; however, these are the three entities that are most often used and focused on. Take some time and research these with your desired professional to identify the best fit for your personal and financial situation. We give our students the professionals, the resources, and the team to copy our structure that we use so they can replicate our successful structure and move forward.

My job is to walk you through the information you need to increase your financial literacy. This will allow you to spend more time with your specific professional to make the best decision based on your personal and financial goals. One particular area of advice that's crucial to cover is how to hold and own long-term assets, such as rental properties, versus how we hold and own rehab assets that we flip.

You will want to have two separate entities to take title and own these different assets:

Entity 1. Owns and takes title to your rehab and wholesale properties that you flip and own short term.

Entity 2. Owns and takes title to your rental and long-term real estate assets that you own for wealth creation and generational wealth that will be passed on to your family, charity, trust, and so on.

It is not smart from a liability standpoint to own your long-term assets in the same entity you use to rehab and wholesale properties. If you get sued—which hopefully will not happen, but very well might—and have all your assets in one entity, then all of those assets are subject to the claim of the lawsuit. This is what makes this separation so essential.

MONEY ALLOCATION STRATEGIES FOR YOUR REHAB PROFITS

People frequently ask me how we should allocate the profits we make from our deals. A rule of thumb that I teach my students about how to account for your taxes, business investments, and personal use is to think of taking the profits you make from a rehab and allocating them into six different buckets for proper planning and growth:

1. 30 percent tax bucket.
2. 20 percent growth capital bucket (for education, trainings, mentors, and coaches).
3. 20 percent operational capital bucket (such as marketing and overhead).
4. 15 percent savings and retirement bucket.
5. 10 percent food, rent, mortgage, and everyday living bucket.
6. 5 percent discretionary and fun money bucket.

You will notice that first bucket, taxes, is the largest. I advise allocating profits from your recent deals into it. By implementing some of the strategies I share, you will be able to reduce a good portion of your taxable income.

The second bucket, growth capital—which involves your own investment into your intellectual assets and other tools and systems to leverage for your business—is the most important investment you can make. Just as you invested in this book, you can take one idea and system I shared in this book and make 100 times the investment in real estate profit.

The third bucket goes directly back to your business to keep it growing and prospering in the form of marketing dollars and overhead needs. You won't be able to continue rehabbing unless you have motivated opportunities (deals) that your marketing dollars and activities have brought in.

The fourth bucket is for your personal savings and retirement. I personally save a lot more than 15 percent from each deal; if you can afford this as well, I suggest you put as much of your profits toward your retirement and savings as you can. The goal of 15 percent is a great start.

The fifth bucket is of course our daily living bucket—paying the bills and putting food on the table. This can be a lower percentage if you are single and have not yet started a family. If you are married with kids, like many of our students are, this will likely be a higher percentage.

The sixth bucket contains money to reward yourself. It might seem frivolous sometimes, but it's very important to remind ourselves why we make so much sacrifice executing this business. I made the mistake early on of not rewarding myself with some discretionary spending on fun things. One of my mentors taught me that we *must celebrate* all wins. I never end up spending 5 percent of my profits on every deal; it usually comes to about only 1 percent. However, the discretionary spending bucket is an important part of the process to have fun and enjoy the efforts of your new business. Any leftover fun money you don't use can go into your savings bucket.

INVESTMENT AND RETIREMENT STRATEGIES[*]

The following wealth building and retirement strategies have allowed me to keep more of the money I have earned as a real estate investor. I've achieved this by using more of the law and code provided to us as business owners and real estate operators.

---

[*]These materials are not intended to be relied upon as the sole basis for any investment decision, and are not, and should not be assumed to be, complete without consulting with a licensed professional. The contents herein and each party that receives these materials should consult its own attorney, business advisor, and tax advisor as to legal, business, and tax advice.

1031 Exchanges

The 1031 exchange tax code is in place to encourage us to keep our money circulating in the economy instead of cashing out and pulling our money out for our private use. A 1031 exchange is when you postpone paying tax on the gain if you reinvest the proceeds in similar property as part of a qualifying like-kind exchange. Realizing the gain deferred in a like-kind exchange under IRC Section 1031 is tax-deferred, but is not tax free.

The IRS wants investors to keep our dollars in the economy; as such, this law encourages us to do this by giving us a tax break on our capital gains bill for the property we are selling. This is done by taking the proceeds of the sold income-producing property and identifying a similar income-producing property or properties of equal or greater value, which allows us to defer our capital gains tax bill. This primarily applies to properties that were bought with the intent to rent or lease for income. So a short-term rehab property typically does not qualify for this tax-deferred scenario. A scenario that *may* qualify is when you buy a property with the intent to rent it and produce cash flow. It is important to work with your qualified CPA to discuss what properties will qualify and which ones will not.

It is good to know about these laws so we can build our long-term wealth faster paying a smaller percentage in taxes as we grow our asset base. Once we have paid our taxes on our rehab profits, we want to invest in passive-income rental assets. At this stage of your wealth-building plan, you can start leveraging and using the IRC Section 1031 to defer taxes and get into higher price point rentals and assets.

Self-Directed IRA Investing

What if I told you that you could be using your 401(k) retirement money, your Roth IRA, or traditional IRA to invest in real estate? You can and *should* be self-directing all of your retirement accounts with a custodian that allows you to facilitate these types of investments.

If you currently have a job that provides a 401(k), you cannot change custodians and access these funds. However, if and when you stop working at that job, you can then transfer from their selected custodian to a self-directed custodian that will now facilitate and allow you to self-direct your money into real estate transactions. (Are you excited yet?)

Few CPAs—and an even a smaller percentage of attorneys—are knowledgeable about self-directed plans. So don't be surprised if your lawyer or accountant hasn't heard of this—or even worse, tell you it can't be done. IRS rules have allowed self-direction since IRAs were created in the mid-1970s. If you go to the IRS website and look at the FAQ's on this topic, you will see this:

> IRA trustees are permitted to impose additional restrictions on investments. For example, because of administrative burdens, many IRA trustees do not permit IRA owners to invest IRA funds in real estate. **IRA law does not prohibit investing in real estate** but trustees are not required to offer real estate as an option.

Typical retirement plan trustees allow investors to invest in stocks, bonds, and mutual funds. The reason Morgan Stanley, Merrill Lynch, Charles Schwab, E-Trade, and so on do not promote self-directing your retirement accounts is simply because *they* don't make any money from this activity.

This is where our financial literacy comes into play. You can simply change custodians from Merrill Lynch to a self-directed custodian. There are many to choose from if you just enter it into an Internet browser. Once you have your retirement account switched over to a self-directed custodian, you can invest in all types of investments. Two that you cannot invest in are life insurance and collectibles.

What is a self-directed IRA?

- A personal savings account for your retirement savings.
- Provides tax-deferred or tax-free savings.
- Allows investment in traditional and nontraditional assets.
- No matter the investment, you have control.

Which retirement accounts can I self-direct?

- Roth IRAs.
- Traditional IRAs.
- 401(k)s from previous employers.
- 401(k)s you create for your new business.
- Solo 401(k)s (more on this in a moment).
- 403(b) plans.
- 457 plans.
- Keogh plans.
- Defined benefit plans.
- HSAs (health savings accounts).

I like to refer to all of these retirement accounts that the IRS encourages us to open as *investment buckets*. Each bucket given to us by the tax code of the IRS has its own tax savings and benefits. Again, the IRS is giving you and I tax breaks to encourage us to save for our own retirement so we will not be dependent on the government for our retirement.

The most important feature that all of these IRA vehicles provide is tax-deferred growth until your retirement. Once you have established accounts that allow you to contribute money to real estate, the next step is to turn around and be a lender. In this scenario, you act as the bank to another investor just like yourself.

Let's compare the tale of two investors, one who utilizes the tools of wealth and invests from an IRA and one who invests out of their personal bank account. Investor 1, who is lending $100,000 out of one of the IRA buckets at 12 percent for five years, will have $181,669.69 at the end of those five years. In this scenario, the annual gains are not subject to tax. This means that each year's interest compounds and grows exponentially. In this example, there were no other contributions to the starting $100,000 investment.

Investor 2 lends $100,000 from a personal bank account at 12 percent for five years. He will have $145,577 at the end of those 5 years. The five-year investment with an assumed 35 percent tax rate looks like Table 21.1.

Because Investor 1 does not have to pay the annual tax on their gains within a protected self-directed IRA, he or she has a total of $181,669.69 at the end of five years. Investor 2, who has to pay taxes annually on the gains because they are not protected in a self-directed account, has a total of $145,577 at the end of five years. So $181,669.69 − $145,577 = $36,092.69 is the difference between the two investors' nest eggs after five years. Investor 2 never learned or executed the tools of wealth and socked away money in a retirement account, so they

TABLE 21.1   Investor 2's Financial Picture

Principal	12%	Gross	35% Tax	Net
$100,000	$12,000	$112,000	$4,200	$107,800
$107,800	$12,936	$120,736	$4,527	$116,208
$116,208	$13,945	$130,153	$4,880	$125,272
$125,272	$15,032	$140,305	$5,261	$135,043
$135,043	$16,205	$151,249	$5,671	$145,577

are forced to invest with their taxable income. However, investor 1 educated himself on the tools of wealth and opened an IRA account and starting putting money in it to invest in the future.

When is the last time you learned one concept that saved you over $36,000? And this is just the tip of the iceberg. You can do rehab deals, wholesale deals, and do entire real estate transactions within these IRAs. Of course, there are very important details and rules to follow on the type of transactions that are prohibited. You want to educate yourself on this topic and work with a professional to get these strategies started and executed the correct way. Some other approaches and types of transactions are explained next.

Captive Insurance

As you build and grow your business, you will have certain risk and business scenarios against which you will want to insure. The conventional insurance market does not provide insurance for every risk that business owners incur. Captive insurance is an alternative to this scenario. A *captive* is an insurance company formed to cover the risks of its parent company. Premiums that the parent operating company pays to a properly structured captive for property and casualty coverage should be tax deductible to the parent company.

In this scenario, a corporation or entity with one or more subsidiaries sets up a captive insurance company as an owned subsidiary. The captive is capitalized and domiciled in a jurisdiction with captive-enabling legislation that allows the captive to operate as a licensed insurer. The parent identifies the risks of its subsidiaries that it wants the captive to underwrite. The captive evaluates the risks, writes policies, sets premium levels, and accepts premium payments. The subsidiaries then pay the captive tax-deductible premium payments. Then the captive, like any insurer, invests the premium payments for future claim payouts. When the year of the at-risk premium is completed, the insurance company can now retain the premium for its own use.

When done the correct way, you could establish and own a captive that your real estate investment business pays premiums to for certain business risks. Once the premium year ends—and if in fact your real estate company did not make a claim on the insurance—then your captive company can invest and direct that premium for its own benefit. The key here is you own the real estate investment company that gets the insurance benefit as well as the business expense of the annual premium. And you own the insurance company that gets to retain the premium after the insured year at risk.

Business owners have been using captive insurance for years. It's not a new code or concept and it has supporting IRS rulings and definitions. Here are the simplified steps of what it looks like to implement a captive:

1. Your asset protection entity or trust sets up a captive insurance company.
2. Your real estate investing entity pays a premium to insure against a business risk to your captive insurance company.
3. Your real estate entity premium is an expense that lowers your adjusted gross income or taxable income. (Captive insurance premiums can be expensed up to $1.2 million.)
4. Your premium has to sit in the captive insurance company for one year and typically 80 percent can be invested in liquid-type investments.
5. After one year, if no claims were made against you, your newly found captive insurance company now owns the premium and can invest that money at that point. At this stage, the gains on that investment are now taxed at dividend rates as opposed to your ordinary income tax rate, as long as you keep the money in the captive insurance company.

The most important step is to identify, prescreen, and find experienced professionals to work with you on the details to see if captive insurance makes sense and can be utilized in your business.

Figure 21.1 depicts an example involving asset protection and entity structure that shows how you can start, own, and participate with the strategies I have shared. This will give a visual illustration of the concepts we have shared for keeping more of the money that we make.

Here are the definitions of the entities in this structure and who benefits from them and how the money flows through this chart.

1. You (star) = You as an individual.
2. Real estate LLC or Corp. (triangle) = The rehab investing entity that you set up to buy and sell properties in.
   a. The profits from this company go to you.
   b. Money made by your real estate company goes to:
      i. Pay you.
      ii. Contribute to the solo 401(k).
      iii. Contribute to the defined benefit (DB) plan.
      iv. Pay premium to the captive insurance company.

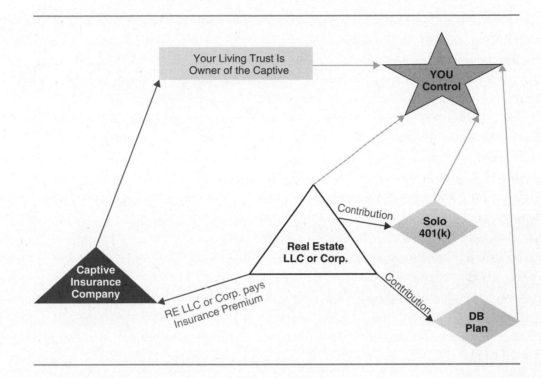

FIGURE 21.1   Asset Protection and Entity Structure

3. Solo 401(k) (Diamond) = The 401(k) plan your real estate company set up for its owner (you) and employee (you). The benefactors of contributions are:
   a. The employee of the real estate company (you).
   b. The owner of the real estate company (you).
4. Defined benefit plan = A retirement plan similar to a pension that your real estate company sets up for its owner (you) and employee (you). The benefactors of contributions are:
   a. The employee of the real estate company (you)
   b. The owner of the real estate company (you).
5. Captive insurance company (shaded triangle) = The retirement company that your real estate company pays premiums to cover insurance risk.
   a. The benefactor of the unpaid premiums is the owner of the insurance company (your living trust).
   b. Money made by the insurance company after holding the premiums for a year can get paid out to the owner of the captive. The owner of the captive is your Trust.

6. Your living Trust (rectangle) = A Trust you have set up for your benefit and long-term assets, wealth, tax, and estate planning.

　a. The benefactor is you. The trust is also the owner of the captive.

　b. Money made and kept in the trust is controlled by you as the trustee for your benefit.

That graphic and the definitions may take a few times to read and look at again before you understand how powerful it is. The main takeaway is that all of the entities and activities in this structure benefit *you*!

Now let's assume that you've made $200,000 of taxable AGI (adjusted gross income or taxable business income) in your real estate investing business by leveraging the IRS code that promotes retirement and business planning as we have discussed. Figure 21.2 shows you how we reduce $200,000 in taxable income to $28,000.

We have a taxable income of $200,000 in this illustration. Assuming a 35 percent tax rate, that is a tax liability or payment due of $70,000 (200,000 × 70 percent). However, in this illustration we implement a solo 401(k), a defined benefit plan, and a captive. By implementing the strategies discussed, our AGI is actually reduced from $200,000 to $28,000. At a 35 percent tax rate that is a tax liability of $9,800 (28,000 × 70 percent). Effectively, we just got to

If you make 200k in Real Estate Income this Year w/ Financial Literacy!

Real Estate Income w/ new BZ's	= $200,000
Solo 401k Contribution	Less ($52,000)
Taxable AGI after 401k Contribution	= $148,000
Defined Benefit Plan***	Less ($20,000)
Taxable AGI after Defined Benefit Cont.	= $128,000
Captive Insurance Premium***	Less ($100,000)
Taxable AGI Income as a BZ's owner	= $28,000

　At a 35% tax rate you owe $9,800 in taxes leveraging IRS sponsored rules to save for your own Retirement

FIGURE 21.2   If You Make $200,000 in Real Estate Income this Year with Financial Literacy

keep $60,200 ($70,000–$9,800) using the knowledge on retirement and business planning we just shared.

Figure 21.3 is one more visual to show the flow of money in the Asset Protection & Entity Structure.

Not only did you save money on your tax bill here, you also control and own each of the buckets into which your company was able to expense the money. Obviously, you need to have enough money here to write checks into each bucket. This is knowledge that many new investors don't implement until year two, three, or four of their investing career. But the longer you commit to making money in real estate, the easier it becomes—and the more money you will make. When you come to that stage, you will be happy you learned about and acted upon these strategies at the start of your investing career.

The information in this chapter should have piqued your interest in learning more of the details about what strategies can and will help you as a business owner. It is critical that you

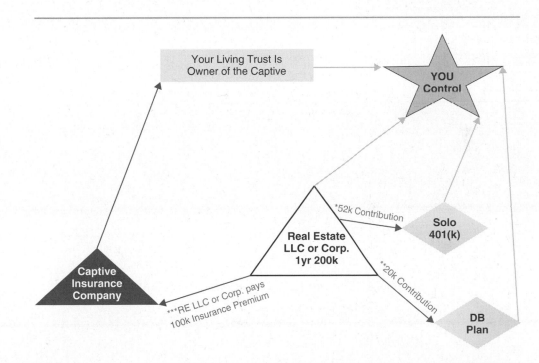

FIGURE 21.3   Asset Protection and Entity Structure 200K Real Estate Earning Example

continue to educate and work with a qualified professional to see if you can put any or all of these strategies to use in your business.

It's not how much money you make but rather how much money you keep. Increasing your financial IQ and getting further education on your own financial literacy will allow you to work smarter and not harder. Continue to learn and educate yourself on these topics. Remember, no one cares about your money more than you.

The Secret to Sustainable Success

Living and Giving with Passionate Purpose

Over the course of this book, I've detailed the ins and outs of how to complete a successful rehab. The final and most important piece of the puzzle, I have found, is living with passion and purpose. When I first started out in this business, I—possibly like many of you—was motivated by money. Through my own experience and what I've seen throughout my years of coaching real estate investors is that living a fulfilled life is ultimately about the impact you have when living your life with passion. It's all about how you grow and improve, the betterment you create for your family and community, and how you can positively change the world around you.

I wholeheartedly believe that each one of us was put on this earth to make a unique difference and create an impact. Many of you reading this book right now will leverage real estate investing as your vehicle to achieve your goals and live your purpose.

Mastering my craft in real estate, being a better husband, improving as a father, and continuing to force growth in every area of my life, day in and day out, are the driving forces in my life. I discovered early on that being motivated solely by money, deals completed, or possessions do not fulfill me. When I ask all of my successful students what they are most proud of as investors, it is the obstacles they have overcome, how they have transformed themselves, given back to their communities, and the excitement they have for the continued journey ahead of them.

The goal of making money alone in real estate is not an enduring motivation. Unless you can focus on something bigger, you will give up the moment you come to your first roadblock. If money is your only motivator, then your "why" isn't substantial enough to get you through the work and tribulations that lie ahead of you in this business.

YOUR IMPACT AS A REAL ESTATE INVESTOR

If each one of us pursues our goals in real estate, we can collectively have a monumental social impact. Rehabbing houses is an extremely powerful way to achieve one of the most significant human drivers: the need to contribute. Our commitment to bettering homes leads far beyond a repaired foundation and new windows. Think about it. Every time we take on a new rehab, we are creating a new home for a buyer to achieve their dream of home ownership to create lifelong memories in. We are improving neighborhoods, removing blighted, ugly houses, and increasing the value of nearby homes. We are creating jobs for all the people we hire to work on the home, adding revenue to our city and town by pulling permits, and stimulating the economy with the purchase of every new cabinet and material we put into our finished rehabs.

On a grander scale, we make profits that allow us to use our resources for the greater good. Being a successful investor gives us more time, energy, and money that we can use to give back. I have discovered that new investors and entrepreneurs, who share a commitment to positively contributing to the world around them, always have better, more enduring success in their business. They are continually looking for ways to give back, support charities, and humanitarian efforts.

PAYING IT FORWARD

People often ask me why I coach and teach real estate instead of focusing on finding more deals for myself. The most rewarding and fulfilling process I can have is helping another investor achieve success through shared knowledge, systems, and experience. However, even more rewarding than that is to see those same investors pursue a higher purpose and a pay-it-forward mentality, showing gratitude by helping others.

Through our philanthropic initiative, FortuneBuilders Gives, my partners, my team, and many of our students have been able to proactively create relationships and opportunities to give back to our communities. Many of our initiatives focus on the areas we are most passionate about—education, children, and housing. We are fortunate to have an amazing community of investors across the country who join us in giving time, energy, and resources to causes and charities near and dear to them. To join forces with us and participate in our causes, please visit us at www.FortuneBuildersGives.com.

FOLLOW YOUR WHY

Ultimately, my hope is that each one of you reading this book use the knowledge I've shared within to start investing in real estate, to achieve success and freedom for you and for your family, and leverage real estate investing as a vehicle to "make a ding in the Universe," as Steve Jobs said.

Ask yourself, what legacy do you want to leave behind? This is your *why*. Follow your *why*, know where you ultimately want to go, and your real estate investing journey will take you to some extraordinary places.

Focus on your passion, be excited about the social impact you will make, and be persistent in your real estate goals. Success leaves clues—so pay enough attention to follow them so you can have the same outcome as many successful real estate investors have before you.

Your new journey begins now.

Index